IMAGES
of America

DeKalb County

Judy Fuson and Ria Baker

ARCADIA
PUBLISHING

ISBN 978-0-7385-9145-2

Published by Arcadia Publishing
Charleston, South Carolina

Printed in the United States of America

Library of Congress Control Number: 2011939560

For all general information, please contact Arcadia Publishing:
Telephone 843-853-2070
Fax 843-853-0044
E-mail sales@arcadiapublishing.com
For customer service and orders:
Toll-Free 1-888-313-2665

Visit us on the Internet at www.arcadiapublishing.com

To our handsome husbands, Eddie and Ricky.
Thanks for your patience and support.

Contents

Acknowledgments

We would like to express our appreciation for the advice, knowledge, and assistance of Tommy Webb, who is the DeKalb County historian and a living book of historic information on our county. We are very grateful for the use of the genealogy room in the Justin Potter Library and the Liberty Historic Room. We would also like to thank the many people who encouraged and assisted us as we searched for pictures and information.

We are grateful to those who opened their doors to us as well as their attics, boxes, closets, and drawers to find the unseen photographs within these pages: Violet Allen, Pat Barnes, Leota Mac Bennett, Denise Brown, Virginia Brown, Gladys Cantrell, Frances Capilinger, Bill and Sue Corley, Geraldine Cook, Genrose Davis, Doyle Evans, Louise Frazier, Jane Avant Fry, Gary Fuson, Wayne Fuson, Annette Webb Greek, Annie Ruth Greer, Kenward Griffith, Mary Ruth Groom, Ed and Gloria Hale, Peggy Huffstetler, Mansell Johnson of Tennessee Tech University (TTU), Marguerite Jones, David McDowell, Debbie Nixon, Ophel Page, Danny and Pat Parkerson, Ron Paschal, Sue Puckett-Jernigan, Robert Robinson, Judy Sandlin, Tom Simpson, Lois Spencer, Cindy Hatton Taylor, Joe Taylor, Tennessee Historic Society, Carol Williams, Billy and Sue Willoughby, Mac Willoughby, and many others. Thank you all!

INTRODUCTION

No one person can carve out and settle the land. This nation, as well as its states, counties, and communities are all a product of many generations. From the American Indians to the first pioneers who arrived full of dreams and lived lifetimes of hard work, our county grew. Men with adventurous spirits, like Adam Dale who settled Liberty, Daniel Alexander after whom Alexandria was named, and Jesse Allen who established transportation across the Caney Fork River, to name a few, have opened the door to this area, bringing others into what is now known as DeKalb County, Tennessee.

DeKalb County was established in 1837 from parts of Smith, White, Warren, and Cannon Counties. The name was taken from Johann DeKalb, a Revolutionary War hero, and the town of Smithville in the center of the county was then formed as the county seat and named in honor of Samuel Granville Smith, a former state senator and secretary of state. Although DeKalb County was not established until 1837, the area had already begun to be settled by the late 1700s. When this land was simply known as the "wilderness," farms, settlements, and plantations started springing up as more and more people were arriving. According to Will T. Hale's *History of DeKalb County*, the area along the Highland Rim, our eastern border, boasted thick wooded areas of black oak, chestnut, hickory, post oak, and white oak, while the valleys led the way with crops. Corn, wheat, flax, cotton, and tobacco as well as some of the finest mules, hogs, and other livestock flourished on farms in the basins and valleys in the western area and in the Caney Fork River Valley.

From the leaders who had a vision and the drive to make their dream a reality, to settlers who put down roots and made a home for themselves in the wilderness known as DeKalb County, we honor you all with this historic picture book. The people who have lived here raising families, fighting to keep us safe through the years, and passing on memories and photographs have all left a great legacy for the generations.

Today, the dreams and hard work continue. The people of DeKalb County are proud of our nation, state, and county. We still raise our families, fight to keep them safe and free, and hope to leave behind something for the future. This book was compiled and written with love and respect to those who have come before us and to help leave something for the future. We want to thank everyone who helped this dream come true.

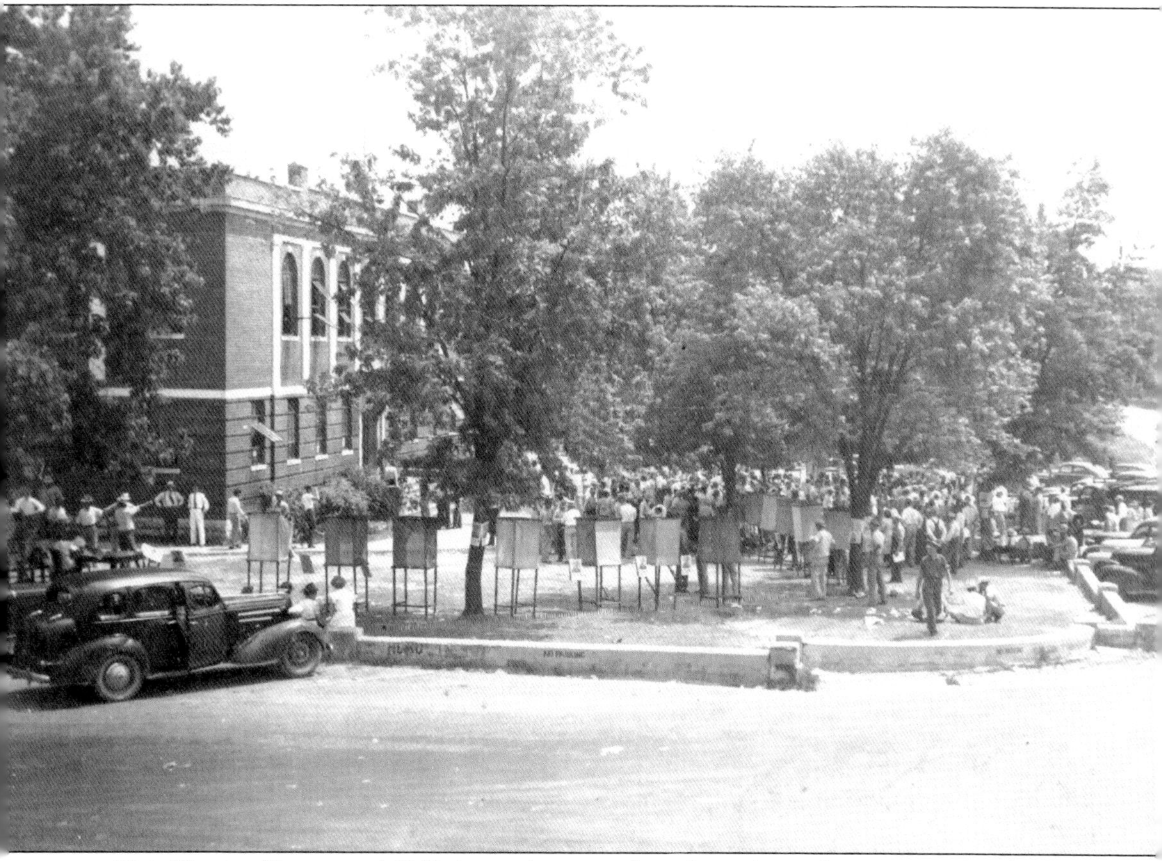

This Election Day around 1940 drew a large number of people on the square at Smithville. At that time, the voting place was set up in the yard surrounding the courthouse, and votes were on paper ballots. (Courtesy of Peggy Huffstetler.)

One

Old-Time Religion

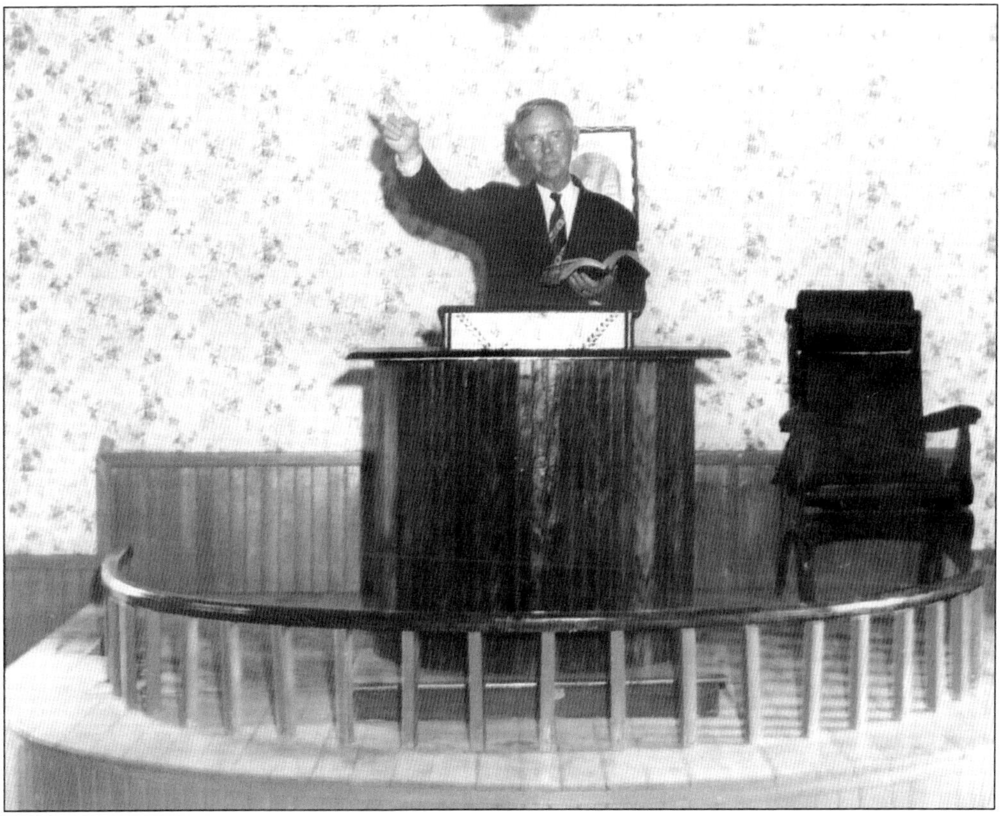

Rev. R.L. Whitlock, a Baptist minister, pastored 10 churches of Salem Association from 1918 through 1946 and in 1925 was pastor of six different churches at the same time—Cooper's Chapel, Elizabeth Chapel, Indian Creek, Providence, Shiloh, and Snow Hill. In early years, many churches met only once a month while sharing pastors. Whitlock pastored Elizabeth Chapel Baptist Church on Holmes' Creek for over 30 years; this picture was taken in that church. (Courtesy of Sue Puckett-Jernigan.)

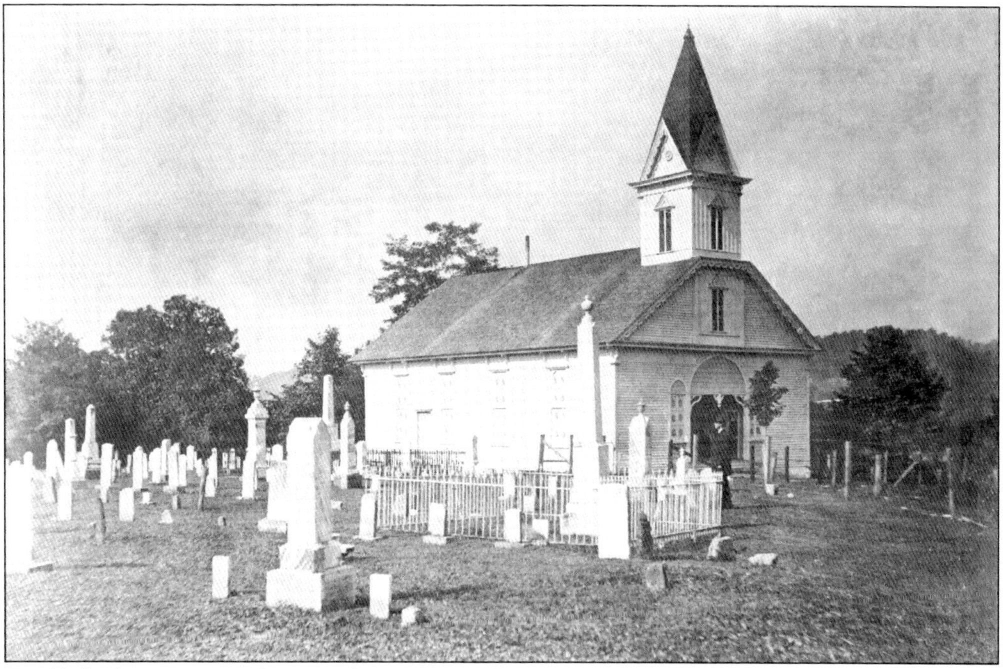

Established in 1809 in Liberty, Salem Baptist Church was the earliest church erected in DeKalb County. The first building of logs was replaced by a frame building in 1849 and later enlarged in 1880 to the frame structure pictured here. Cantrell Bethel, who had helped establish a church in Brush Creek in 1802, later established Salem and served as the pastor for the first 28 years. (Courtesy of Kenward Griffith.)

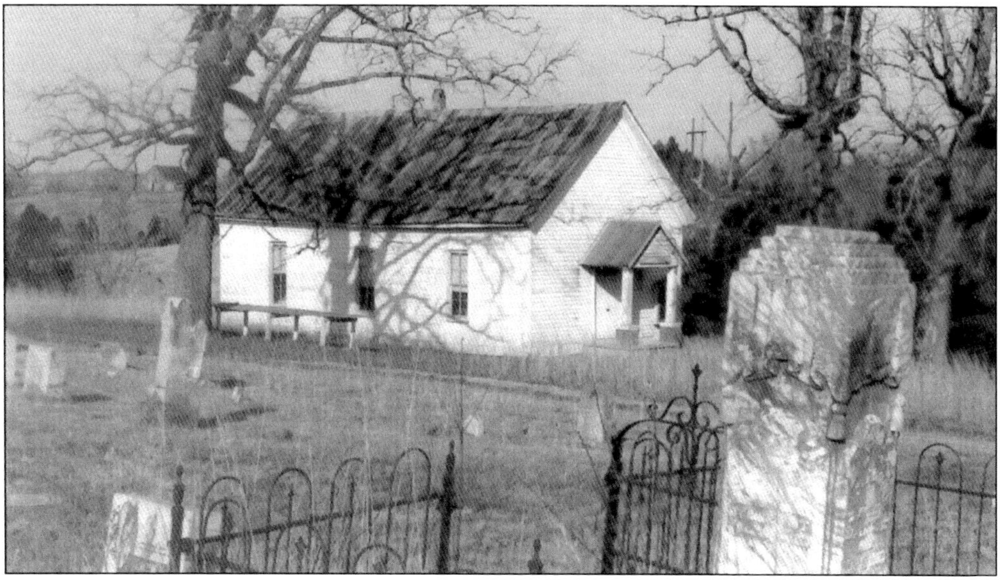

The Bildad Baptist Church on Sink Creek south of Smithville was also organized in 1809 by Cantrell Bethel, who served as pastor of this church from 1809 to 1814. This church eventually became known as Old Bildad when some members divided into the church now known as New Bildad Primitive Baptist in 1854. This church building is still standing; however, no members are now alive. (Courtesy of Tommy Webb.)

Established in 1813, Alexandria Methodist was the first of this denomination in DeKalb County. This frame building was erected in 1885. At the time it was built, it had an upstairs with outside entrance, which was used as a schoolroom. Over the years, it has been remodeled and is still used by the present congregation. (Courtesy of Alexandria Methodist Church.)

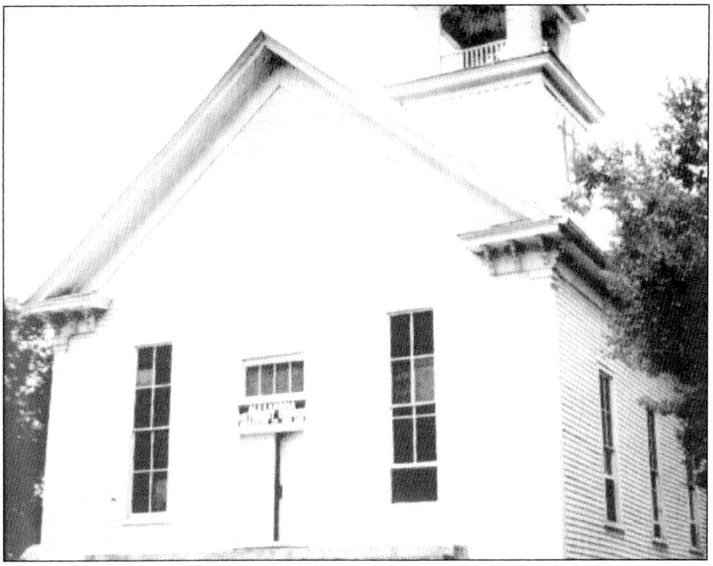

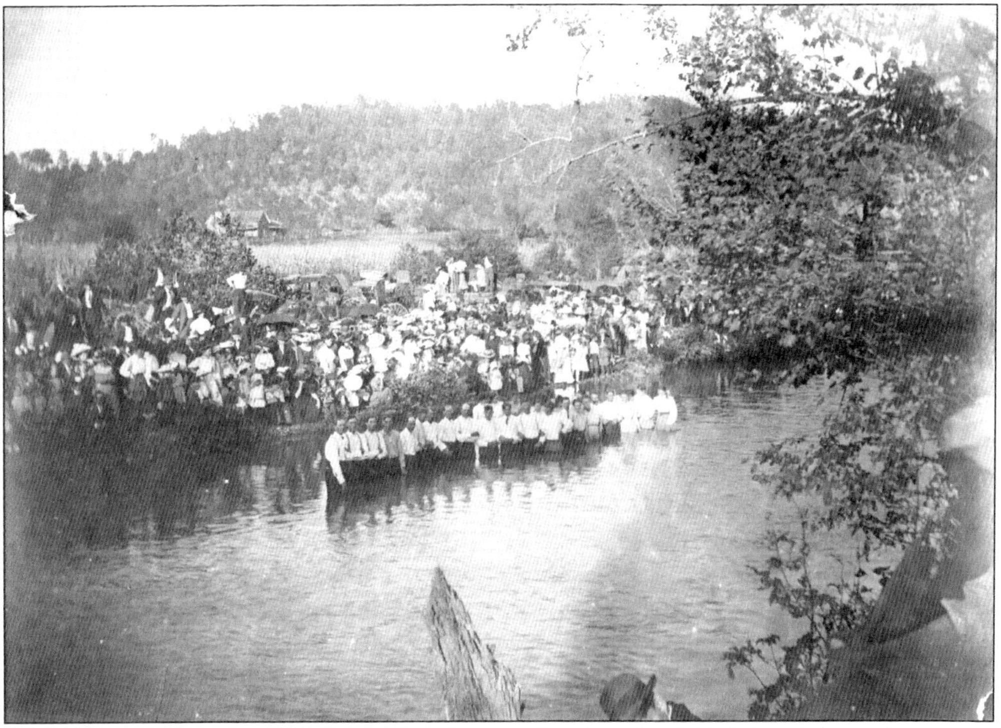

A baptism of about 30 people from Mt. Zion Baptist Church in Smith Fork Creek drew a large crowd around 1900. Located on Lower Helton between Temperance Hall and Alexandria, the church was established in 1851 as another arm of Salem Baptist Church. (Courtesy of Ron Paschal.)

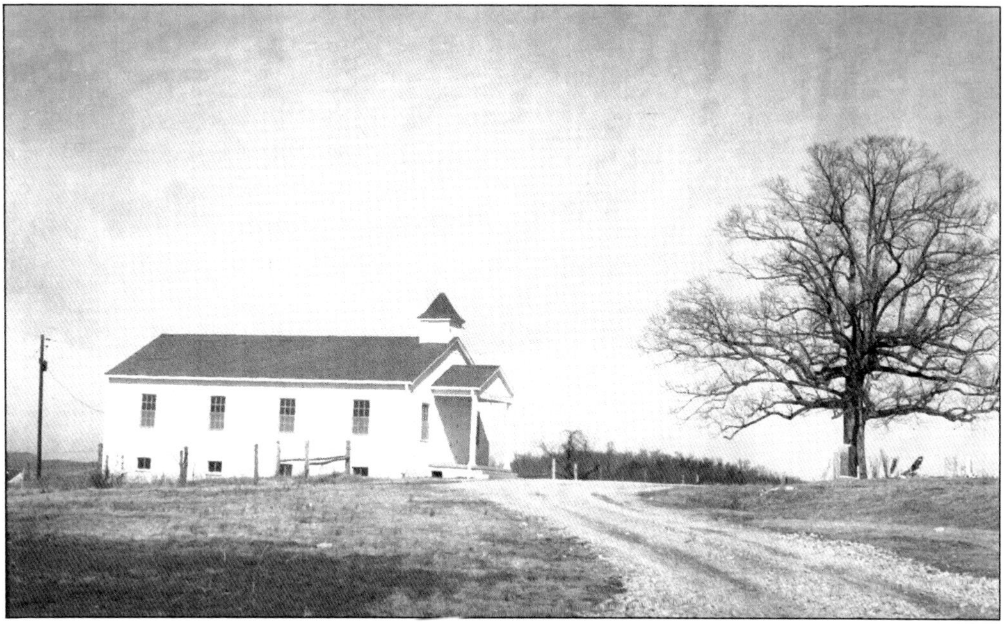

Located two miles east of Alexandria, New Hope Baptist Church was established in 1818 as an arm of Salem by William Dale, a younger brother of DeKalb County's first settler, Adam Dale. William Dale served as first pastor of this church until 1835. This church has been destroyed twice by tornados in 1928 and 1955. This photograph shows the church rebuilt after the last tornado. (Courtesy of Ria Baker.)

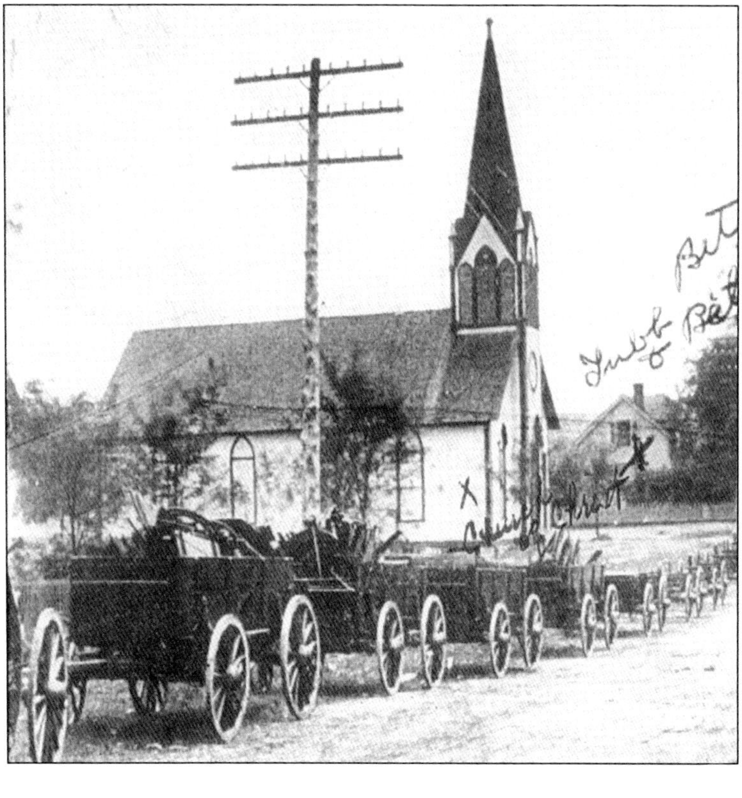

This church in Alexandria was the first Church of Christ in the county, formed in 1835. This building was constructed in 1858 on the turnpike where the present rock building was erected in 1935 after this building burned. The wagon train going by the church is from the Roy & Jones Buggy & Wagon Company, as they were transporting these wagons into town for sale. (Courtesy of Ria Baker.)

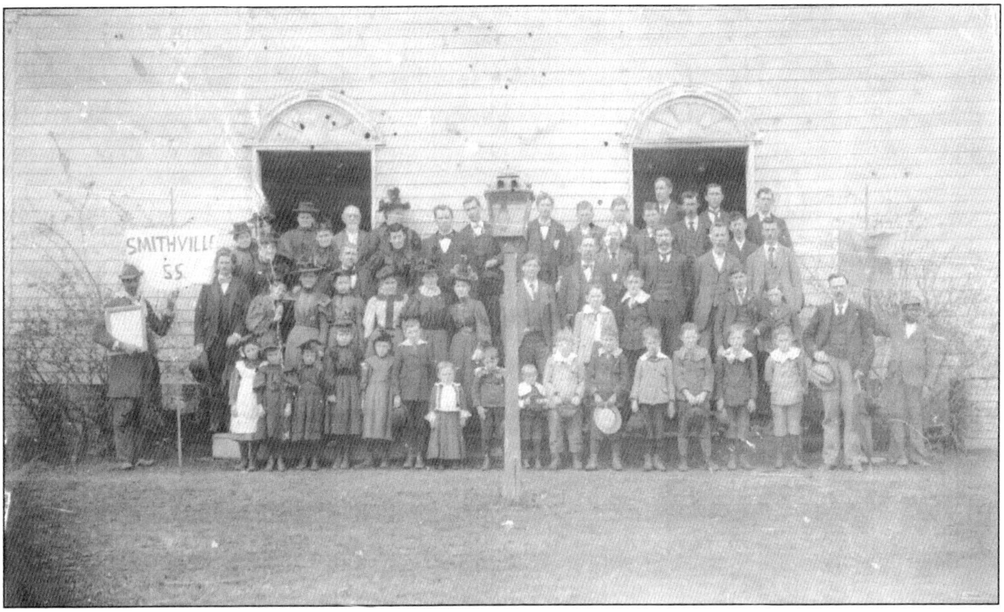

The first church of any kind to be established in Smithville was the Methodist Church in 1838. It was located on Fourth Street at that time. It was later moved to the present location where this large frame building was built after 1870. This picture shows a Sunday school group of 1901 in front of the church. (Courtesy of Justin Potter Library.)

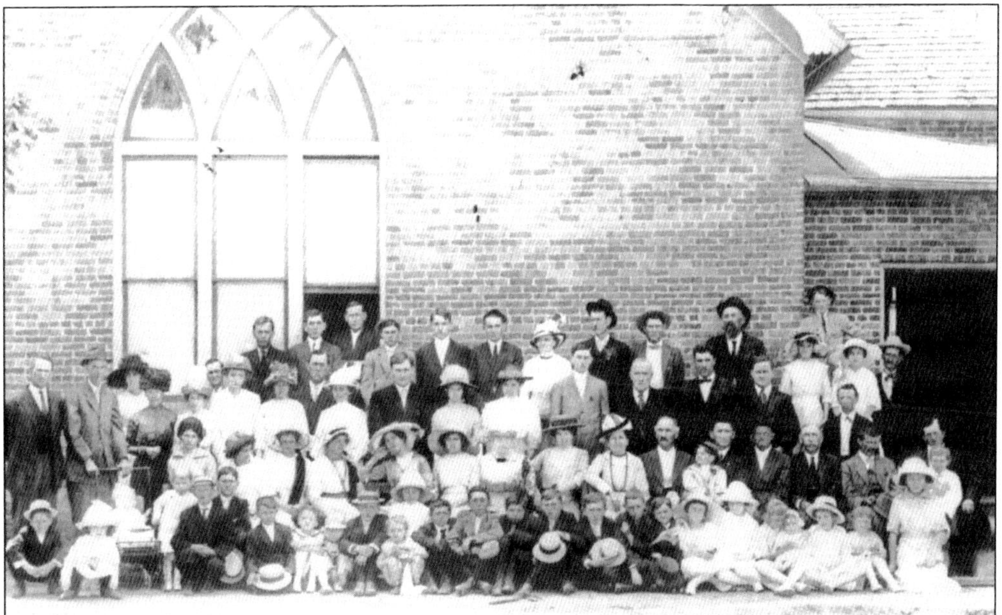

Here is the Smithville Church of Christ congregation on Easter Sunday 1912. This church was established in 1868 by Jeff Boles, Leo Boles, and J.M. Kidwell, who began by preaching in the courthouse. This building was erected in 1902, but as the congregation increased, they outgrew it and built a new one in 1971 on Dry Creek Road on the west side of Smithville. (Courtesy of Justin Potter Library.)

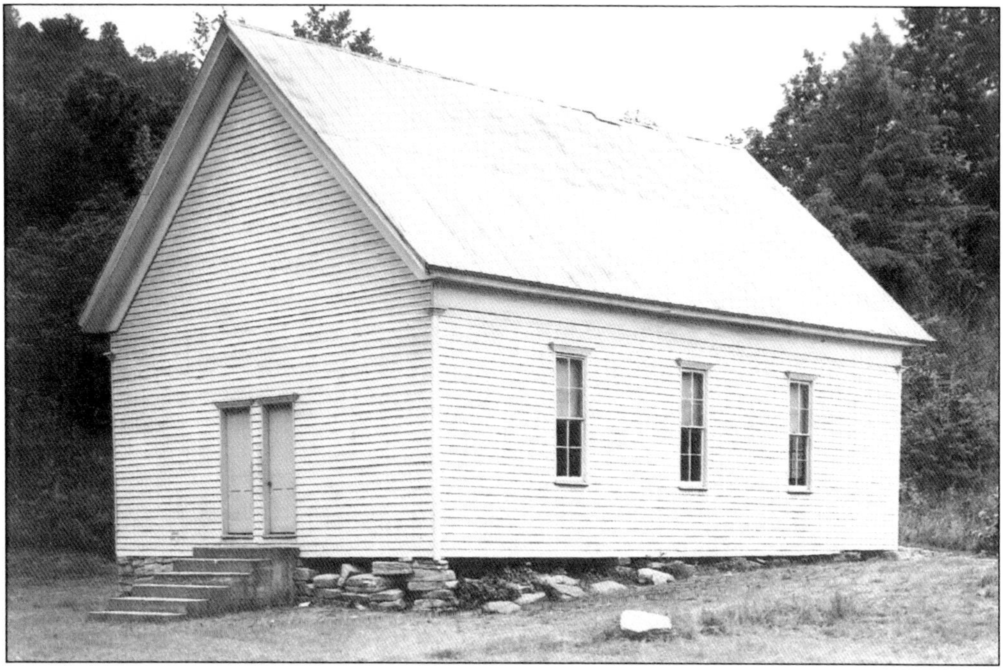

Indian Creek Baptist Church was also established in 1844 as an arm from Salem. For the first four years, it was called Caney Fork Church, but the name was later changed to Indian Creek. The first building was a log structure used for more than 50 years and later moved and used as a school. This building was erected around 1900 and was moved to Hurricane Ridge in 1947 when Center Hill Dam was built. It is now somewhat remodeled and known as Indian Creek Memorial Baptist Church. A group of people present for the last meeting in July 1946 is pictured below before the temporary disbanding because of the dam construction. The oil lamp hanging from the ceiling of the old church on the creek is now hanging in the new structure on Hurricane Ridge. (Both, courtesy of Sue Puckett-Jernigan.)

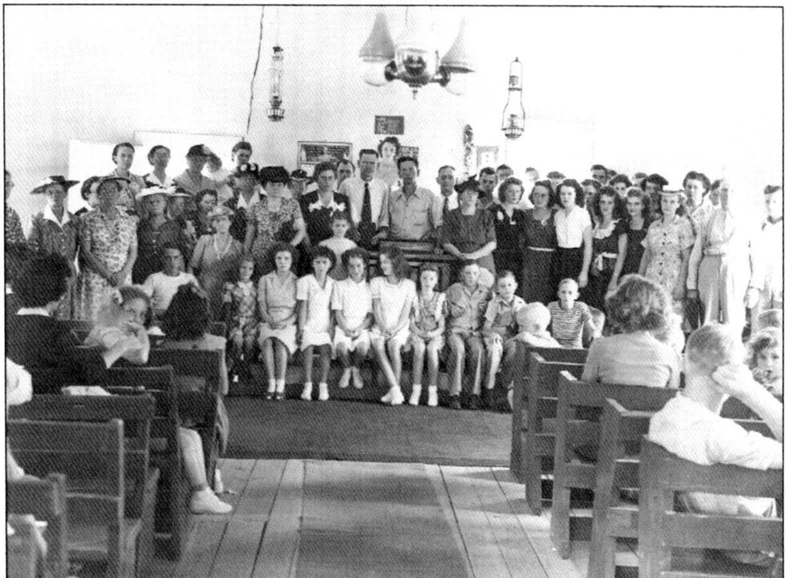

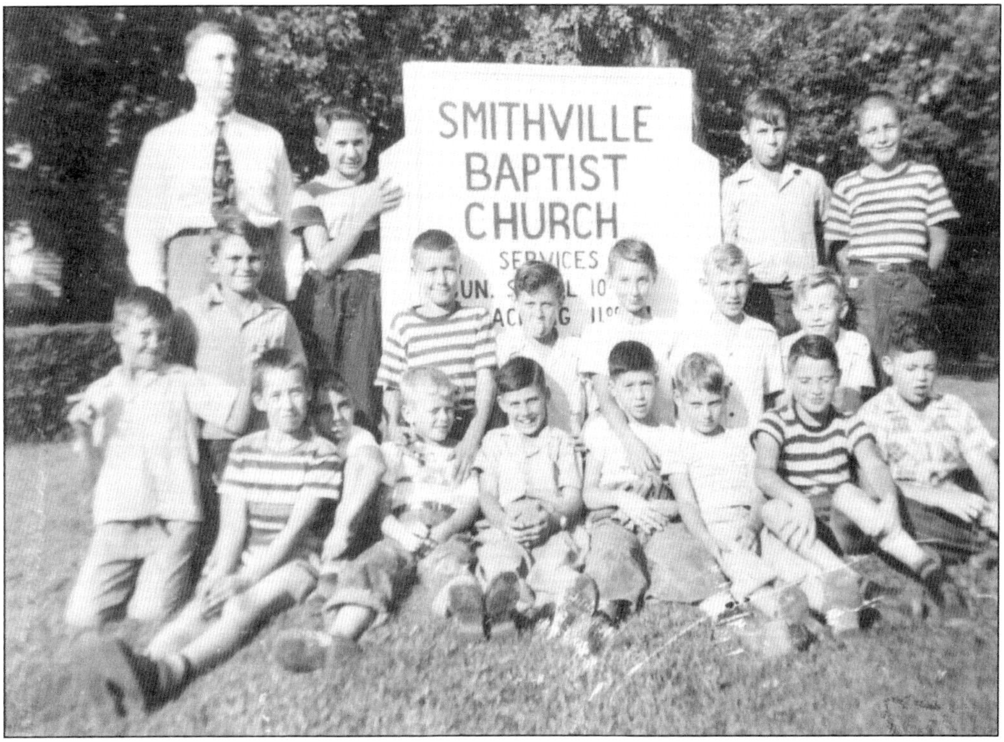

Here are the Royal Ambassadors with pastor D.W. Pickelsimer in 1949. They include, from left to right, (first row) unidentified, Nickie Roy Smith, Will Herman Smith Jr., Kenneth Moore, L.M. Murphy, Gaylor Pickelsimer, Dean Whitt, Bethel Thomas, and Carter Braswell; (second row) Boyd Malone, Jewel Murphy, Bobby Dale, Gordon Certain, W.J. Tramel, and Charles Dale; (third row) Brother Pickelsimer, Joe Mason, Joe Windham, and Billy Judd Murphy. (Courtesy of Marguerite Jones.)

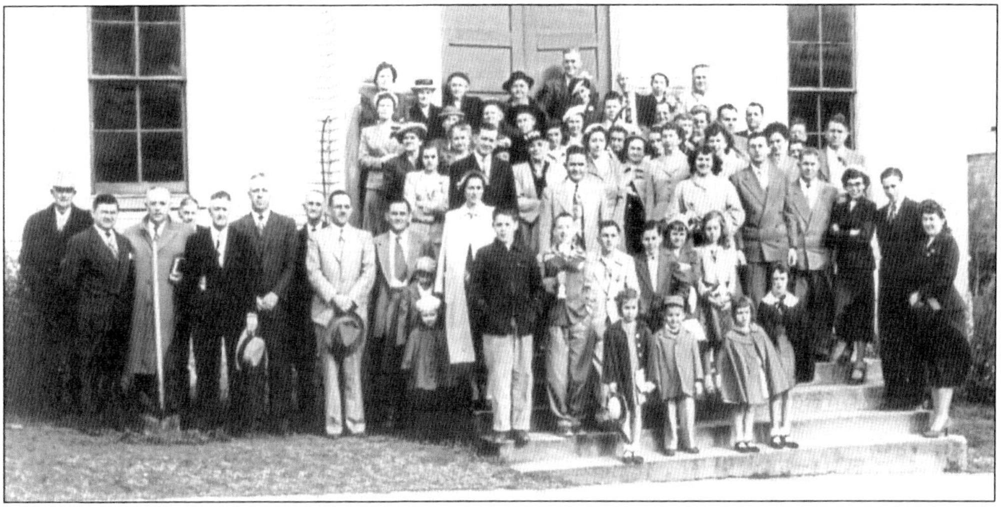

Smithville First Baptist Church was established in August 1844 by Methodist church elders John Bond, Archamac Bass, and Jesse Allen. The first house of worship was erected about 1858, and the building shown here was constructed in 1902. The congregation pictured here is participating in a ground breaking in March 1952 for the construction of the present-day church. (Courtesy of Justin Potter Library.)

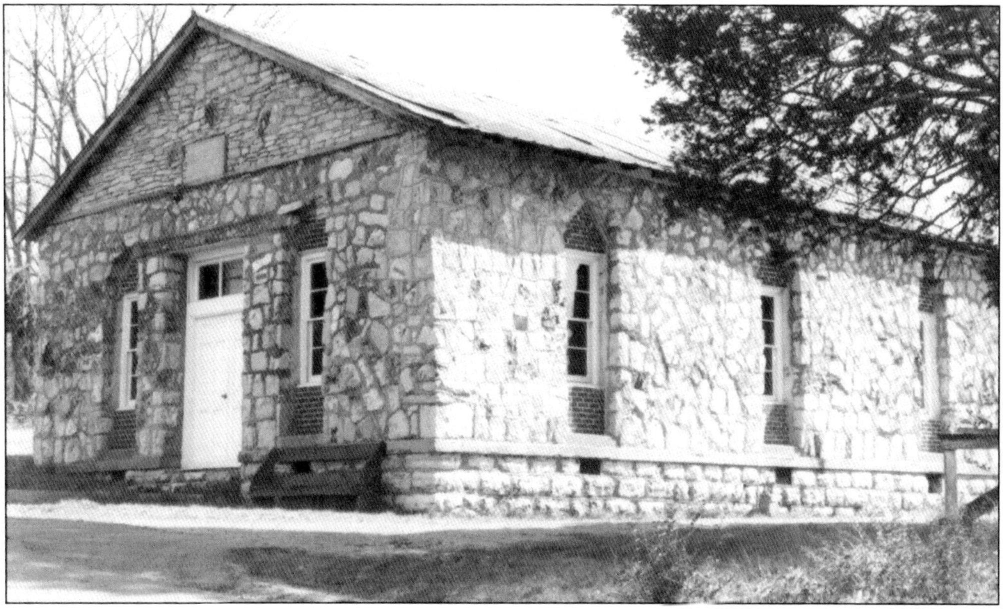

Seay's Chapel Methodist Church in Alexandria was the county's first black congregation, established just after the Civil War in 1869. Located at the end of Cemetery Street in Alexandria, this building is now owned by the city of Alexandria and used by another church. The original church burned around 1929 and was rebuilt in 1931, as seen here. (Courtesy of Thomas G. Webb.)

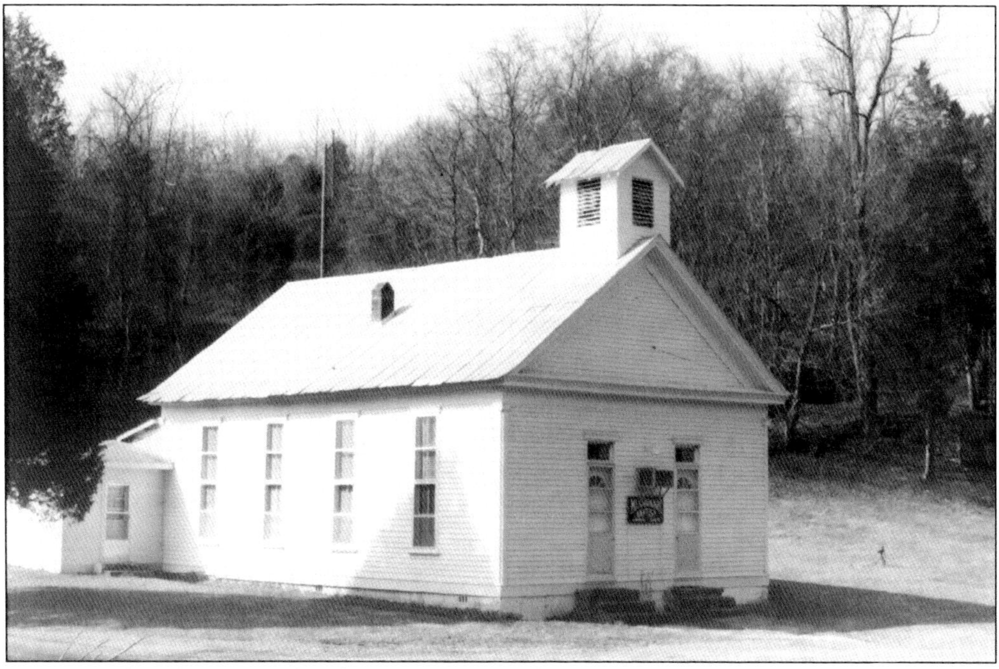

Cooper's Chapel Baptist Church on Dismal Creek north of Liberty was established in 1880 and named in honor of Methodist Isaac Cooper, who helped construct it and was eventually baptized into this church, becoming a faithful Baptist. This picture was taken in 1976 and shows the first addition to the original building made on the back side in 1965. (Courtesy of Thomas G. Webb.)

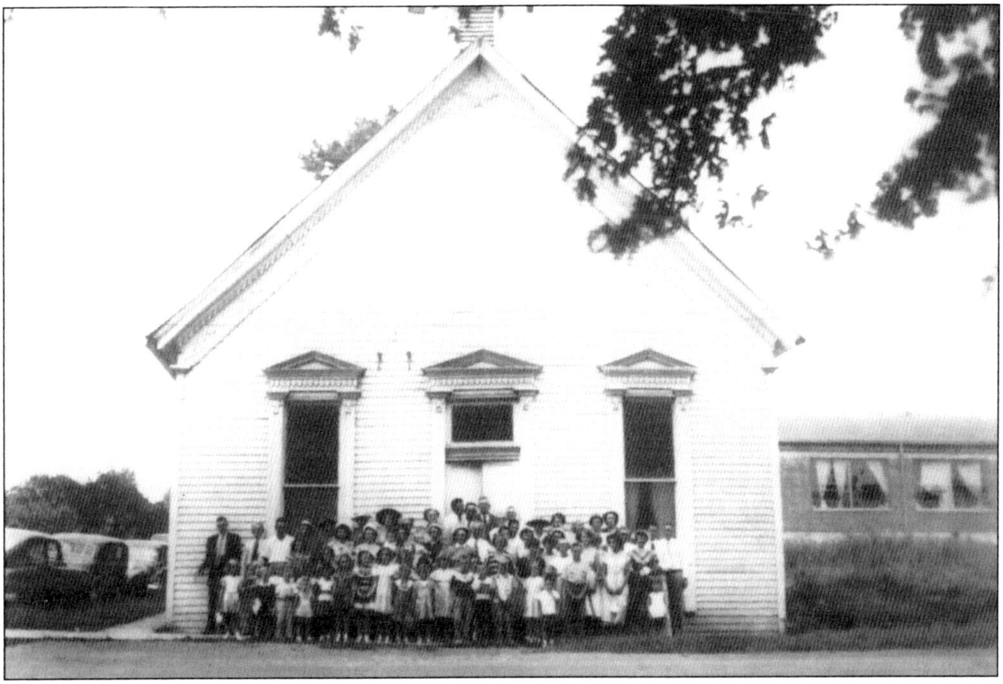

Above, the Smithville Cumberland Presbyterian Church stands with its congregation around 1951. This church was established in 1873 by Rev. Jesse Hickman, and a lot was purchased for $75 in 1879 on which the church building was completed in 1886. Below is a Vacation Bible School group of the Smithville Cumberland Presbyterian Church on May 31, 1946. Teachers Clara Jennings (left) and Rosa John Twilla (right) are standing at the sides of the children, and pastor Reverend Denning is standing in the fourth row, fourth from left. Some children identified are Bethel Thomas Jr. and David Foutch (sitting in the first row on the left), Linda Estes and Linda Hendrixson (second row, fifth and sixth from left) and Fay Johnson (second row, far right). (Above, courtesy of Justin Potter Library; below, courtesy of Denise Brown.)

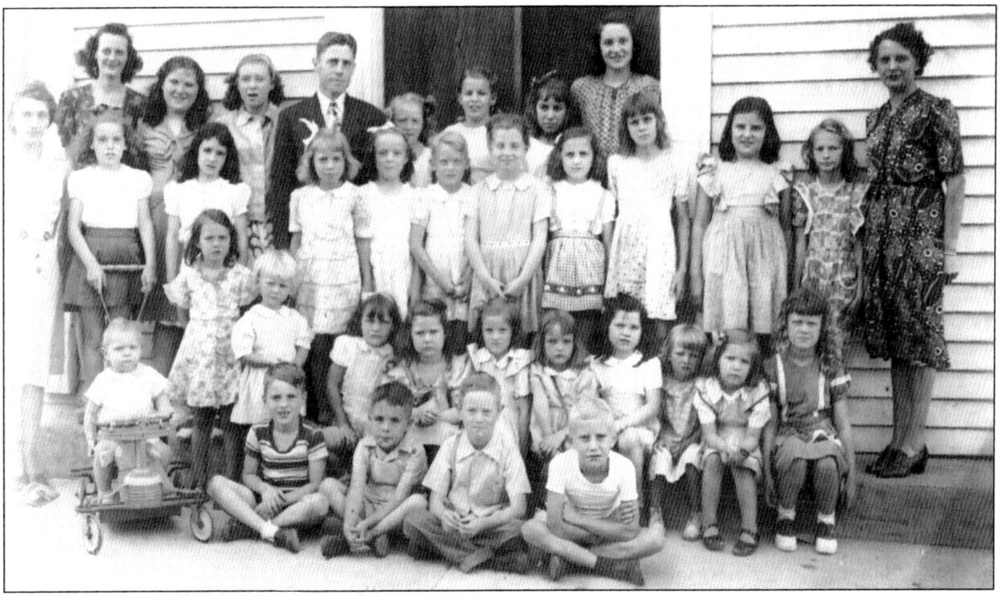

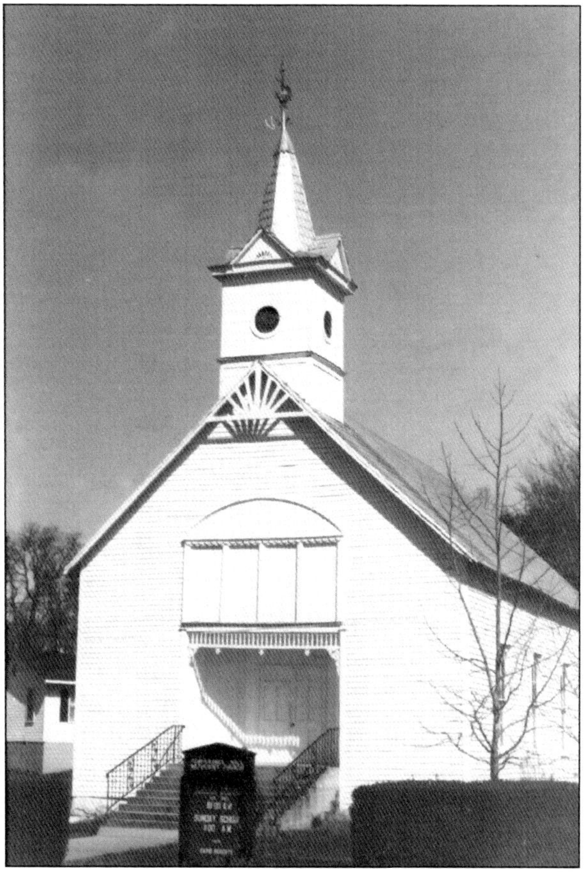

Temperance Hall Methodist Church was established in 1873. The original church building was of logs and was located on Cedar Hill just northeast of the present church. A new frame building was erected around 1890 and was later destroyed by fire. This beautiful old building was rebuilt at the same place after the fire and has remained in use for over 100 years. (Courtesy of Thomas G. Webb.)

The Dry Creek Baptist Church congregation is assembled at the creek in front of the church in 1902. This church was organized in 1886, and the building was erected in 1889 when the nearby Round Hill Church decided to combine with it. It was destroyed by a storm in 1928, rebuilt on a more convenient location, and was moved and rebuilt at the present location around 1950. (Courtesy of Louise Frazier.)

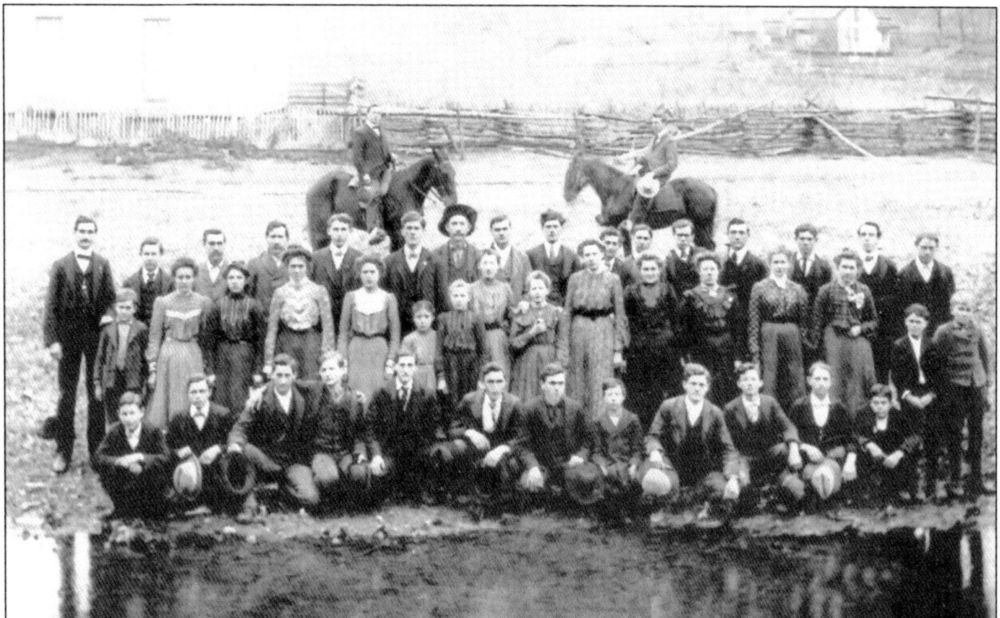

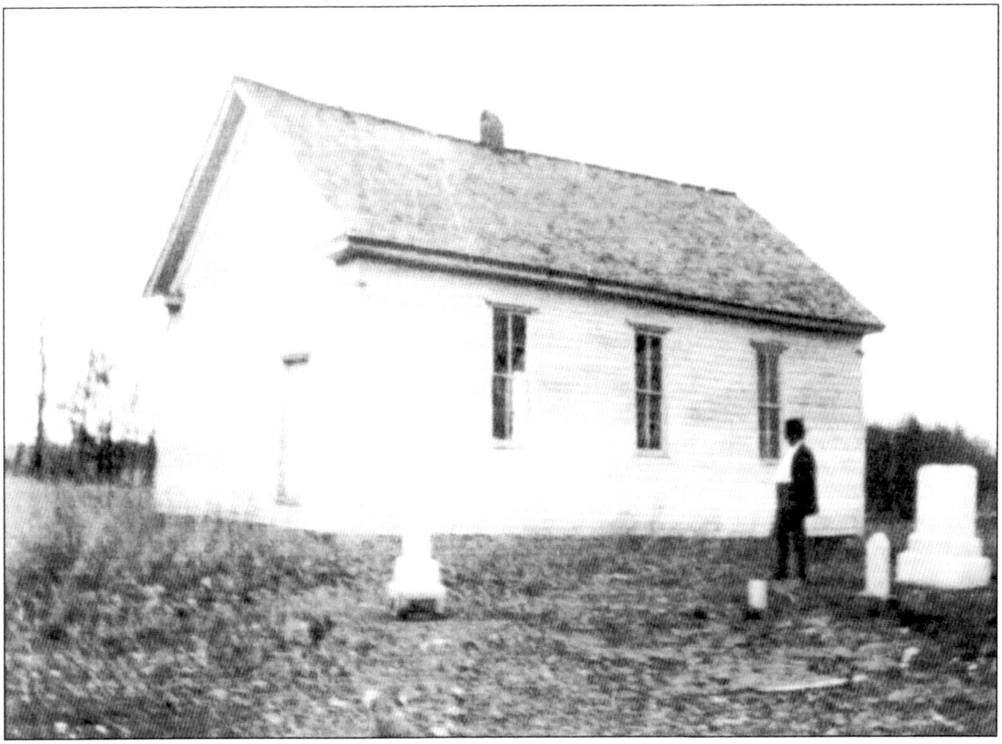

Above is the Snow Hill Methodist Church around 1918. Originally called Man Hill Methodist, this church was established in 1883 and located on Man Hill Road just off Snow's Hill. The name was changed to Snow Hill Methodist in 1893 when this new church was built and moved onto Snow's Hill after the old one had burned. Both sites were given by the Tom Haas family. Pictured below is the dedication of the new building of Snow Hill Methodist Church in April 1927; it was rebuilt at the present location after the old church building was torn down in October 1926. (Above, courtesy of Justin Potter Library; below, courtesy of Gwynn Hendrixson.)

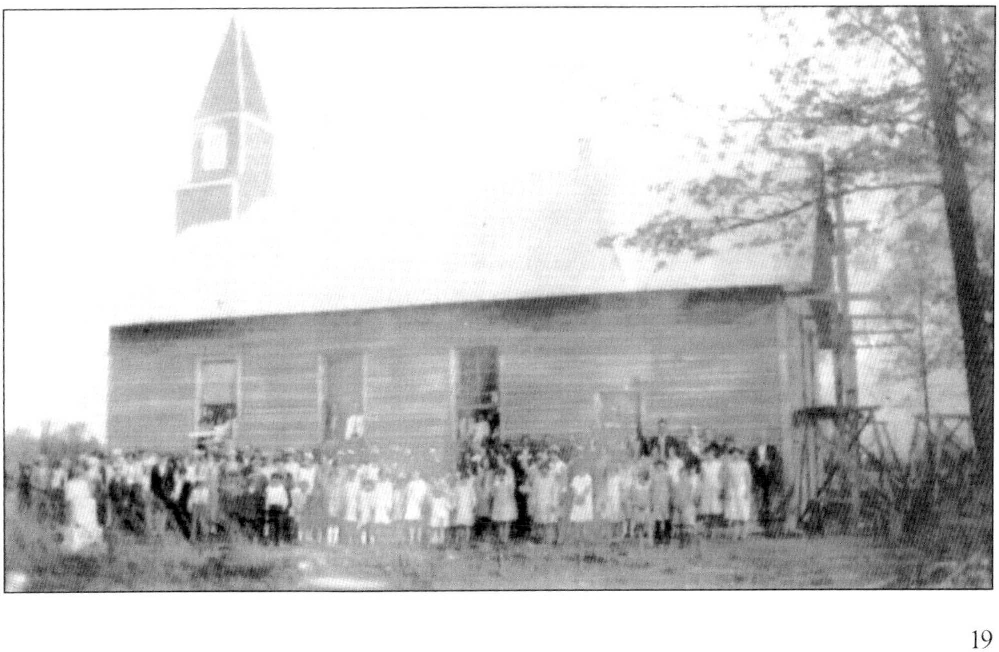

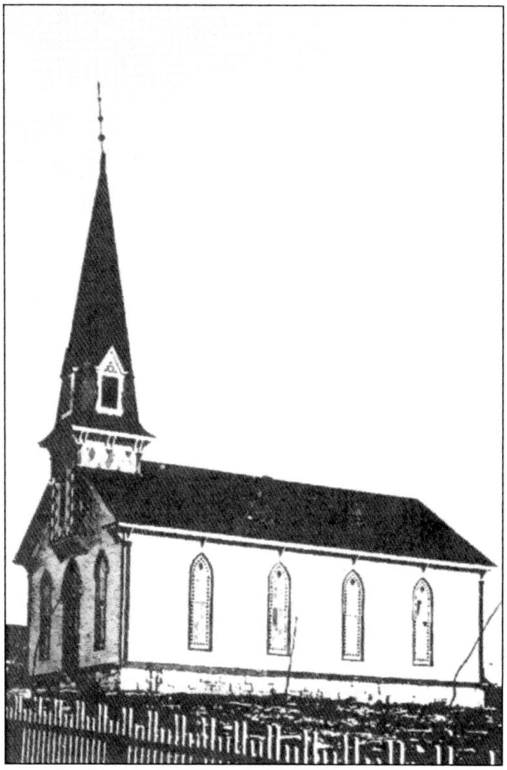

This postcard shows the Alexandria First Baptist Church, called "one of the neatest houses of worship in this entire section of country" by J.H. Grime in his *History of Middle Tennessee Baptists*. This church was established in January 1887 after a doctrinal debate between elder J.B. Moody, editor of the *Baptist Gleaner*, and Dr. T.W. Brents, a leader of the local Campbellites (Church of Christ). The town of Alexandria was mainly dominated by Methodists, Campbellites, and a few Presbyterians. The Cumberland Presbyterians offered the people who wanted to establish a Baptist church the use of their house of worship until they could construct a building. After the first beautiful church building of the Alexandria Baptists was struck by lightning and destroyed, the structure pictured below was erected in 1914 and stood until the present building was reconstructed around 1974. (Both, courtesy of Alexandria First Baptist Church.)

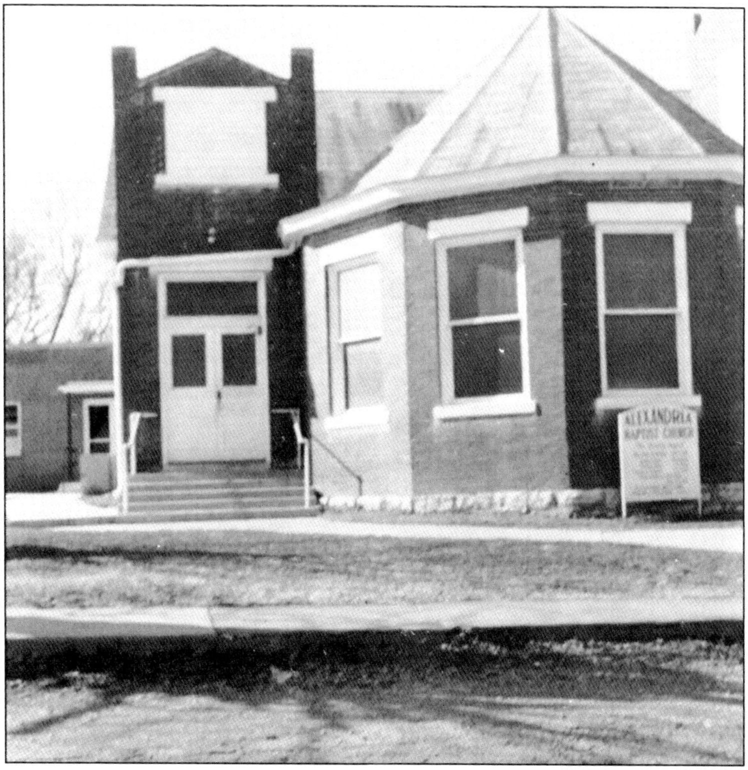

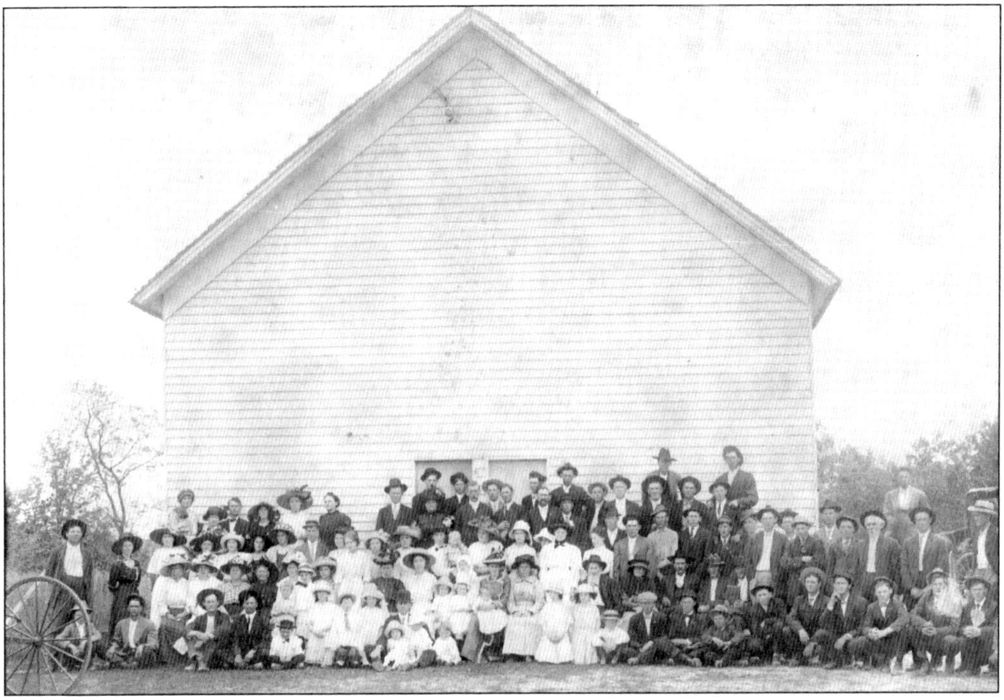

Pictured on May 4, 1913, the Snow Hill Baptist Church was established by Elders J.H. Davis, A.J. Waller, and D.C. Taylor in 1897. It was located in the Snow's Hill community about five miles west of Smithville. The charter members came from other nearby churches, most of which were in Indian Creek and Dry Creek. A.J. Waller was the first pastor; Rev. J.L. Mason is pictured here. (Courtesy of Judy Fuson.)

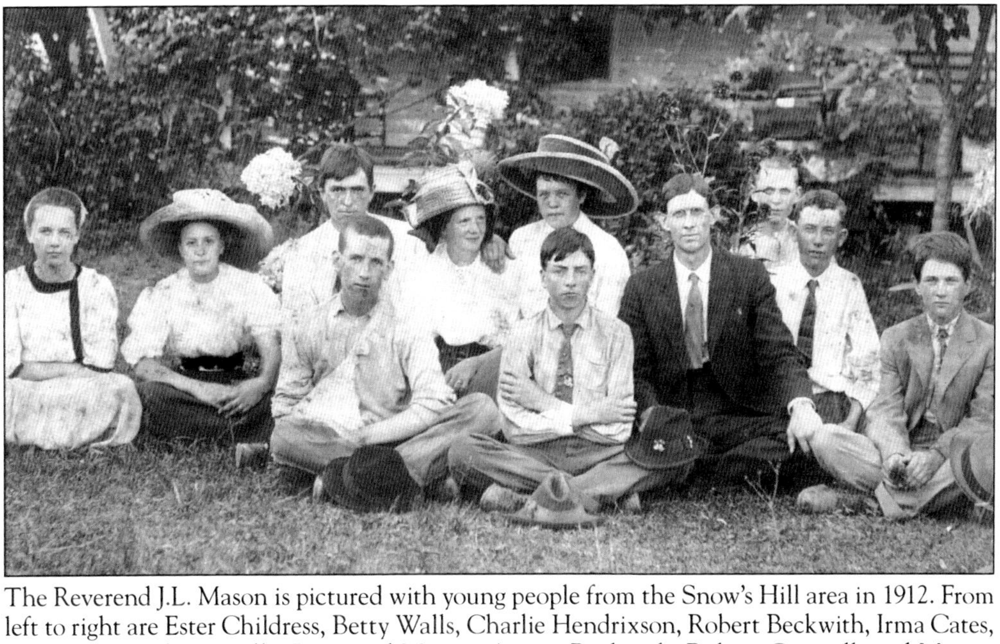

The Reverend J.L. Mason is pictured with young people from the Snow's Hill area in 1912. From left to right are Ester Childress, Betty Walls, Charlie Hendrixson, Robert Beckwith, Irma Cates, Pearl Keith, Falson Walls, Reverend Mason, Anson Beckwith, Robert Cantrell, and Martin Taylor. (Courtesy of Judy Fuson.)

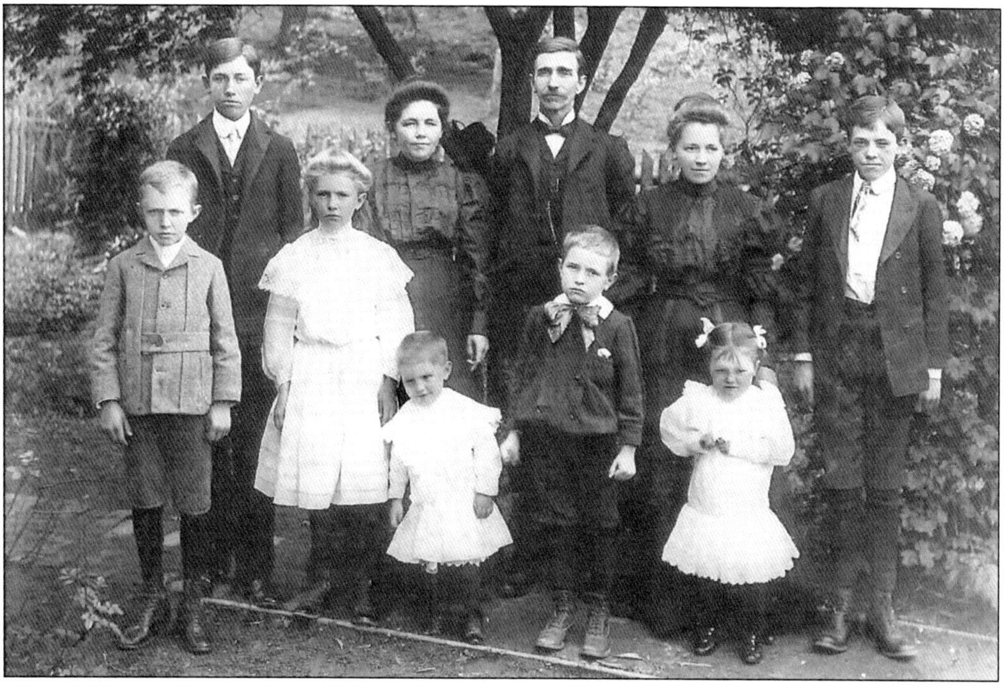

Rev. W.P. Banks, a Methodist preacher in this county in the early 1900s, is pictured with his family. Banks was a circuit pastor in the area for 16 years before he retired because of bad health. He died in 1914 at the age of 57. (Courtesy of Tom Simpson.)

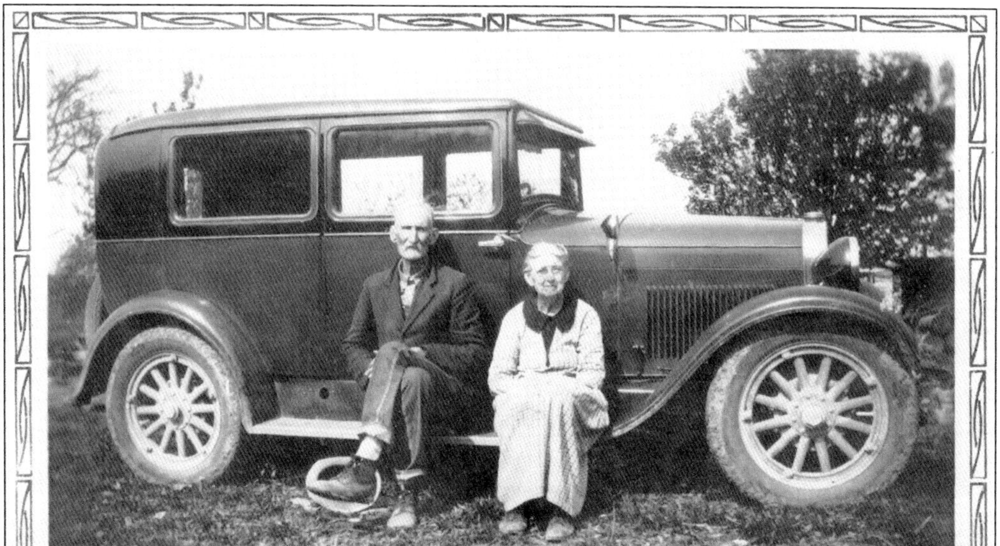

Reverend Steven and his wife, Laura Fuson Robinson, are sitting on the step board of a son-in-law's car in April 1932. His own mode of transportation was always horse and buggy. This couple was married in 1883 and had 17 children. He was called to preach and later ordained by Cooper's Chapel Baptist Church in 1897, pastored churches, and helped establish Cave Springs and Elizabeth Chapel. (Courtesy of Robert Robinson.)

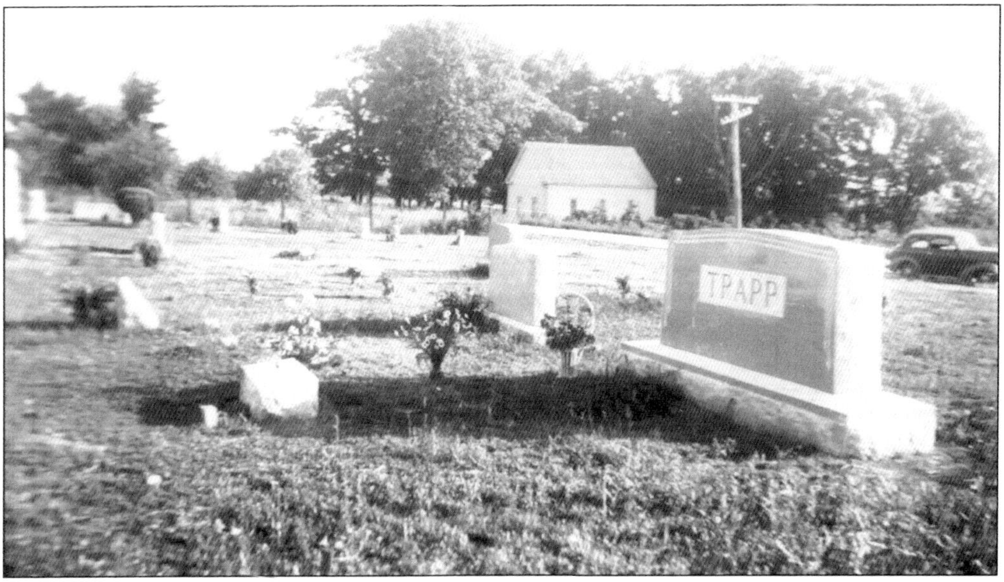

This is the early part of the Whorton Spring Cemetery, which was started in 1929, with the Whorton Spring Baptist Church in the background. This church was organized in 1889, and this building was completed in 1904 and used until a brick building was erected in 1956. (Courtesy of Carol Williams.)

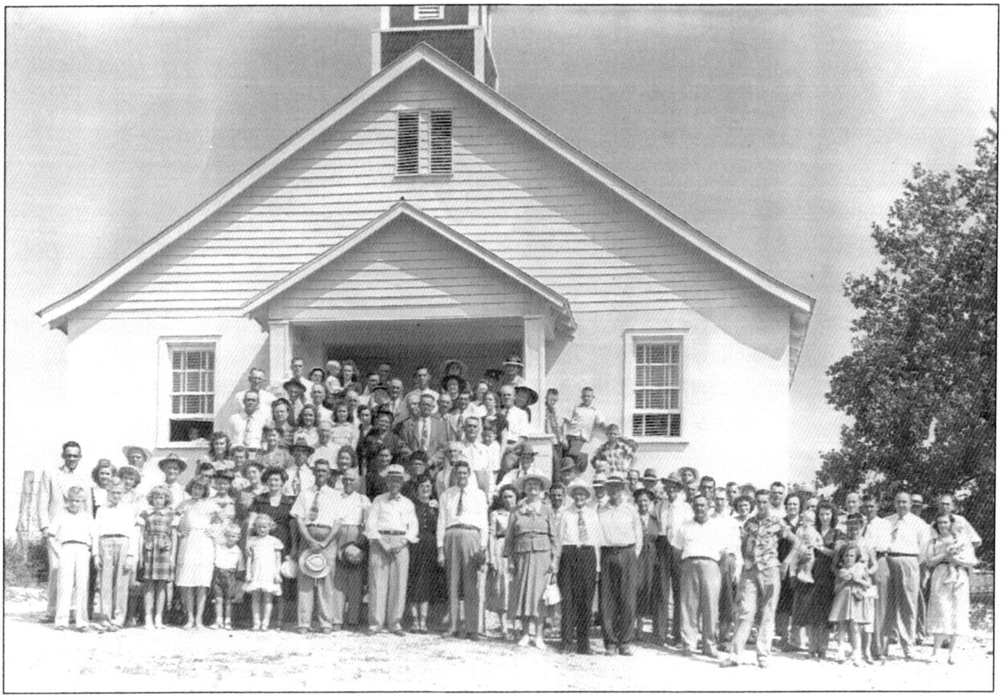

The Dale Ridge Chapel Baptist Church's new building is pictured at the dedication in 1951. Starting as a community church with both Methodists and Baptists attending, the church was organized on June 5, 1949, after the Baptist participants outvoted the Methodists. It was moved off the hill to another location on the same road in 1990 and renamed Memorial Missionary Baptist Church. (Courtesy of Sue Puckett-Jernigan.)

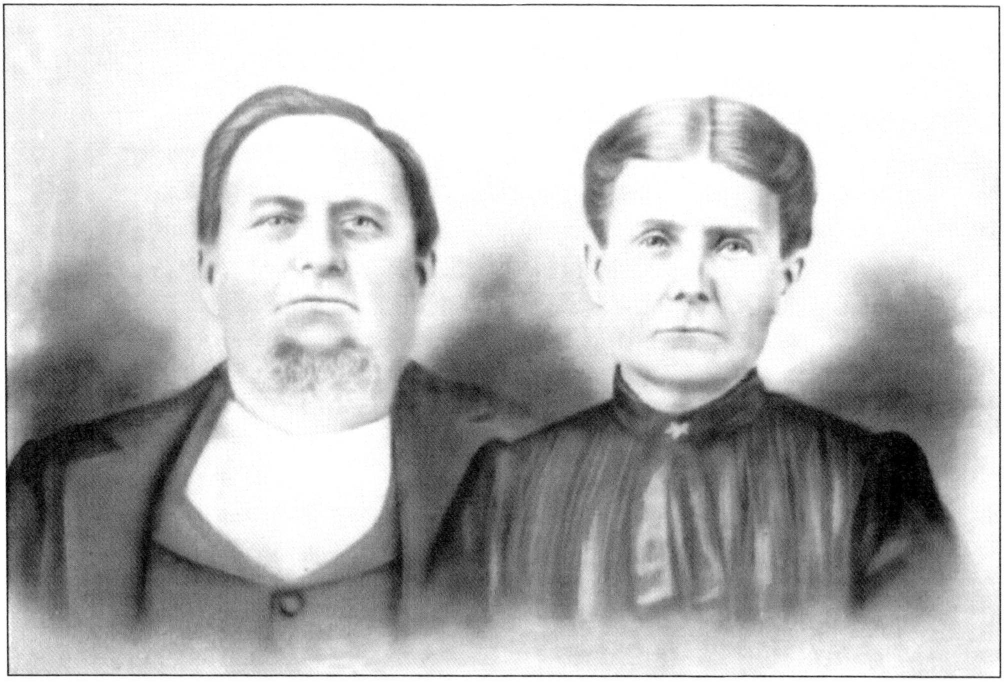

Elizabeth Jane Taylor's family provided land for a church to be built on Holmes' Creek in 1901. The church was then named in honor of her as Elizabeth Chapel Baptist Church. Pictured above are Elizabeth and her husband, David J. Taylor. The church was disbanded in 1947 when Center Hill Lake was being formed but was reorganized and rebuilt just north of Smithville in 1952. Below is a picture of the congregation present for the dedication of the new Elizabeth Chapel Baptist Church. Many upgrades and additions have been made in this church since that time, and it is still in operation with many more members. (Both, courtesy of Ophel Page.)

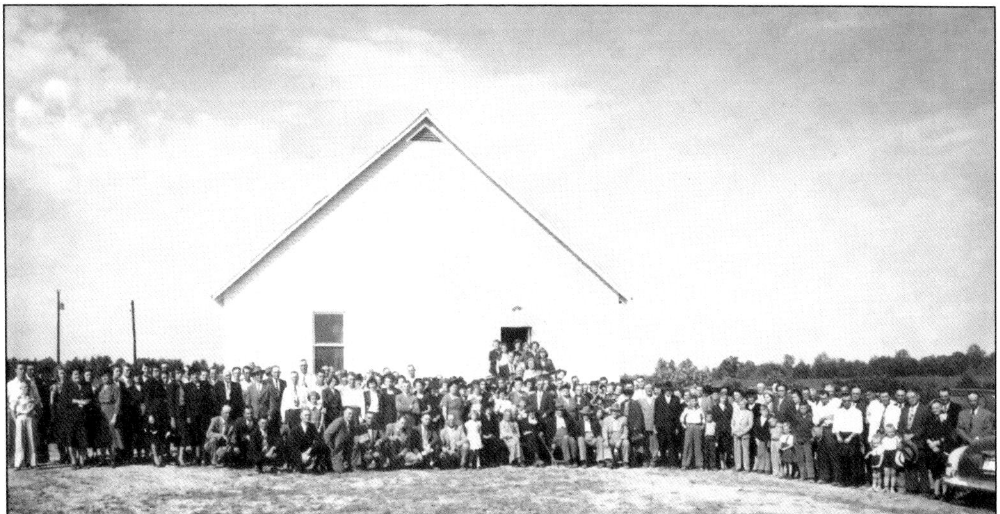

Two

Reading, 'Riting, 'Rithmetic, and Recess

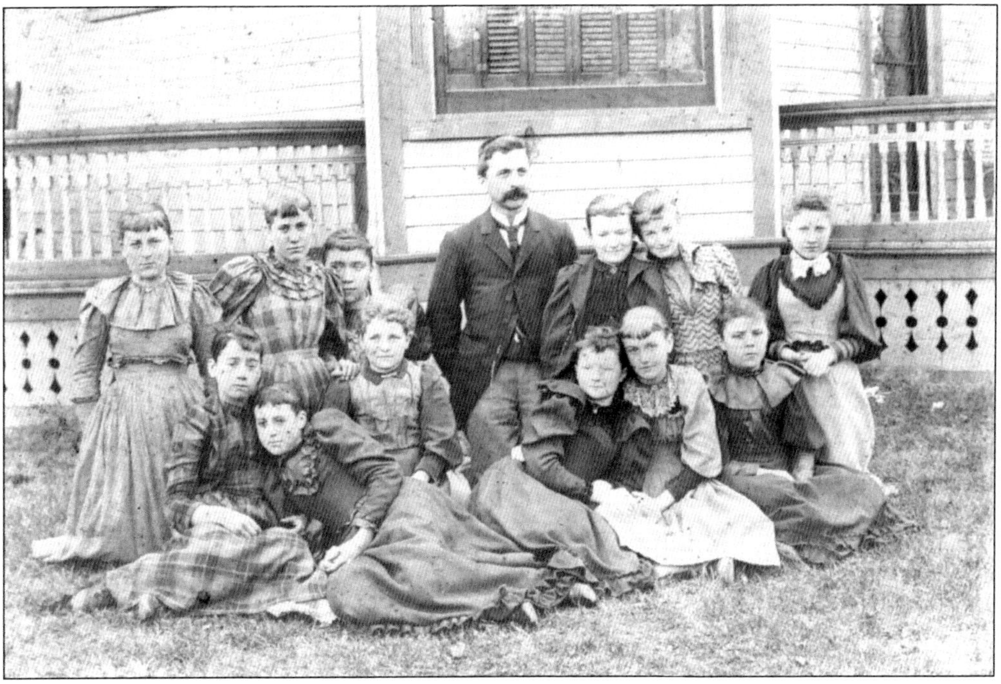

Shortly before the Civil War began, two female academies were established in the county, one in Alexandria and another in Smithville. These young ladies were known as the "Girls of Alexandria" and attended the Alexandria Female Academy in the 1880s. There is no documentation of the exact closing date, but it was still in use in the late 1890s. (Courtesy of Bill and Sue Corley.)

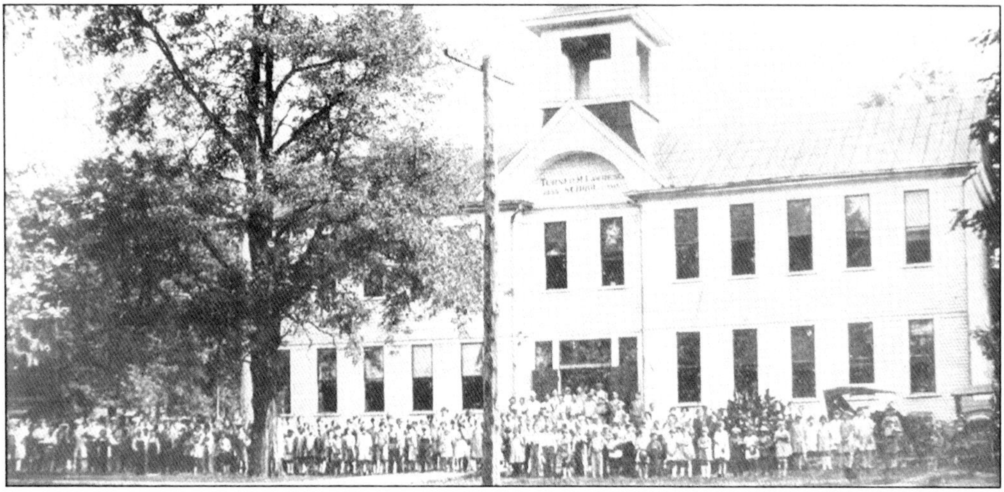

Turner M. Lawrence School was founded in 1856. The photograph above was made in 1939 when there were 223 students enrolled. Below, in front of the T.M. Lawrence High School in 1921 are the following students from left to right: (first row) Marlon Ford, Lunsford Reeves, Marvin Nixon, Wayne Tarpley, Haskel Foutch, Robert Lester, Phillip Walker, Turney Evans, and J.D. Martin; (second row) Julie Rollins, Laurine Hearn, Clemmie Foutch, Ella Buterbaugh, Avo Vandergriff, Frances Henley, Ruth Stark, Lanna Mai Oakley, Elizabeth McMillen, Ida May Huffman, and Elendar Marler; (third row) Janet Bone, Bernice Neal, Virginia Lester, Astra Belle Stark, Mary Robinson, Elizabeth Rutland, Lottie Garrison, Zelma Dinkins, Alberta Highers, and Monte Lee Sneed; (fourth row) Johnnie Curtis, James McMillen, Phocian Wright, Campbell Davis, Mr. Lumley (teacher), Alton McMillen, Clyde Sampson, Truman Stark, Grace Davis, and Miss Mina Lumley (teacher). (Both, courtesy of Ria Baker.)

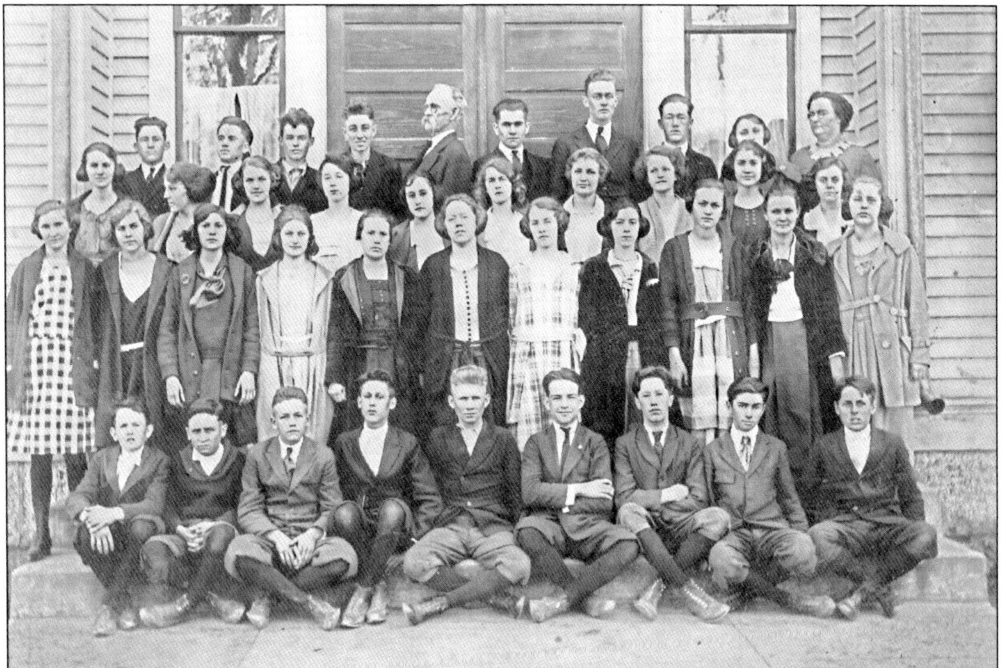

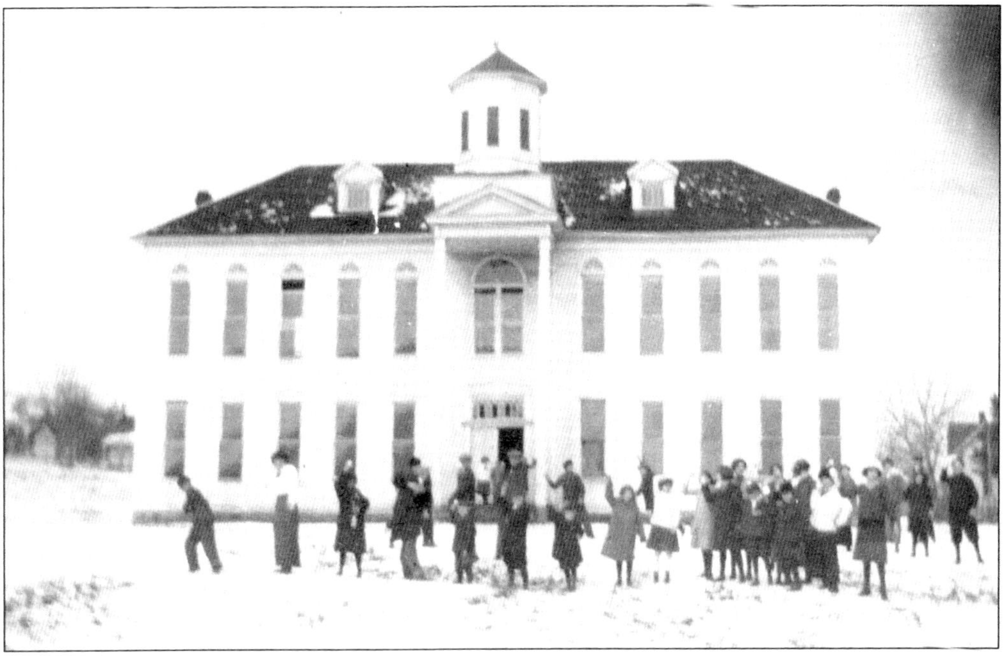

After a fire destroyed the first building, this rebuilt, bigger-and-better Liberty Masonic Academy in Liberty was recorded to have about 100 pupils in the late 1890s. Tuition to attend was $1–$2.75 per month, depending on grade level. The picture above was taken on a snowy day in 1917. Below, these unidentified teens, posing on the Liberty Academy School steps, are enjoying a Coca-Cola. Coke used the amber bottle with the paper label shown here in the very early 1900s. (Both, courtesy of Liberty Historic Group.)

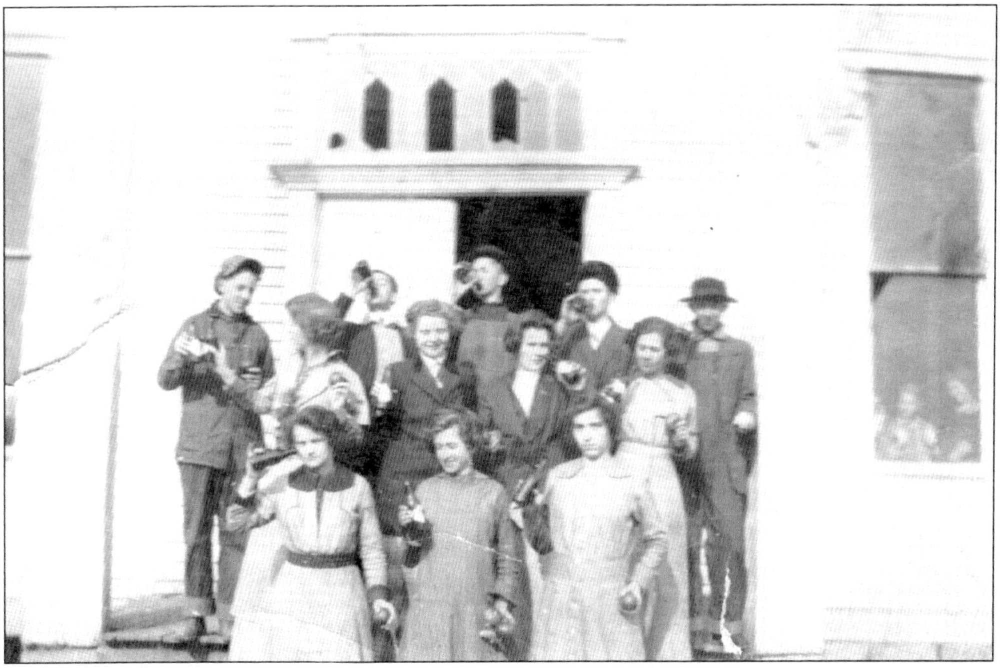

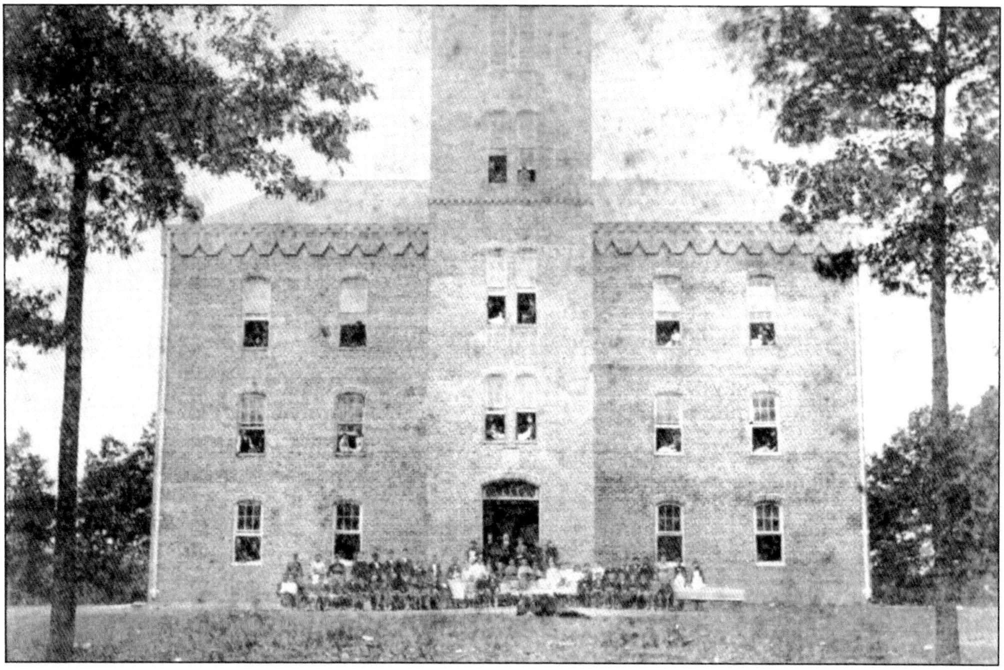

Pure Fountain College in Smithville was built of brick in 1883. It stood three stories tall with a five-story tower and was expected to be a "pure fountain of knowledge," thus its name. Tuition was $5 per month per pupil. The first year, the school had 200 pupils, including the primary grades. This building burned in 1898. (Courtesy of Justin Potter Library.)

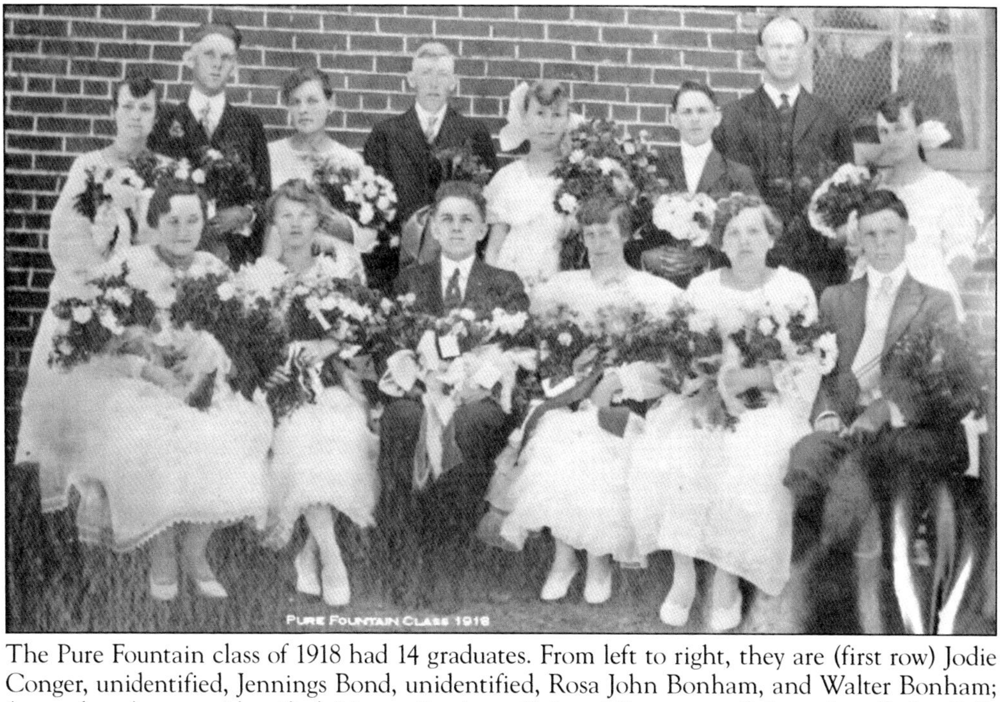

The Pure Fountain class of 1918 had 14 graduates. From left to right, they are (first row) Jodie Conger, unidentified, Jennings Bond, unidentified, Rosa John Bonham, and Walter Bonham; (second row) two unidentified, Macon Bonham, Robert Thompson, Calysta Atwell, Joe Bell, G.U. Edmonson (principal), and unidentified. (Courtesy of Justin Potter Library.)

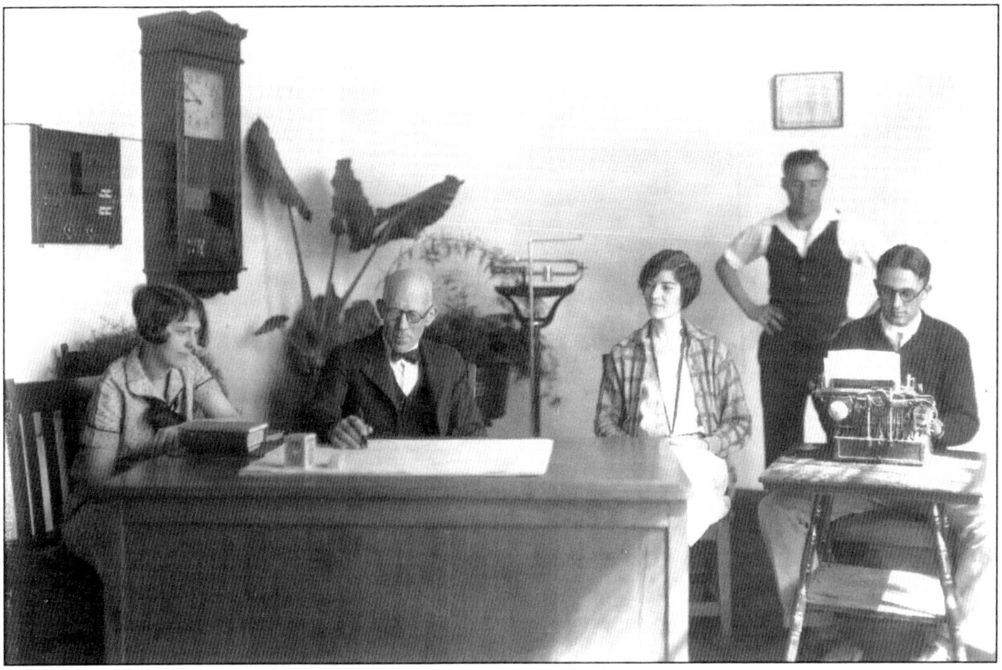

The picture above was taken inside the Smithville High School office about 1930. Z.P. Beachboard (seated at the desk) was principal at that time. Below, the cast of young actors at the high school in Smithville is posing for the camera in 1928. They include, from left to right, (first row) Gladys Gray, James Ford, and Mamie Hendon; (second row, sitting) Ana Louise Beachboard, unidentified, and Mary Hooper; (third row, standing) two unidentified, Joe L. Evins, Royce Givens, unidentified, John Robinson, Phillip Turner, T.J. Potter, and unidentified. (Both, courtesy of Justin Potter Library.)

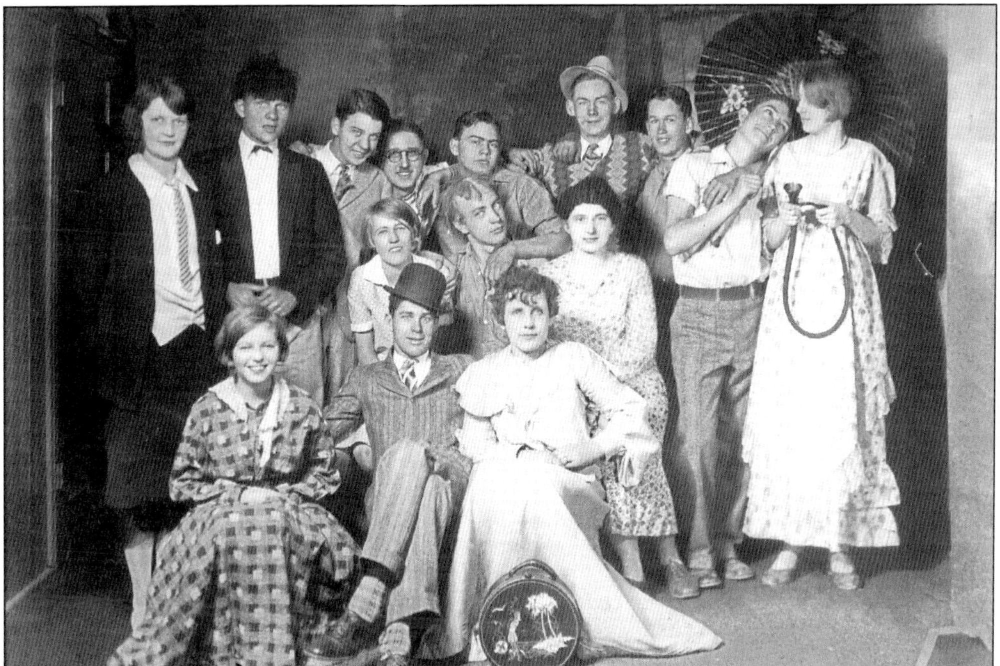

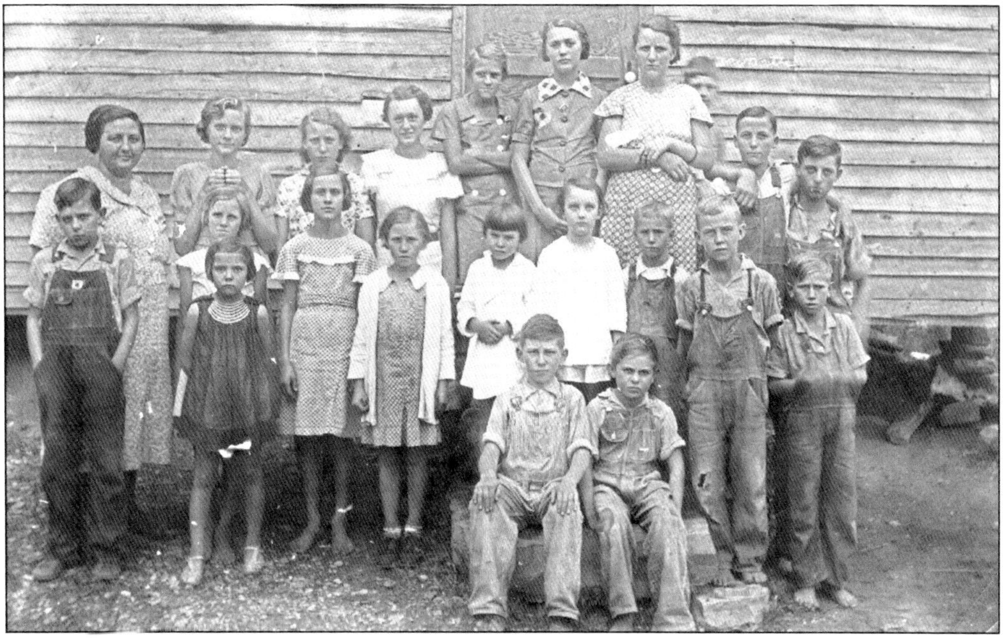

The Cave Springs School was located at the head of Indian Creek. The students pictured here in 1936 are, from left to right, (first row) Cliea Robinson and Carl Turner; (second row) Pete Parker, Billie Sue Tramel, Jo Close (in front of Billie), Francis Vanatta, Ruth Robinson, Claudia Robinson, Bobbie Jewel Spencer, Eugene Vanatta, J.C. "Buck" Vanatta, and Hoyte Close; (third row) Flora Thompson (teacher), Roberta Turner, Audrey Taylor, Verla Spencer, Druse Close, Retha Spencer, Freda Page, Charles Page, James Tramel, and Clyde Turner. (Courtesy of Geraldine Cook.)

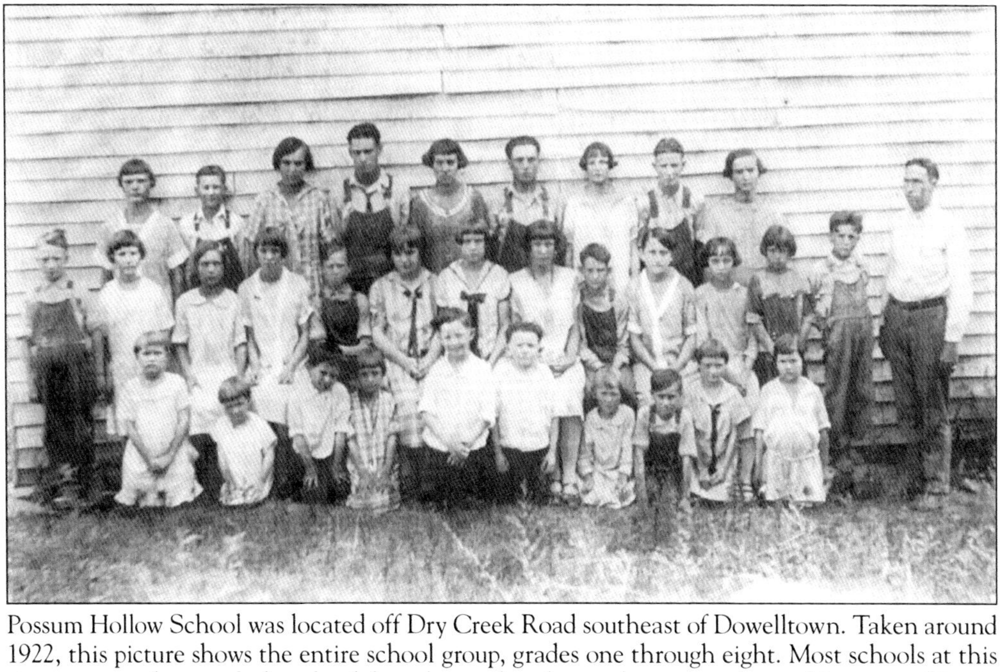

Possum Hollow School was located off Dry Creek Road southeast of Dowelltown. Taken around 1922, this picture shows the entire school group, grades one through eight. Most schools at this time were used not only for school, but also as churches and meeting places. (Courtesy of Justin Potter Library.)

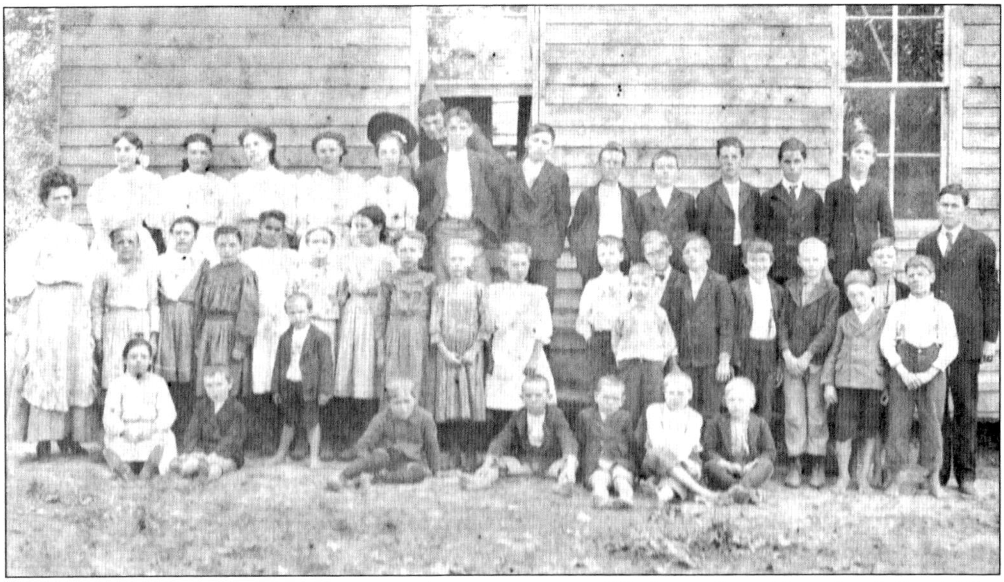

The Crossroads School in 1905 was near the intersection of Highway 83 and Dry Creek Road. The students include, from left to right, (first row) Harzonia Keith, Willie Alexander, Tom Ervin, Jim Keith, Morgan Keith, Harvie Braswell, and Arthur Robinson; (second row) Altie Evins (teacher), Sarah Keith, Betty Walls, Amanda Patton, Della Ervin, Betty Alexander, Basel Alexander (in front of Betty), Pearl Keith, Noveila Braswell, Lela Braswell, Cora Ervin, Thurston Walls, Jim Walls, Everett Beckwith, Isaac Keith, William Cantrell, Olmer Stanley, Anson Beckwith, Clay Clayborn, George Braswell, and teacher Ceasar Webb; (third row) Carrie Mullican, Hattie Robinson, Daisy Ervin, Lula Ervin, Emily Beckwith, Burchard Jones (inside at window with dunce cap on), John Taylor, Bob Keith, Robert Cantrell, Johnnie Alexander, Robert Beckwith, Willie Beckwith, and Riley Walden. (Courtesy of Judy Fuson.)

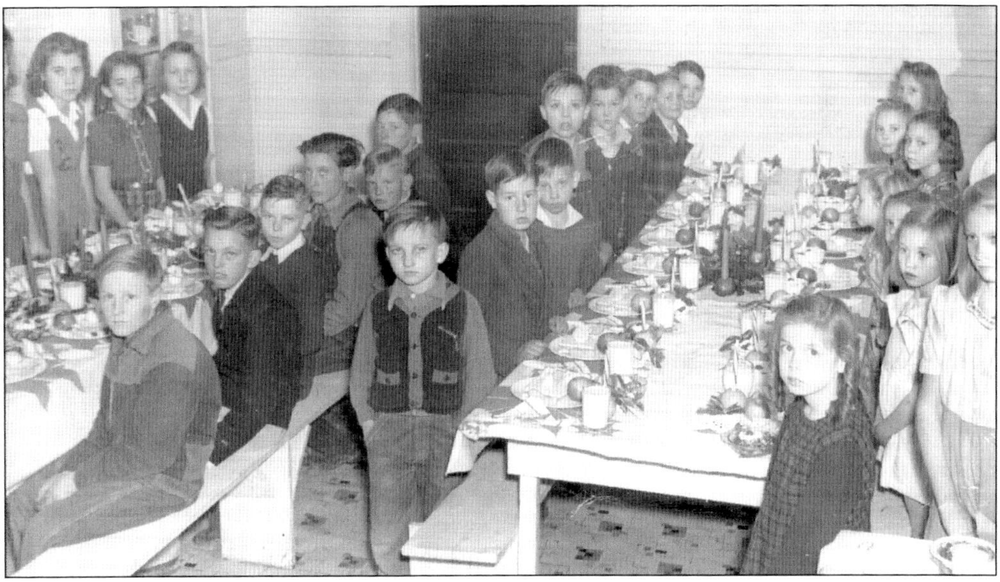

The Blue Springs School children shown here with their best clothes and manners had Christmas dinner provided by Save the Children Federation (SCF). Notice the tables set with tablecloths, napkins, and glassware. (Courtesy of Justin Potter Library.)

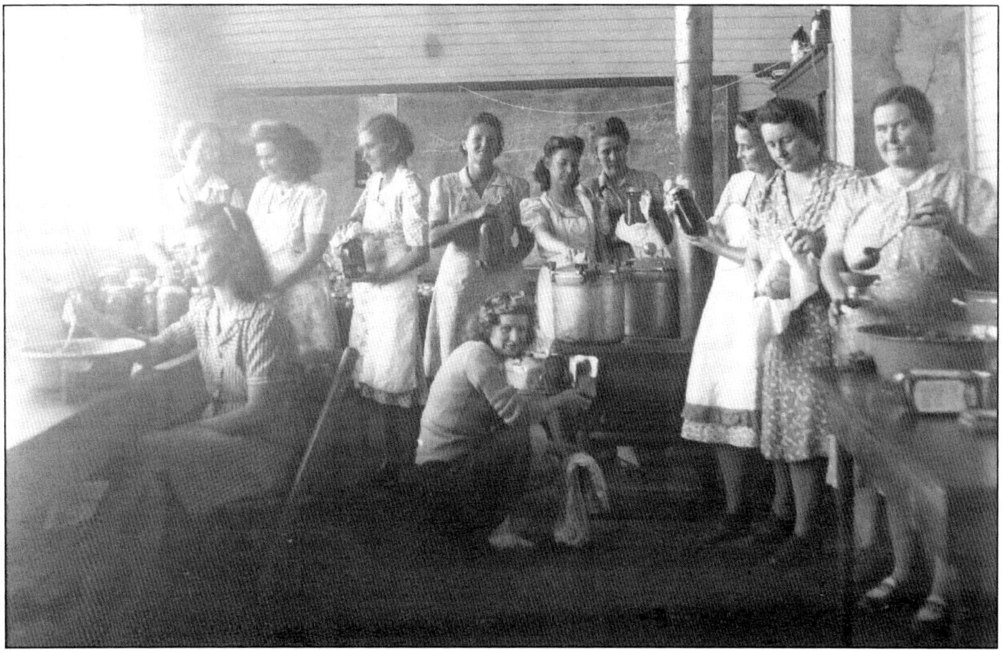

The SCF also sponsored canning for children's lunches. Around 1945, mothers of Keltonburg School children shown here volunteered their time and efforts to can food grown in the school garden. They canned 900 quarts of food and grew 40 bushels of potatoes in the school garden. (Courtesy of Justin Potter Library.)

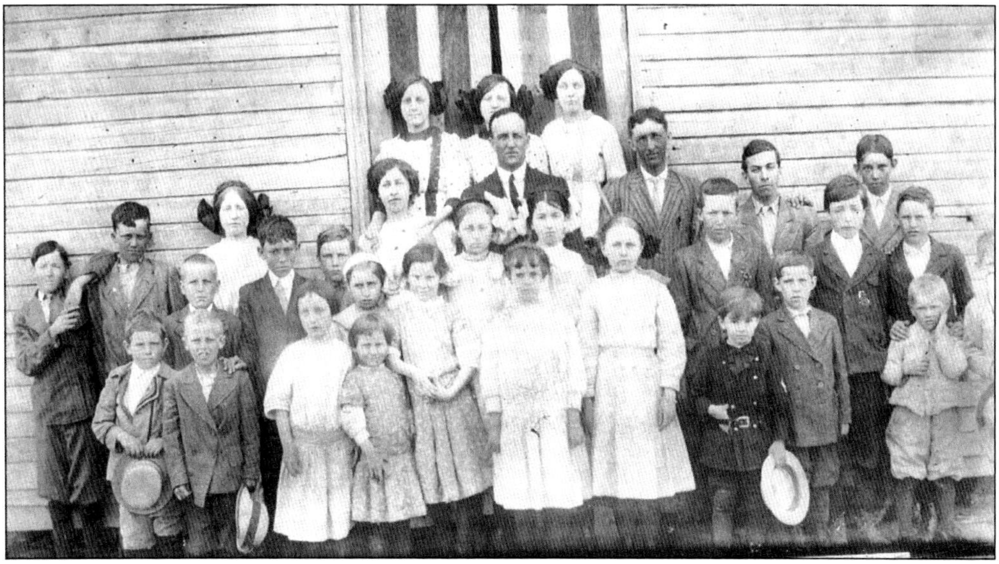

Pictured in about 1912, Four Corners School was located at Forks of the Pike near the present intersection of Highways 96 and 70. Pictured from left to right are (first row) two unidentified, Maude Groom, Robbie Hicks, ? Groom, ? Groom, Monte Lee Henley, Turney Evans, unidentified, Gilmore Campbell, and John Campbell; (second row) Paul Groom, Dolphin Vanatta, unidentified, ? Groom, Georgia Hicks, Eula Allen, Grady Evans, and Dury Cooper; (third row) Berry Stevens, Hoyt Evans, Loi Evans, Matt Bratton (teacher), Garland Evans, Dawson Griffith, and Irby Oakley; (fourth row) Lena Groom, Carrie Groom, and Fannie Groom. (Courtesy of Doyle Evans.)

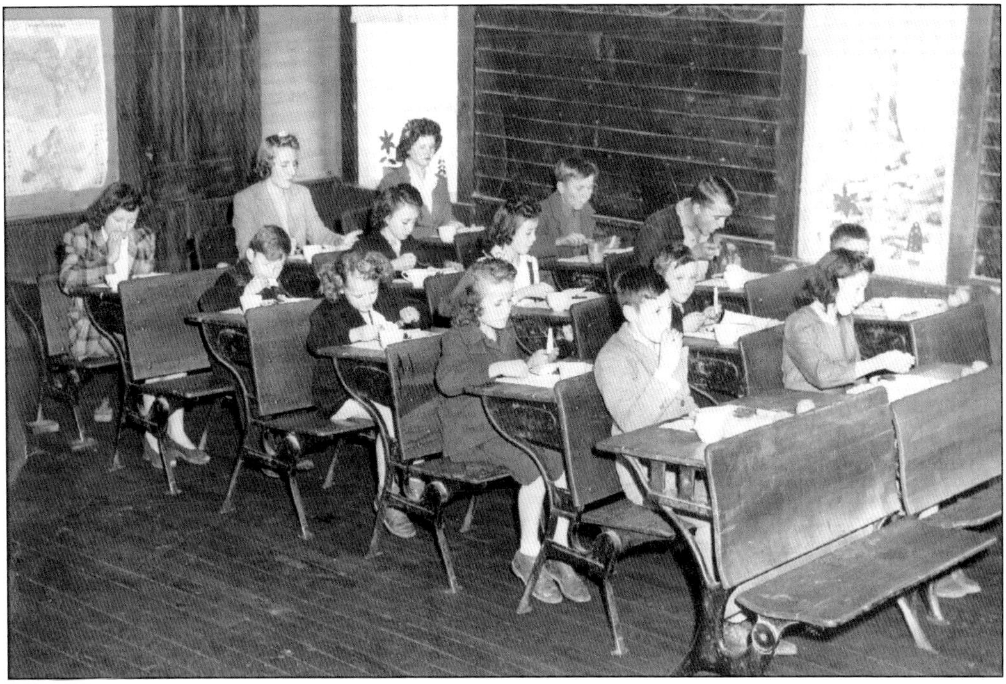

This picture taken in December of 1945 at Bildad School shows the class eating at their desks. Without a cafeteria, the students used their desks for both eating and studying. (Courtesy of Justin Potter Library.)

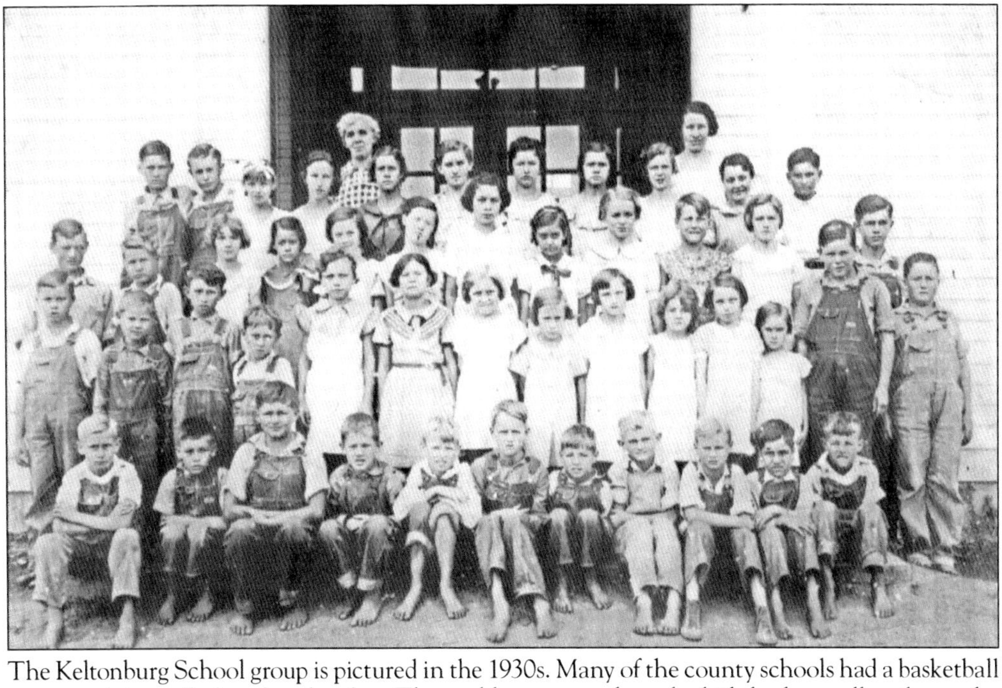

The Keltonburg School group is pictured in the 1930s. Many of the county schools had a basketball team, and they all played each other. The problem came when the kids had to walk miles to the neighboring school for a game. Some laughingly said they were too tired to play when they finally got there. (Courtesy of Justin Potter Library.)

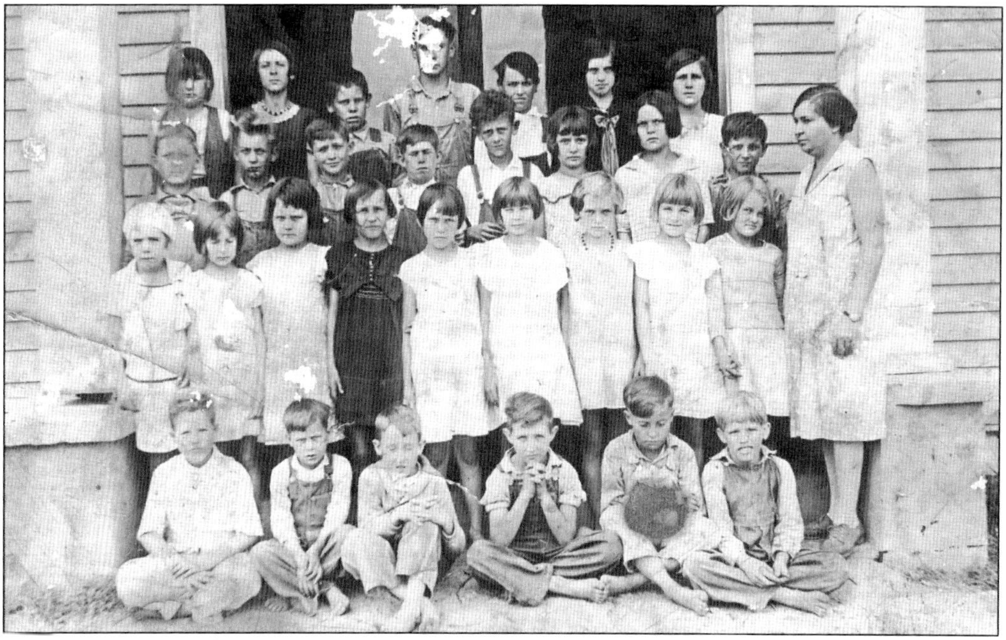

A Snow Hill School group is pictured around 1930. From left to right are (first row) Thomas Russel, James Tramel, Jack Taylor, Glenn Hale, Austin Rhody, and Roy Hendrixson; (second row) Evie Hendrixson, Ruth Beckwith, Bonnie Pearl Keith, Francis Wilson, Ola Wilson, Ruby Tramel, Elizabeth Davis, Ruby Lee Robinson, Zula Davis, and teacher Lilly Trapp; (third row) Paul Vanderpool, John Vanatta, Othel Smith, Haskel Tramel, Thomas Hobert Robinson, Elsie Snyder, Annie Vanderpool, and Vernon Hendrixson; (fourth row) Bertha Hendrixson, Ovaline Hendrixson, George Keith, Shelie Allen Rhody, W.J. Tramel, Frances Evins, and Eva Hale. (Courtesy of Ruth Taylor.)

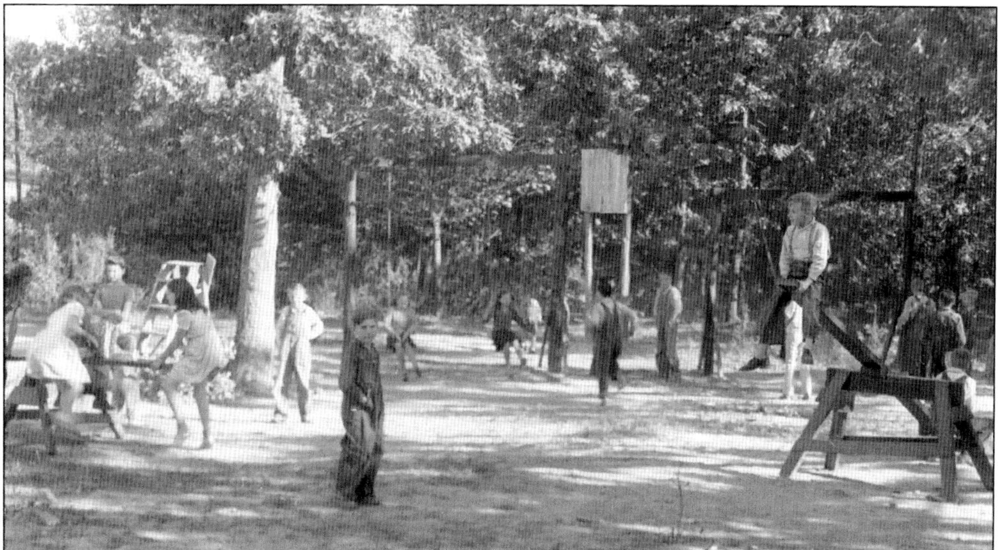

This picture from about 1945 shows the children of Bright Hill School enjoying a beautiful day on the playground. Recess was a much anticipated time when little ones played while the older groups socialized, and teens sometimes got their first kiss. (Courtesy of Justin Potter Library.)

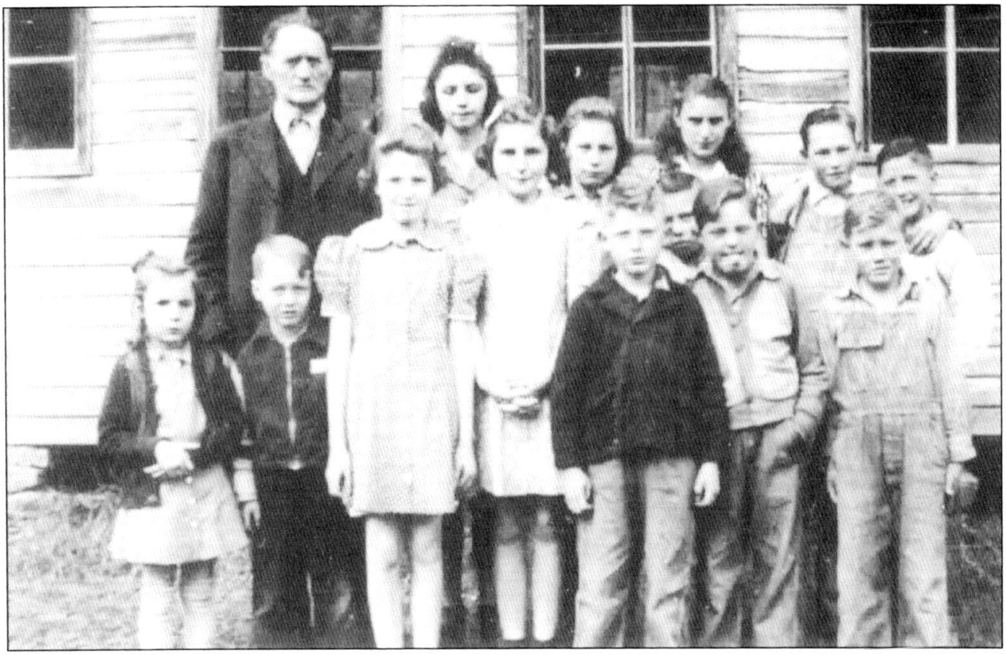

The Red Hill School on Indian Creek is pictured in 1944. From left to right are (first row) Barbara Page, Gordon Ray Spencer, Marie Walker, Bobby Jean Walker, James Fuson, Dan Turner, and Don Turner; (second row) teacher Dave Spencer, Claudine Walker, Alene Page, unidentified, Ruby Page, Joe Mullican, and unidentified. (Courtesy of Wayne Fuson.)

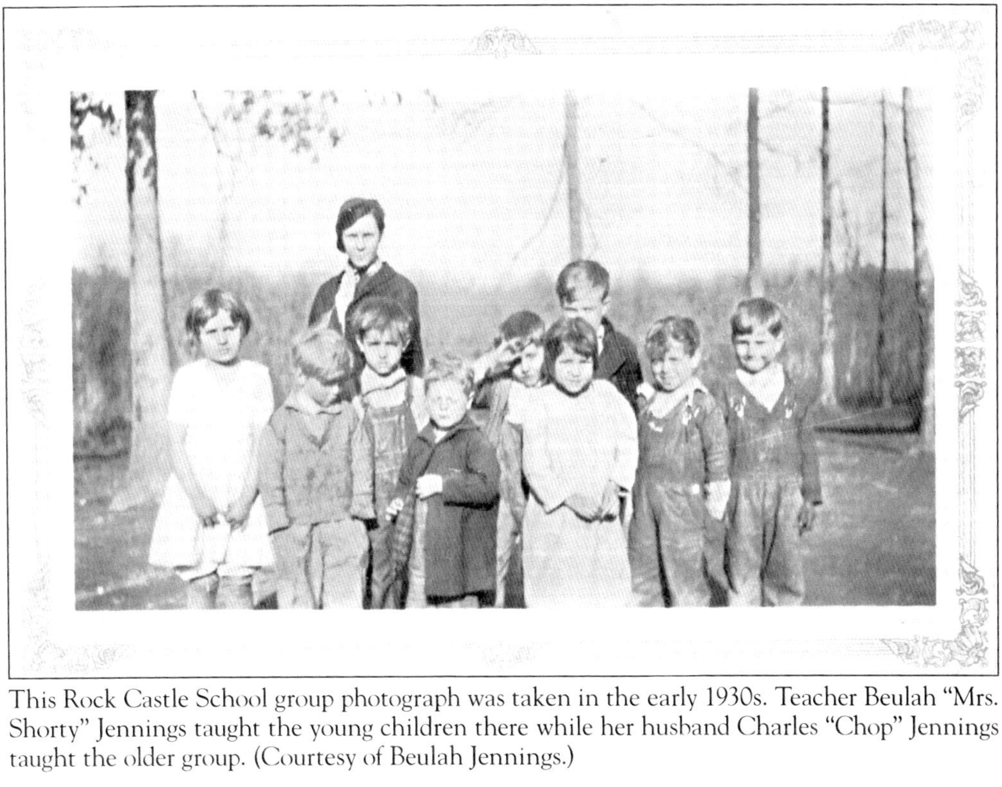

This Rock Castle School group photograph was taken in the early 1930s. Teacher Beulah "Mrs. Shorty" Jennings taught the young children there while her husband Charles "Chop" Jennings taught the older group. (Courtesy of Beulah Jennings.)

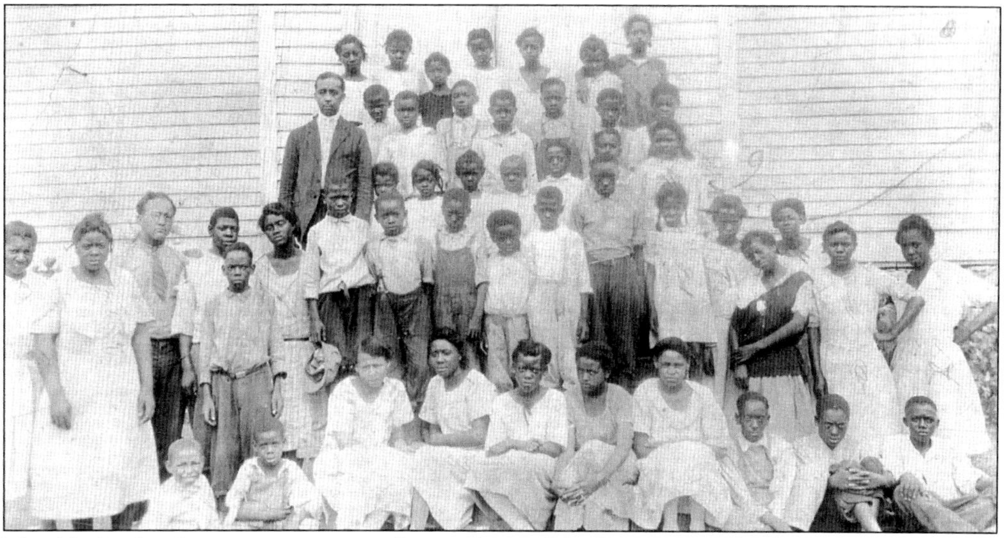

This black school group picture was taken in front of the first Seay Methodist Church at the top of Cemetery Street in Alexandria. The original school building, located just to the south of the church, was a small, one-room school with an Odd Fellows lodge above. It burned just before this picture was taken around 1925. James Moore, the little boy standing beside the teacher, recalled both the school and church. (Courtesy of Ria Baker.)

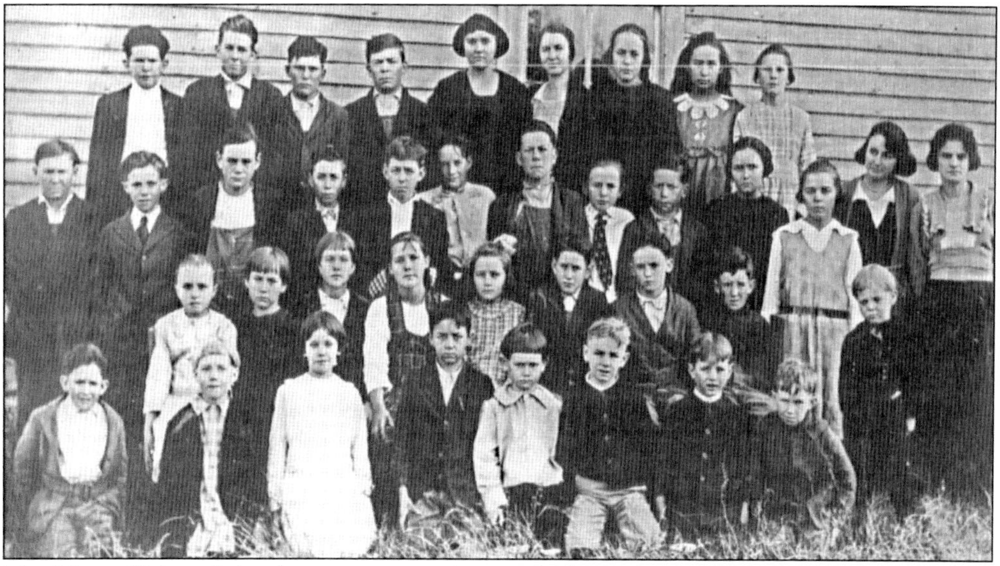

The Upper Helton School group just southeast of Alexandria in 1921 includes, from left to right, (first row) Jimmy C. Rowland, Ruby Nell Rowland, Robbie Scott, Robert Tenpenny, Carl Foutch, J.T. Crowder, Frank Prichett, and Carl Prichett; (second row) Alene Rowland, Dixie Mai Willoughby, Vera Dale Rowland, May Davis, Willie Mai Robinson, Valace Rowland, Willie Floss Woodlin, Earl Prichard, and unidentified; (third row) Hudson Roberts, Clyde Rowland, John Anderson, Ivan Prichard, Elmo Loring, Brad Anderson, Bill Willoughby, Alvie Foutch, Marvin Willoughby, Gladys Campbell, Ruby Robinson, and teachers Lorene Cantrell and Maurene Wood; (fourth Row) Frank McMillan, Dib Robinson, Paul Berry, Thurman Robinson, Bonnie McMillan, Lanna Bell Crowder, Lela Victoria Foutch, Lorene Rowland, and Clara Dale Robinson. (Courtesy of Justin Potter Library.)

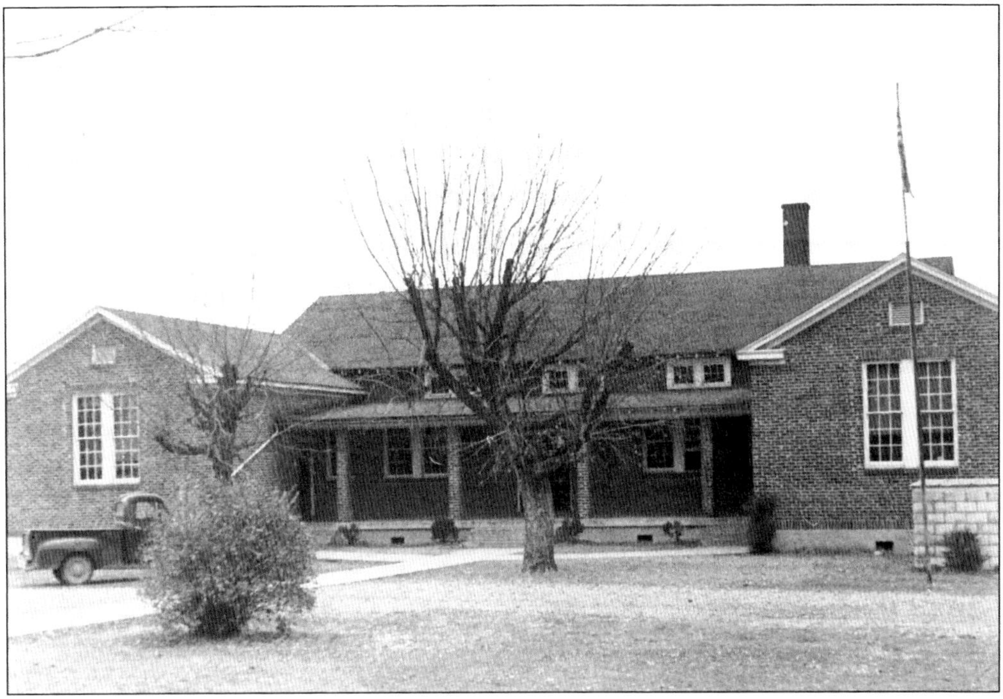

Located on West Main Street, Alexandria Elementary School was built about 1938 and was used at that time along with the old T.M. Lawrence High School. Grades one through eight were taught here until 1974 when the Alexandria, Liberty, and Dowelltown schools were consolidated in the new DeKalb West School on Highway 70 near Liberty. (Courtesy of DeKalb County Department of Education.)

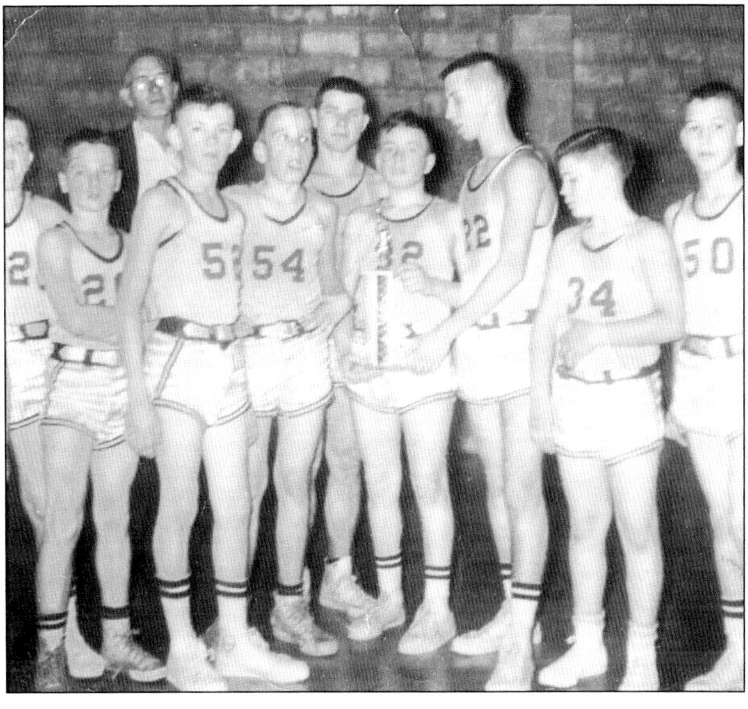

The Alexandria Elementary School boys basketball team was a tournament winner in 1964. Shown from left to right are Greg Lewis, Bill Jennings, coach Charles "Chop" Jennings, Richard Lewis, James Hale, Bob Jennings, Danny Parkerson, Jim Brown, Bobby Hall, and Burford Byers. (Courtesy of Danny Parkerson.)

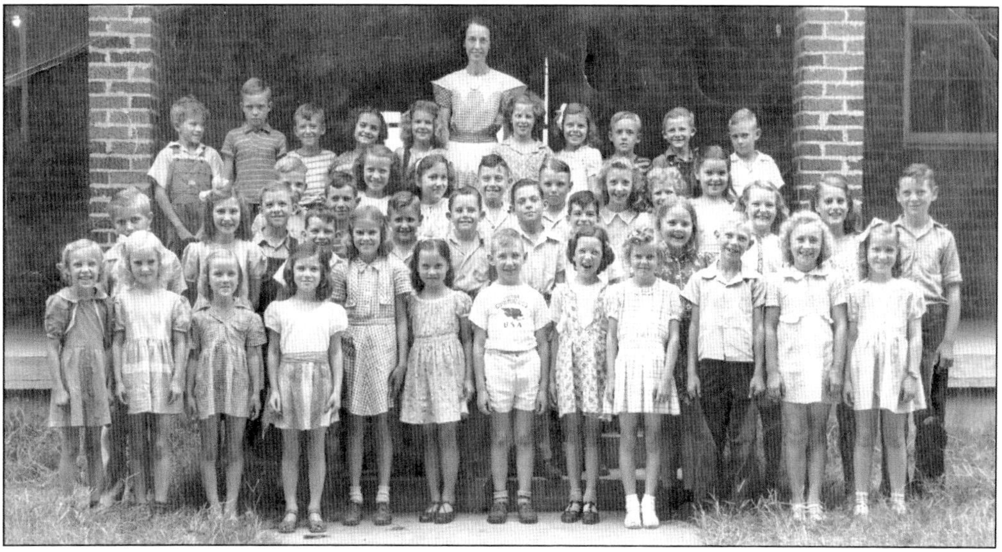

This is Alexandria Elementary School's first and second grades in 1947–1948. Pictured from left to right are (first row) Edna Mai Burton, Joan Malone, Helen Malone, Lyna Charles Kitchings, Betty Sue Wauford, Mary Lou Fitts, Bobby Christian, Shelby Jean Willoughby, Cathleen Fleming, Jerry Self, Faye Vantrese, and Judy Curtis; (second row) unidentified, Betty Jo Malone, Joe Turner, Russell Redrick, Harold Pittman, Jimmy Dodd, Lawrence Harrison, Edward Wayne Avant, Mary McPherson, Freda Rose Davenport, unidentified, and David Bain; (third row) Clarence Thomas Davenport, Joe Foutch, Peggy Hooper, Polly Dinges, Ronny Nerren, Don Edward Sandlin, Barbara Dodd, Judy Foutch, and Judy Wright; (fourth row) Willie Farless, James A. Gibbs, Tommy Lowe Curtis, Mary Elizabeth Bolton, Louise Grandstaff, Jimmie Mai Curtis, Daris Jennings, Ray Donald Thomas, Nolan Turner, and Sam Foutch. Standing at the rear is teacher Drucie Hopkins. (Courtesy of Mac Willoughby.)

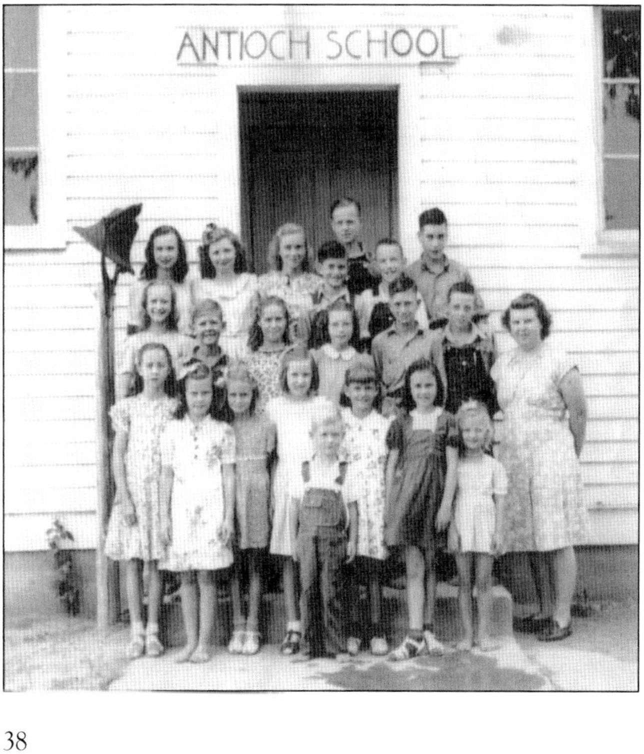

The Antioch Elementary School was located on Antioch Road past Keltonburg in the southeastern section of the county. Pictured here in 1947 are, from left to right, (first row) Joyce Green, Barbara Ann France, Orthana Adcock, Eva Barnes, Richard Pedigo (in front of girls), Loretta Pedigo, Fay Green, and Barbara Hellen Judkins; (second row) Anna Cantrell, LeRoy Pedigo, Betty Ruth Cantrell, Janice Green, Earl Adcock, Billy Adcock, and Hazel Ray (teacher); (third row) Loretta Cantrell, Euola Barnes, Elsia Green, Earl Dean France, James Green, and Clamon Cantrell; (fourth row) Harold Cantrell. (Courtesy of Justin Potter Library.)

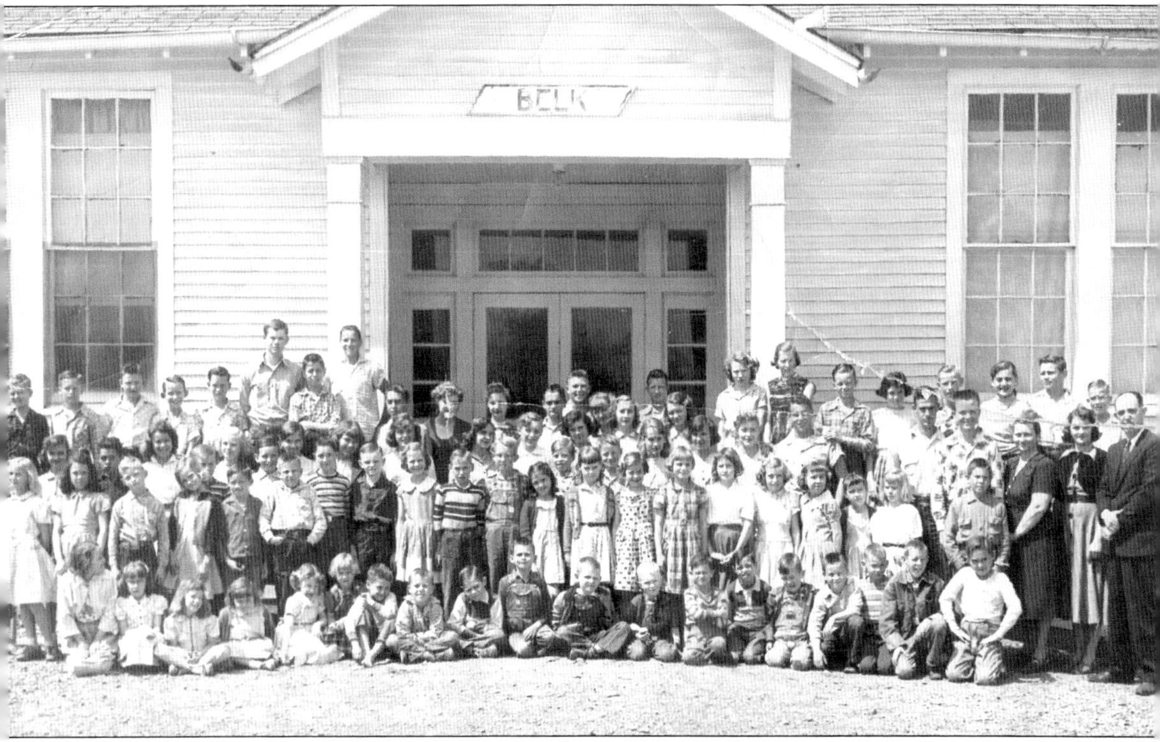

The Belk School located in the southeastern corner of the county was in operation from 1928 through 1972. The people in this community were very supportive of this school, which also became a powerhouse in sports. Many children passed through these doors into all walks of life. This picture was taken around 1955. From left to right are (first row) Vidadel Usrey, Diane Adcock, unknown, Phyllis Jaco, Katherine Wright, unknown, Cantrell Jones, Dwain Young, Lonnie Pack, Roy Ray, Harvey Barnes, Jerry Wright, Repsie Pedigo, George Roller, Ronnie Pedigo, Eddie Green, Larry Green, Tom Green, and Willie Cantrell; (second row) Marie Beshearse, unknown, Harold Blankenship, Elaine Adcock, Bruce Wright, Don Bandy, Roger Jones, Jerry Ray, Sandra ?, Gary Young, Aubrey Wright, Brenda Cope, Anthony Adcock, Carol Adcock, Phillip Adcock, Diane Walker, Janie Barnes, Thelma Cantrell, Mildred Gillette, Helen Jaco, Peggy Griffin?, Iva Griffin?, and Johnny Green; (third row) Glenda Young, Betty Jaco, Johnny Roller, Christine Adcock, unknown, Faye Beshearse, Brownie Barnes, Ann Cantrell, Retha Usrey, Ann McCormick, Joanna Jaco, Elaine Young, Patricia Ray, Ruby Cantrell, Helen Cantrell, Elsie Wright, Noah Usrey, Mildred Adcock, Kenneth Johnson, Royce Turner, Bobby Wright, Mary Cantrell (teacher), Edith Adcock (teacher), and Elzie McBride (teacher); (fourth row) Kenneth Beshearse, Eugene Wright, Justin Barnes, Joe Wright, David Adcock, Elmer Adcock, Grady Ray, Harold Luna, Mac Redmon, Gertrude Hawkins, Helen Judkins, Billy Cantrell, J.B. Blankenship, Joyce Hawkins, Charles Adcock, Eva Dean Wright, Beulah Simpson, Larry Wright, Linda Ray, Edward Young, Sandra Judkins, and Joe Adcock. (Courtesy of Pat Barnes.)

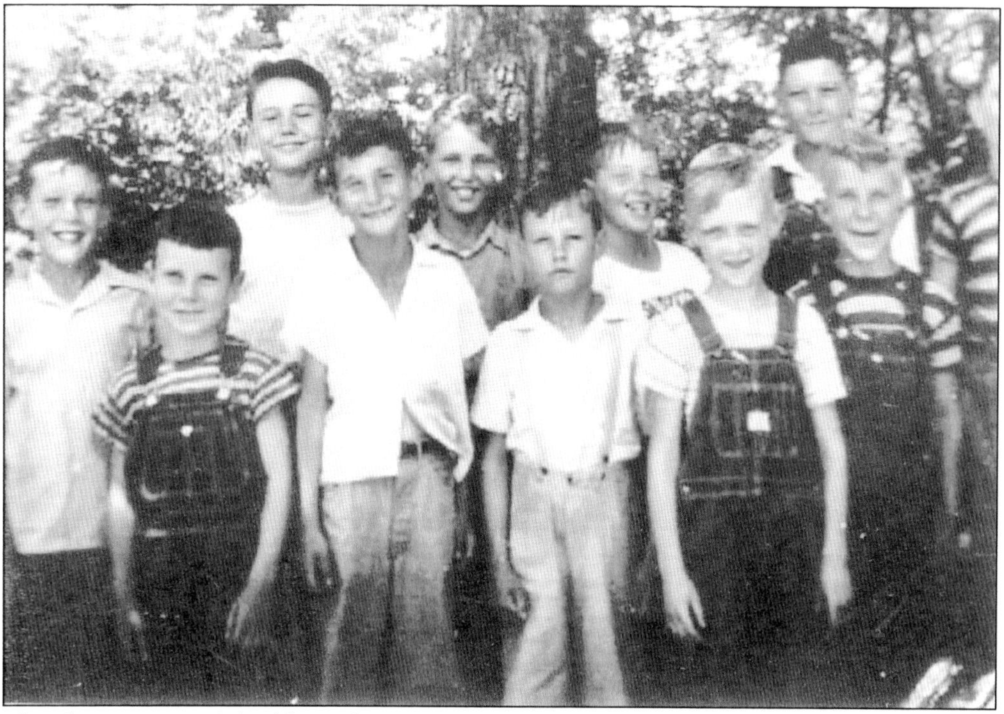

The Chestnut Grove School located on Hurricane Ridge west of Smithville seemed to be a segregated group. The boys pictured above around 1946 are, from left to right, (first row) Arthur Redmon, W.J. Page, Junior Fuson, and Mitchell Jones; (second row) unidentified, Aubrey Dean Snyder, Taft Snyder, unidentified, Willie Lee Fuson, Bobby Redmon (in front of Willie Lee), and Billy Redmon (cut off). The Chestnut Grove girls pictured below around 1944 are, from left to right, Betty Sue Hill, Barbara Fuson, Alene Page (behind Barbara), Pauline Mullican (visitor), Gladys Fuson, and Bobbie Fuson. (Above, courtesy of Wayne Fuson; below, courtesy of Gladys Cantrell.)

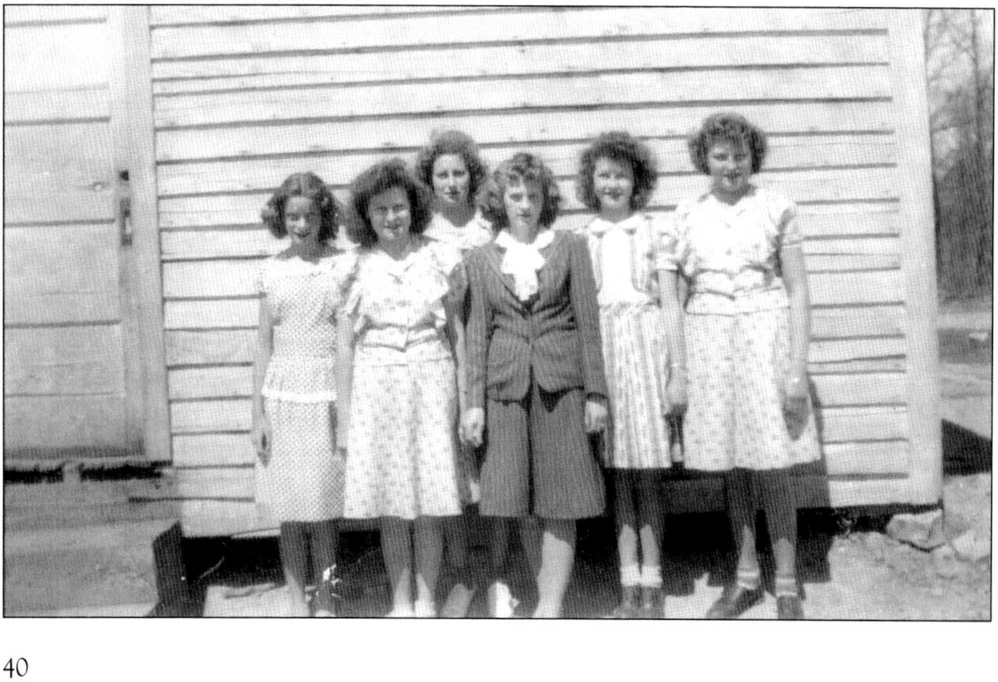

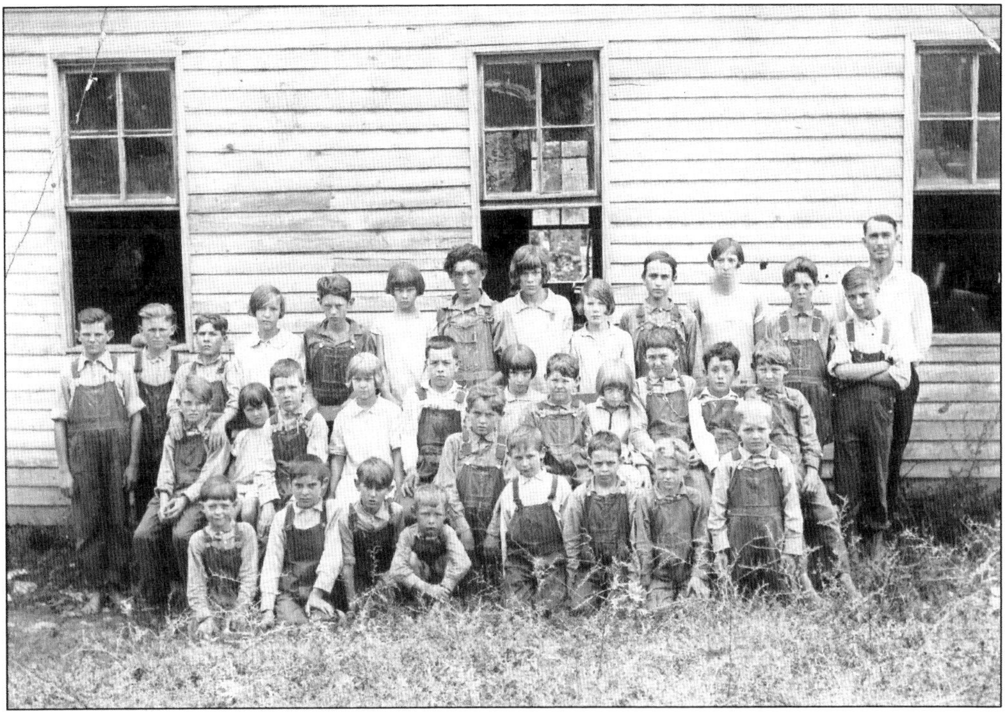

Pictured around 1940, the Coconut Elementary School was located on Coconut Ridge Road, north of Smithville. (Courtesy of Gary Fuson.)

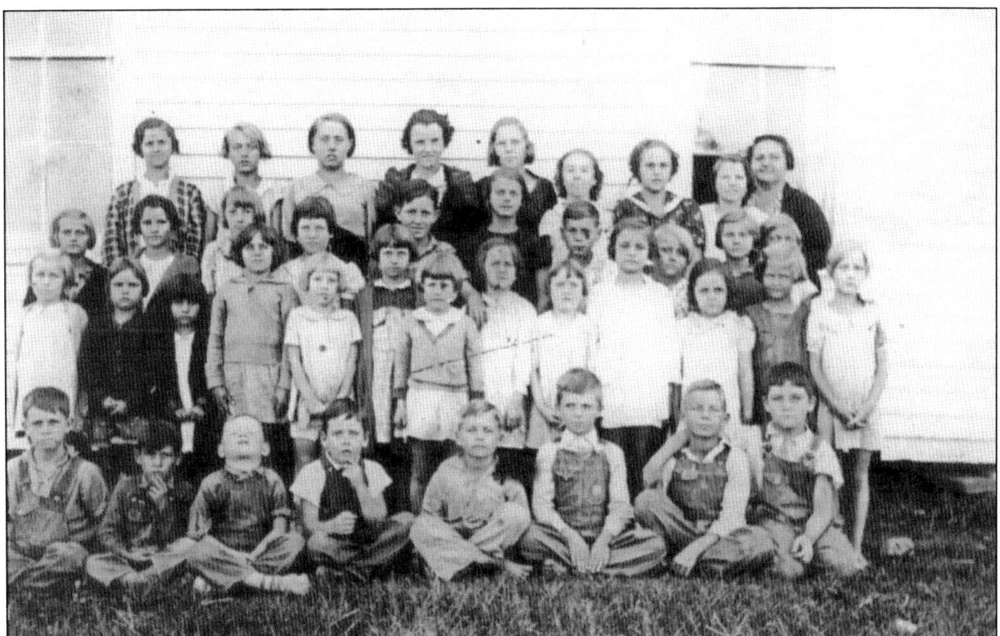

Corley Springs School was located three miles west of Smithville. This group picture was taken in 1940 with teacher Flora Thompson teaching grades one through eight. (Courtesy of Justin Potter Library.)

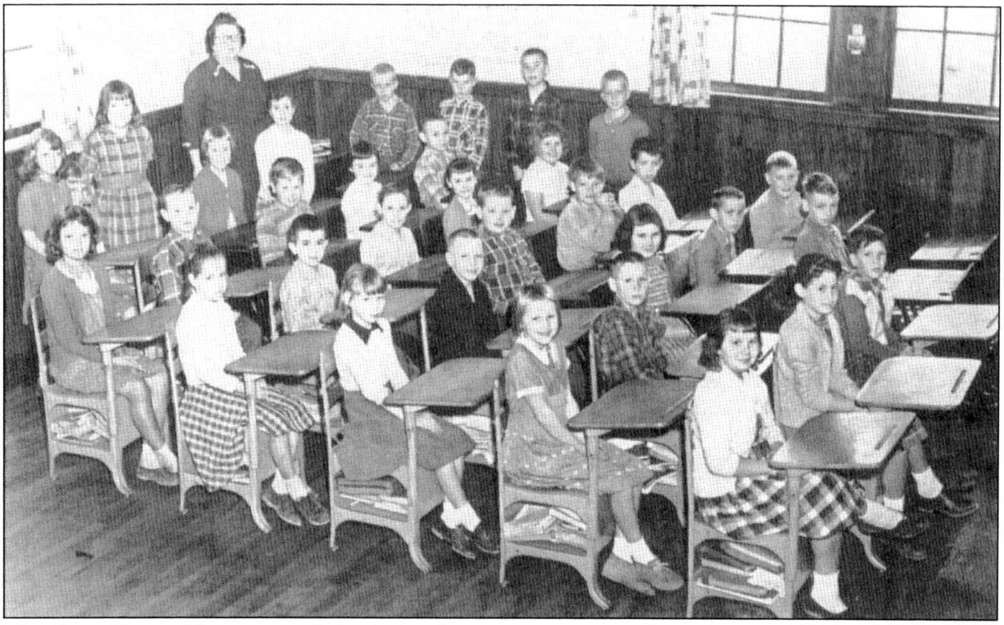

The Dowelltown Elementary School third and fourth grade class in 1961–1962 is pictured here with their teacher Lois Vandergriff. On April 16, 1974, the school was destroyed by a large tornado along with most of the town. It was at this time that the DeKalb West School was built combining Alexandria, Liberty, and Dowelltown into one school teaching kindergarten through eighth grade. (Courtesy of Justin Potter Library.)

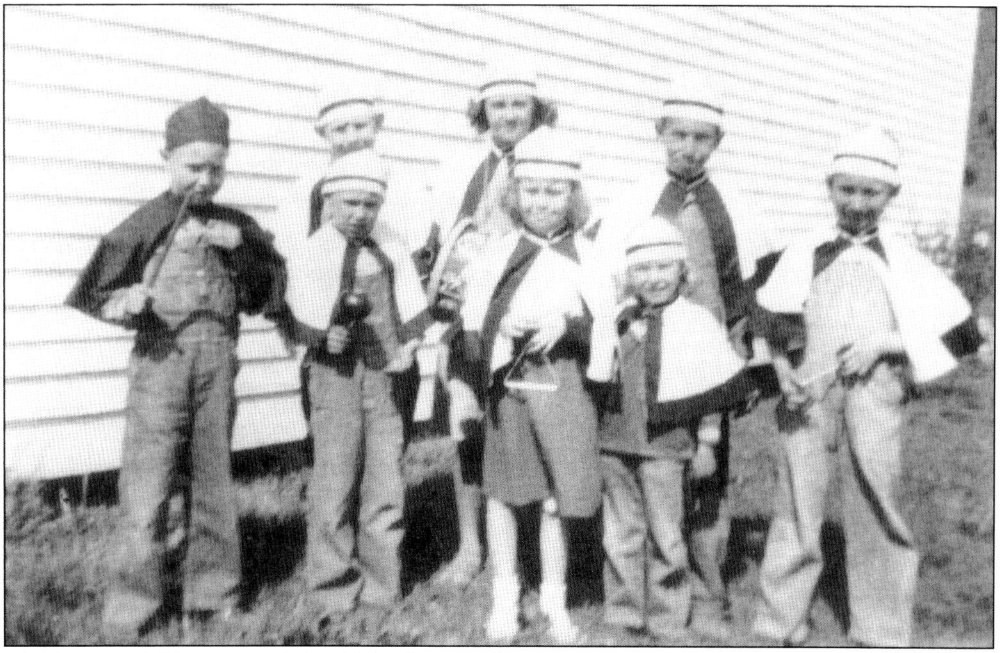

The Dry Creek Elementary School Rhythm Band was formed in 1949 by Jane Vandergriff. Pictured from left to right are (first row) Teddy Edge, Joyce Hendrixson, and Judy Frazier; (second row) leader Joe Ronald Frazier, Kenny Edge, Betty Sue Barret, John L. Frazier, and Bob Earl Fuston. (Courtesy of Louise Frazier.)

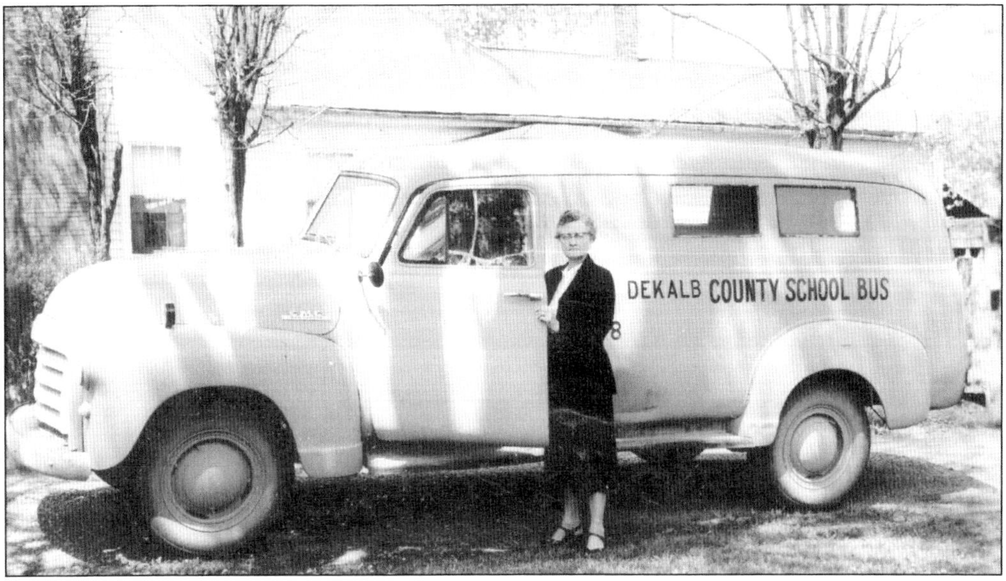

Willette Anderson drove a "little school bus" in Dowelltown and Alexandria for 25 years beginning in 1931 with a privately owned van. In later years, the county school system supplied one for her to drive. (Courtesy of Ron Paschal.)

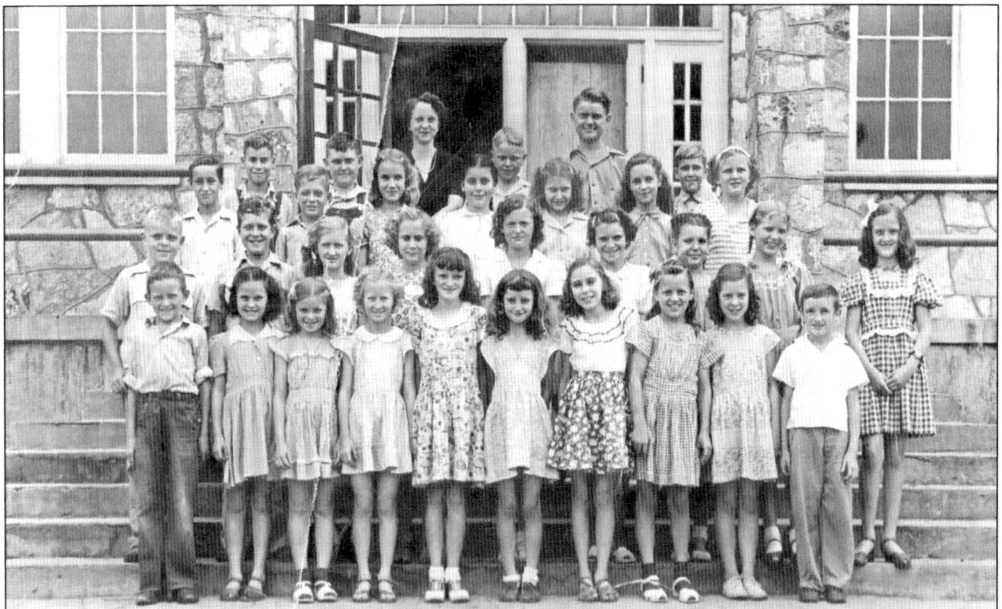

A Liberty Elementary School group from about 1946 is pictured here. From left to right are (first row) Jimmy Mullinax, Mary Campbell, Marie Hayes, Mary Brown Herman, Ruby Nokes, Lavelle Robinson, Glinda Adkins, Joyce Adamson, Marjorie Smith, and Sam Martin; (second row) Robert Pistole, J.D. Thomason, Jo Ann Hayes, Mary Ann Malone, Lavonne Saddler, Minnie Cummings, Mary Hobson, Jenny Goggin, and Mary Lou Givans; (third row) J.T. Pursell, Roger Corley, Nonnie Bell Barrett, Jane McCullough, Majorie Smith, teacher Irene Hancock, Helen Martin, Ralph Parton, Henretta McDuffy, Robert Thomas, James Anderson, Billy Moss, and Jim Roy Derting. (Courtesy of Liberty Historic Group.)

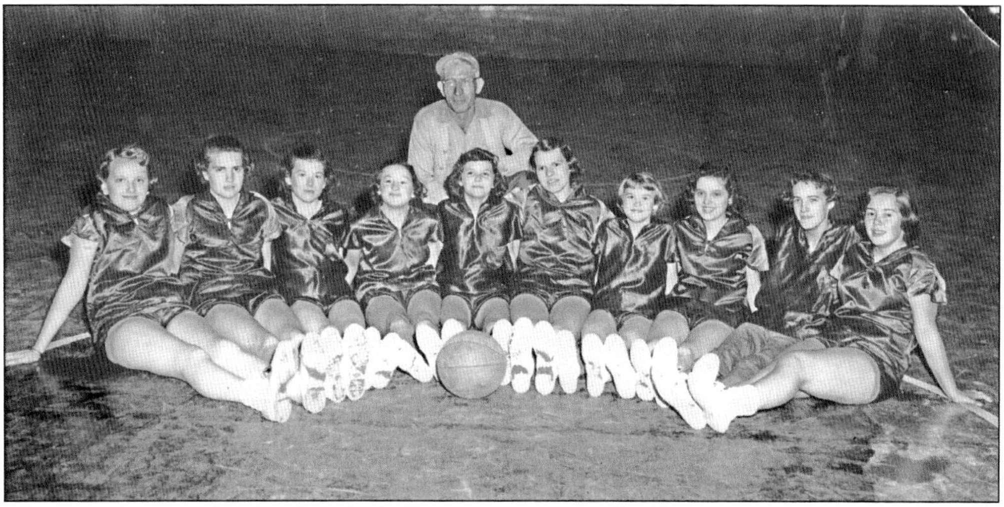

This is a Liberty High School Basketball team in 1956, coached by Charles Jennings. From left to right are Diana Fite, Jo Frankie Hobson, Dinah Howard, Martha Smith, Janet Foutch, Charlotte Robinson, Ruth Hayes, Maxine Davenport, Sarah Jennings, and Margret Ann Robinson. (Courtesy of Liberty Historic Group.)

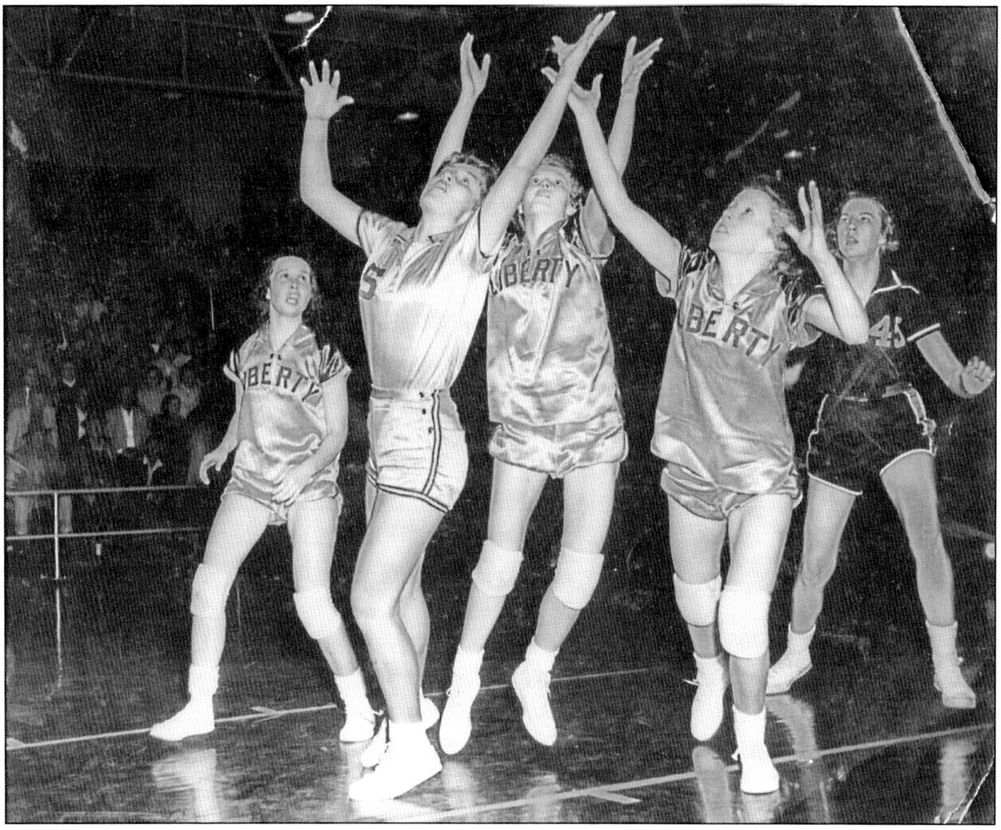

Smithville High and Liberty High were bitter rivals. Although located in the same county, these two schools played hard against each other twice a year with one game at each school. Shown here is one of the girls' basketball games in the mid-1950s. (Courtesy of Marguerite Jones.)

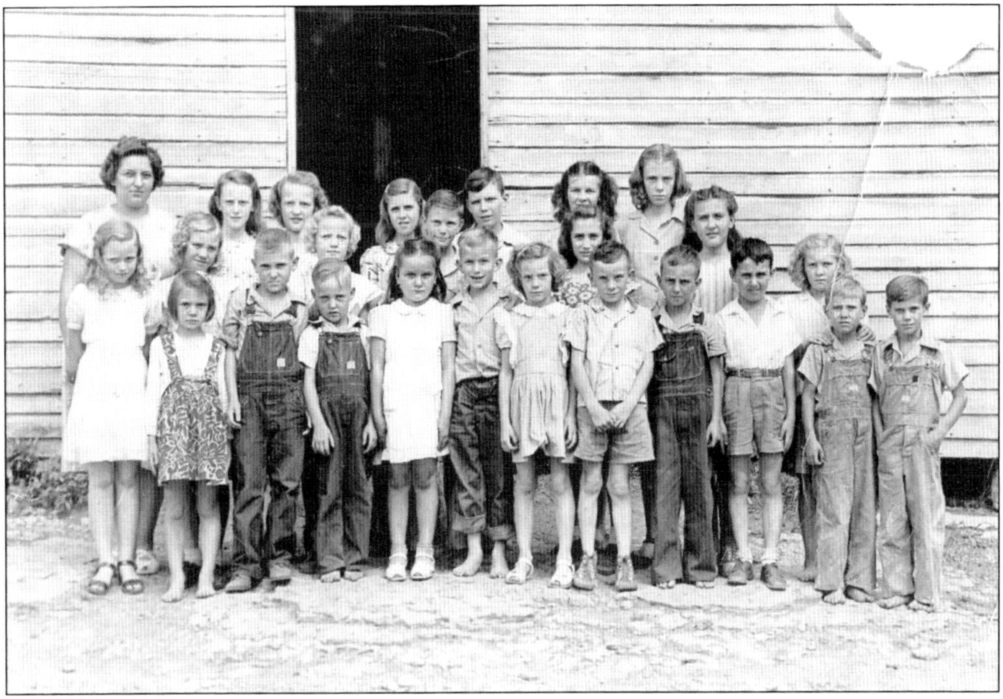

The Lower Helton School in the late 1940s had one teacher, Jo Nell Amonett Curtis. Judy Close and her brother Benny Close are in the first row, sixth and seventh from left. (Courtesy of Liberty Historic Group.)

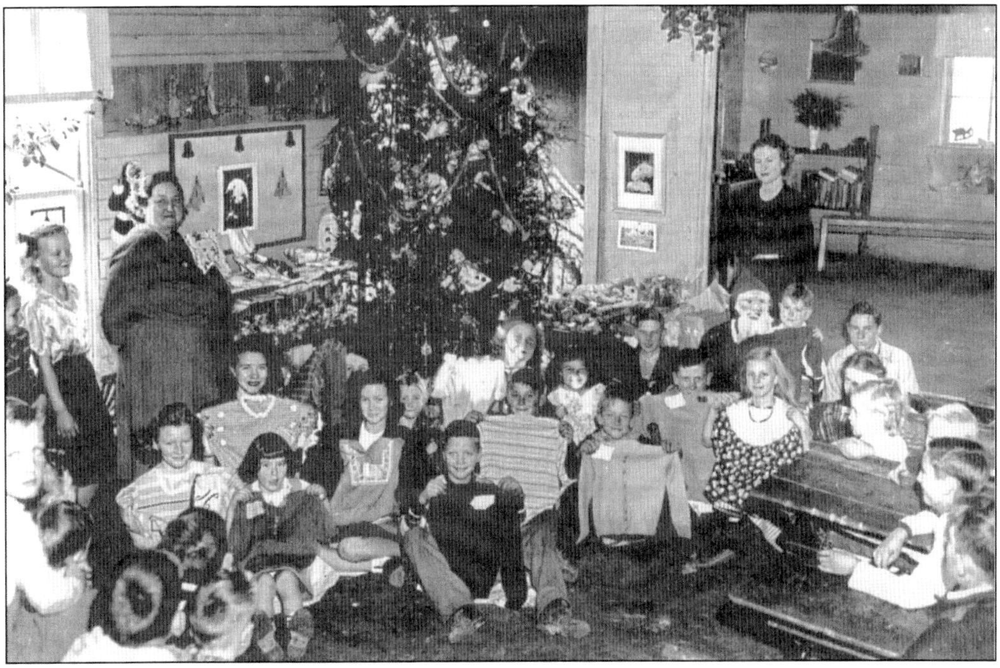

The Oak Grove School received money to buy presents for the children in 1947. This picture shows them enjoying their Christmas holiday. Flora Thompson was the teacher of this class. (Courtesy of Justin Potter Library.)

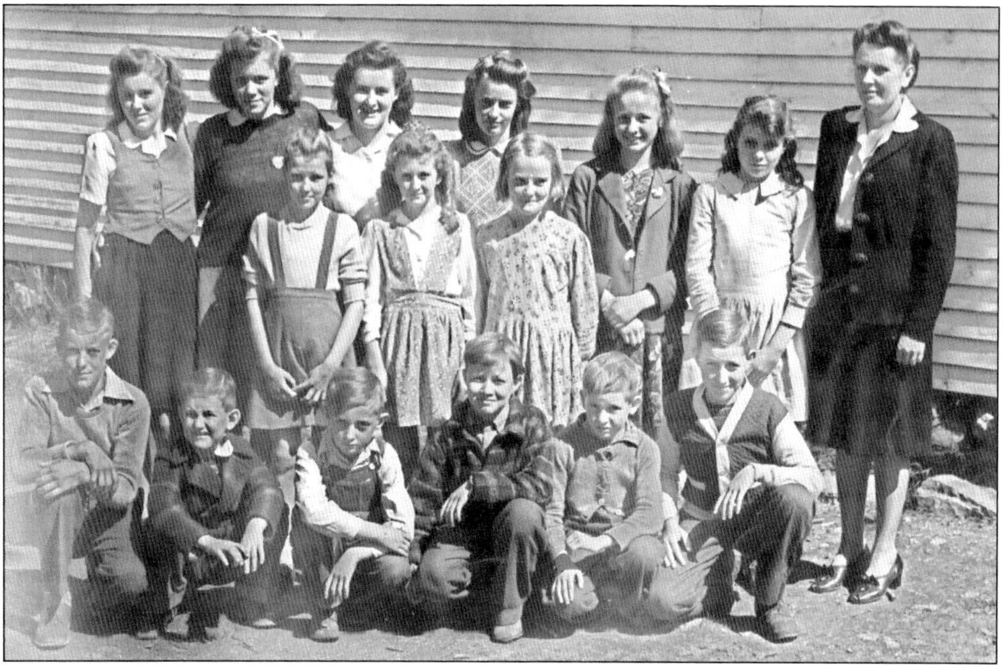

Pack School was at the head of Holmes' Creek. Shown around 1944, this group includes, from left to right, (first row) Ophel Page, Omrie Allen, Billy Jack Pack, Hubert Ferrell, Jimmy Taylor, and Joe Greer; (second row) Helen Braswell, Hazinel Pack, and Barbie Dale Johnson; (third row) Erma Dell Page, Dorothy Greer, Barbara C. Page, Christine Johnson, June Taylor, Georgie Dean Pack, and teacher Lucille Ferrell. Below is a view inside the Pack School at the same time, with Ferrell at the front of the room. (Above, courtesy of Ophel Page; below, courtesy of Justin Potter Library.)

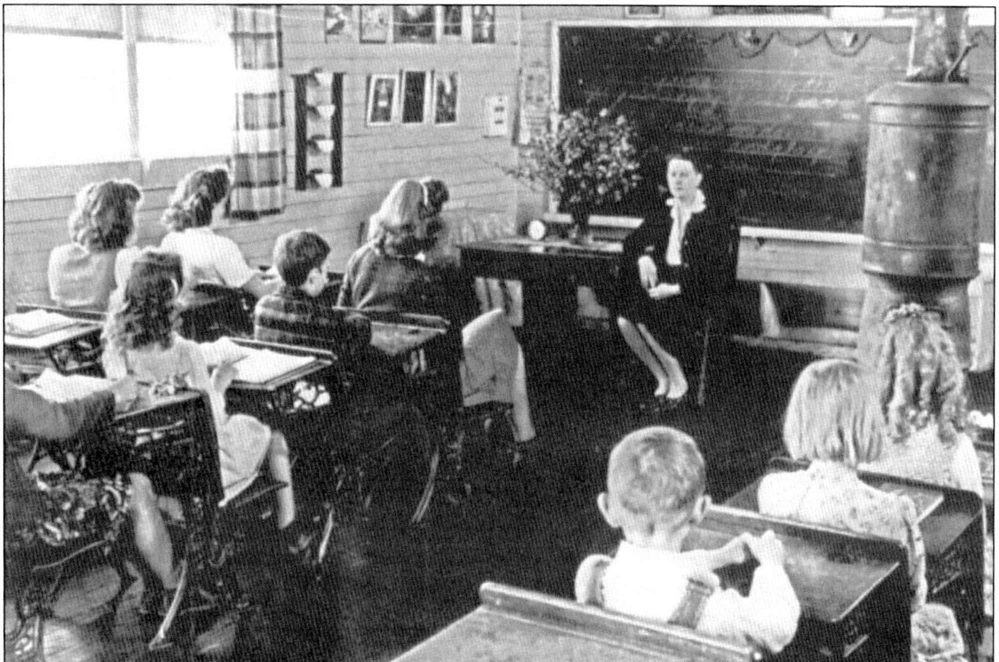

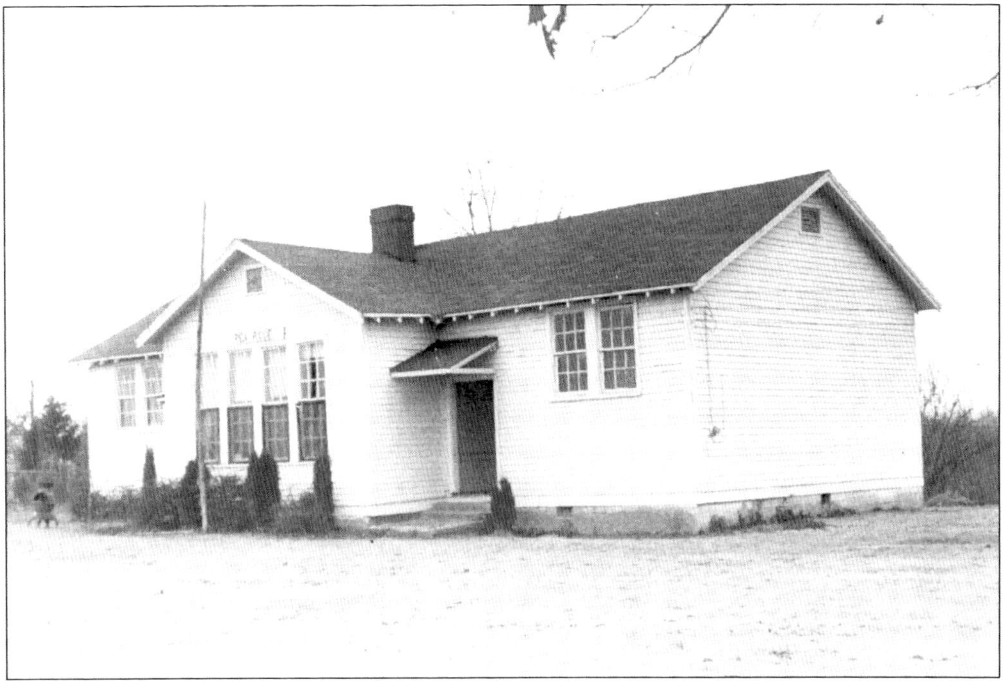

The Pea Ridge School was built about 1948. Blue Springs, Midway School, Mahathy Hill, and Cross Roads were also built with the same plans, making these schools all look-alikes, at least on the outside. (Courtesy of DeKalb County Department of Education.)

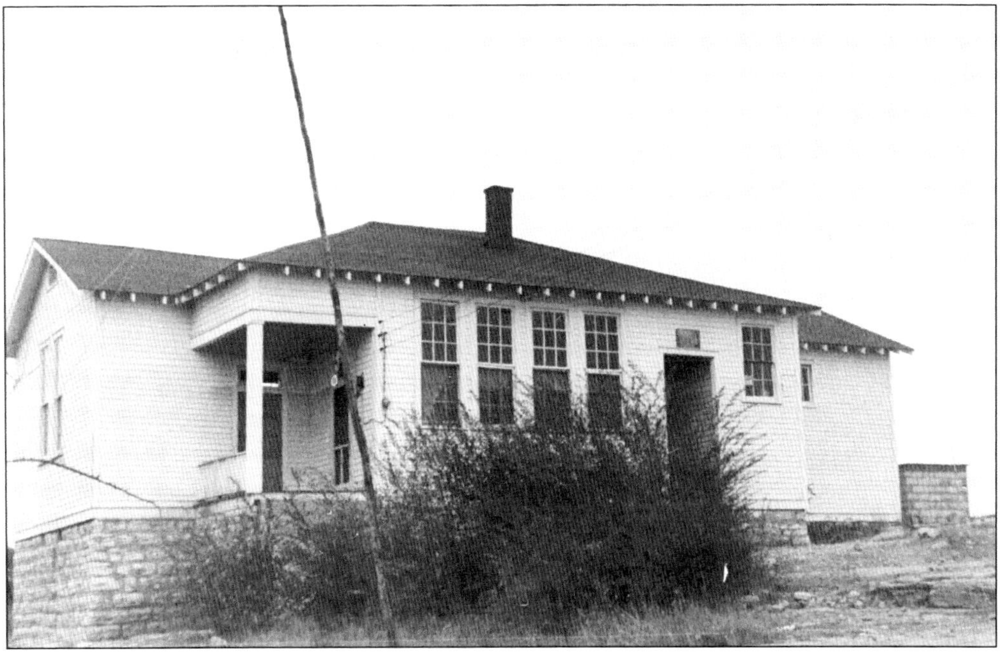

Rosenwald School in Alexandria was built in 1927–1928 and cost $4,048. Julius Rosenwald, owner of Sears Roebuck and Co., created a grant program to help build schools for African Americans; this school was built with his help. It closed after desegregation and was sold at public auction in the 1970s. It no longer stands. (Courtesy of DeKalb County Department of Education.)

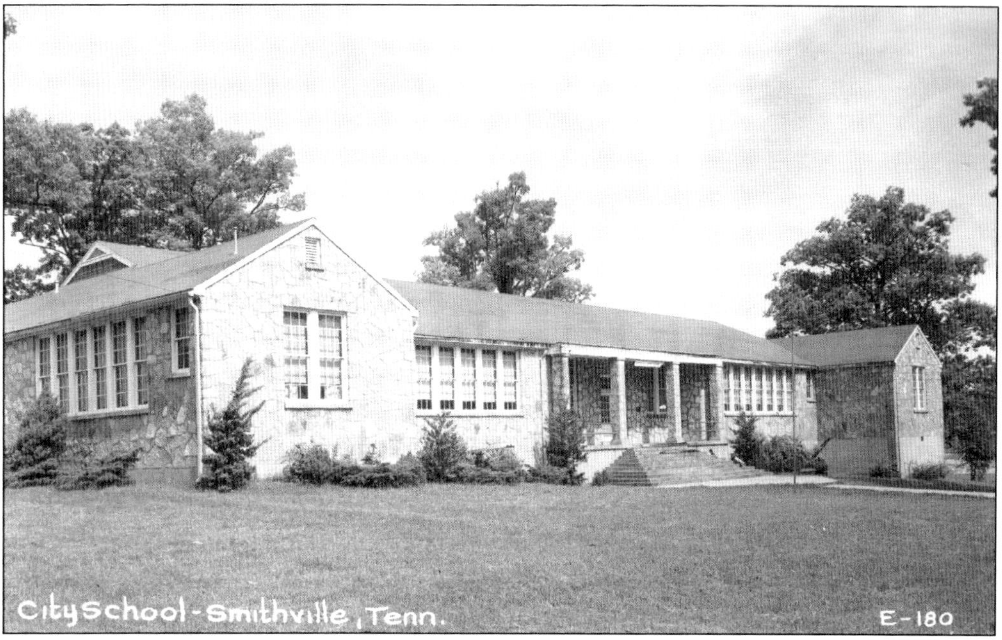

Smithville Elementary stood on College Street in Smithville, and was built in 1939 as a Works Progress Administration project. Stones from the area were used for this building as well as for Dowelltown and Liberty Schools. (Courtesy of Carol Williams.)

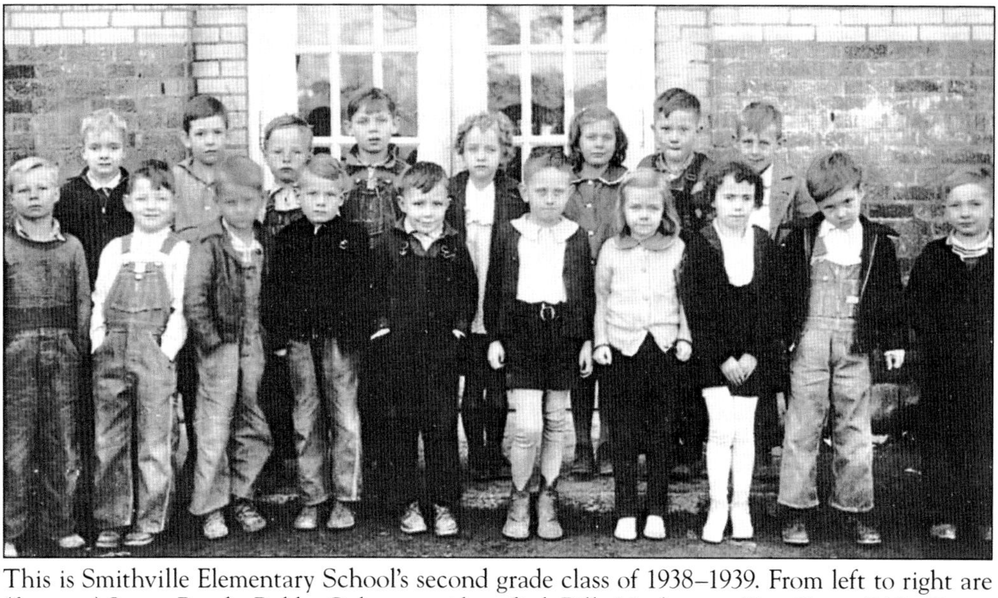

This is Smithville Elementary School's second grade class of 1938–1939. From left to right are (first row) James Bandy, Bobby Colvert, unidentified, Billy Vanhooser, Don Terry, Eddie Royce Cantrell, Jo Ann Masters, Jean Murphy, Ned Harney, and Ozias Conger; (second row) Charles Foster Dearman, Billy Jack Allen, Tolbert Summers, Morris Driver, Rava Nell Cantrell, Dora Mangrum, Jack Hooper, and Jack Wagner. Their teacher was Mrs. John Hayes, not shown. (Courtesy of Justin Potter Library.)

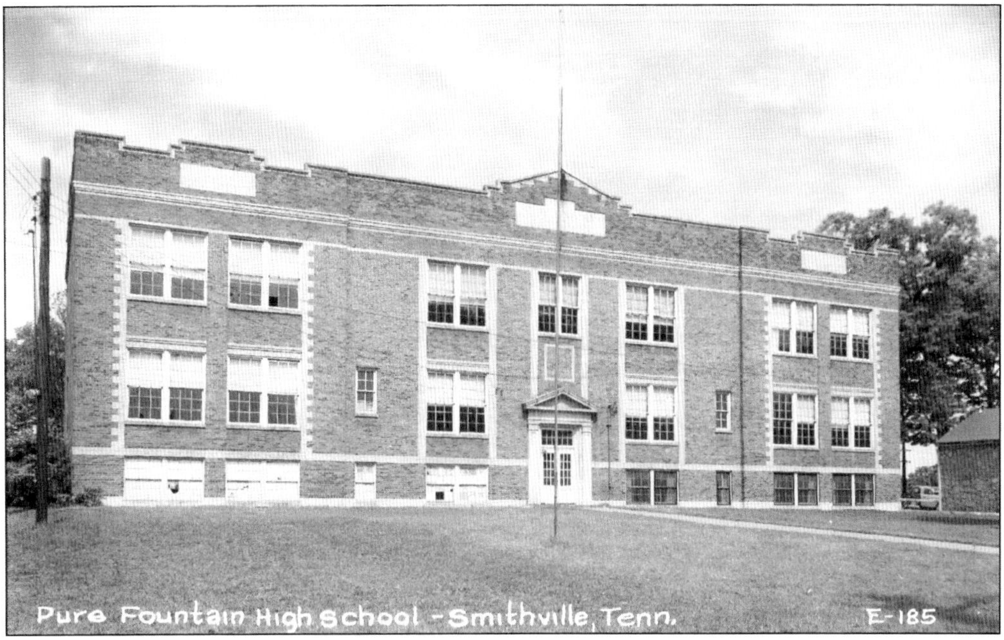

In 1929, the state mandated each county to have a county school. Therefore, Pure Fountain became DeKalb County High School. Although it was always called Smithville High, it was officially DeKalb County High School. (Courtesy of Carol Williams.)

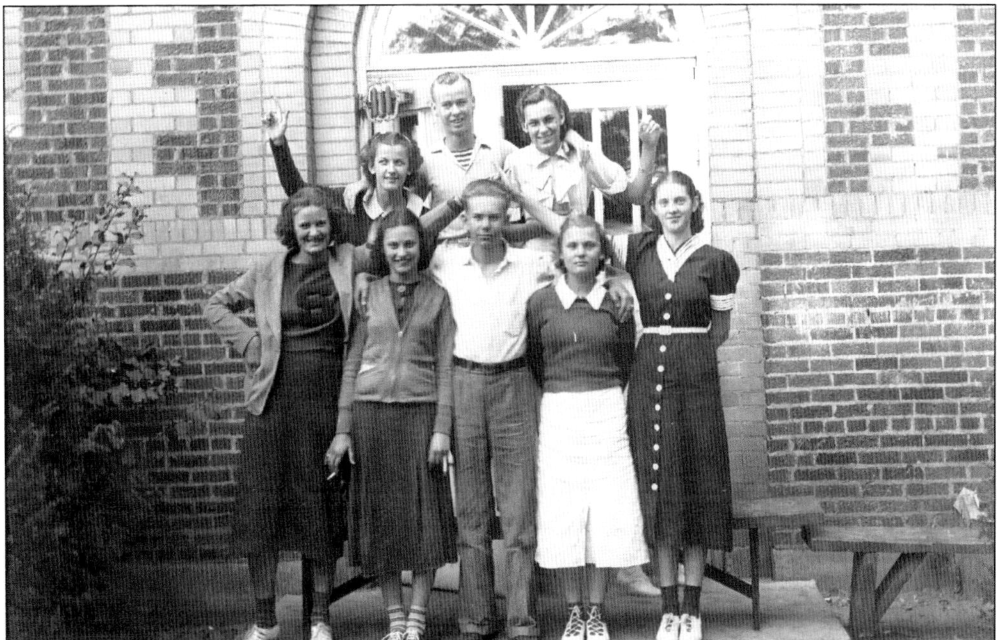

Here is a group of friends at Smithville High School in about 1937. From left to right are (first row) Vada Taylor, Caroline Trapp, unidentified, Dean Paris, and unidentified; (second row) Helen Willoughby, Harold Ratliff, and Louye Smith. (Courtesy of Carol Williams.)

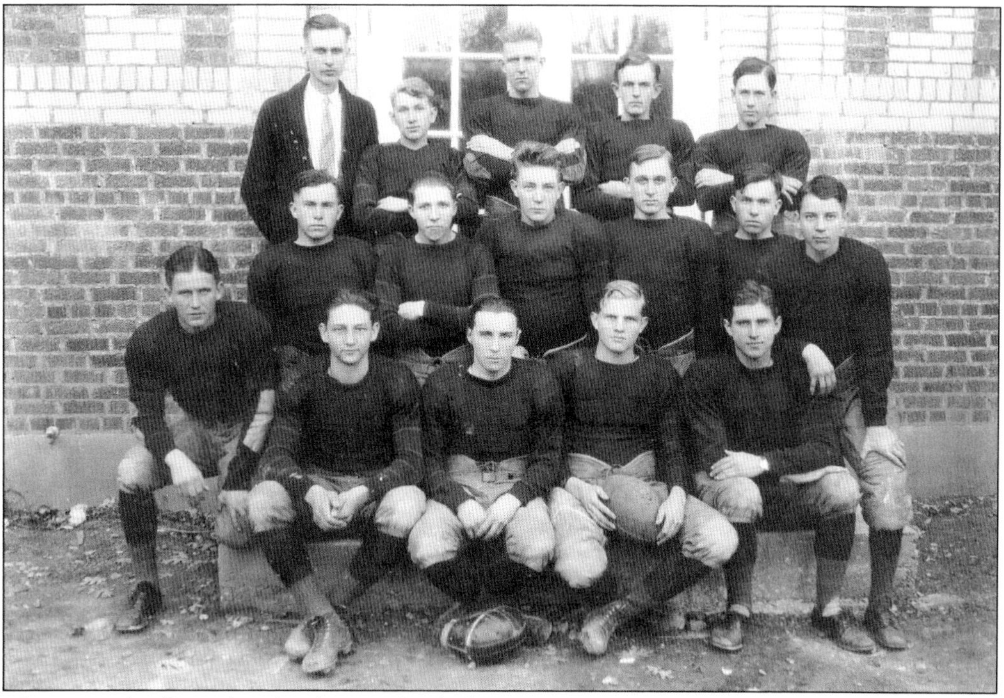

This is Smithville High School's 1927 football team. Although many young men played football, only Smithville had a team in the early years. Pictured from left to right are (first row) unidentified, Charles Taylor, unidentified, Ed Bell, and unidentified; (second row) Jewel Young, unidentified, Grant Roy, Royce Givens, Ewel Young, and Joe Evins; (third row) coach Charles Hill, Fain Potter, C.M. Loring, and two unidentified. (Courtesy of Justin Potter Library.)

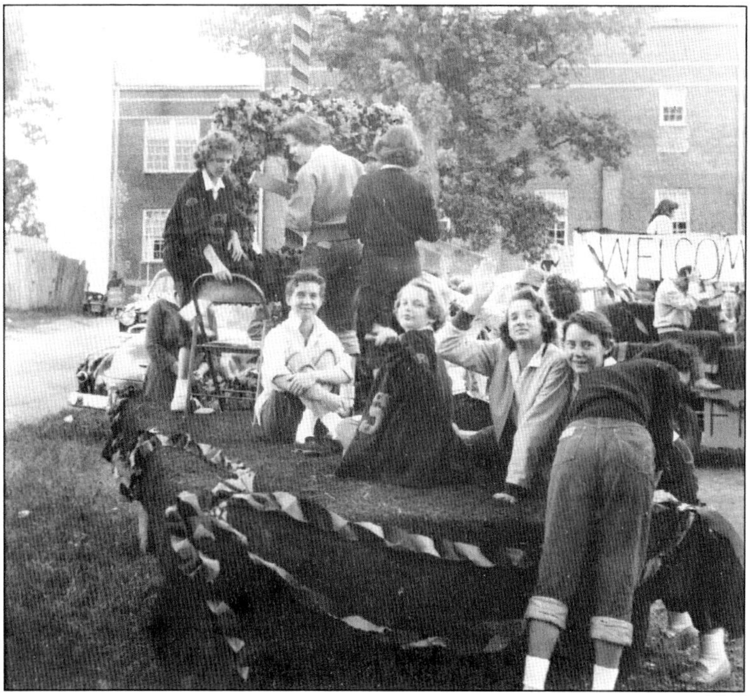

Members of the Tigerette Club at Smithville High School are working on a 1956 homecoming float. Those facing the camera are, from left to right, Barbara Love, Becky Ford, Linda Hendrixson, Delma Vanhooser, and Nina Cantrell. (Courtesy of Marguerite Jones.)

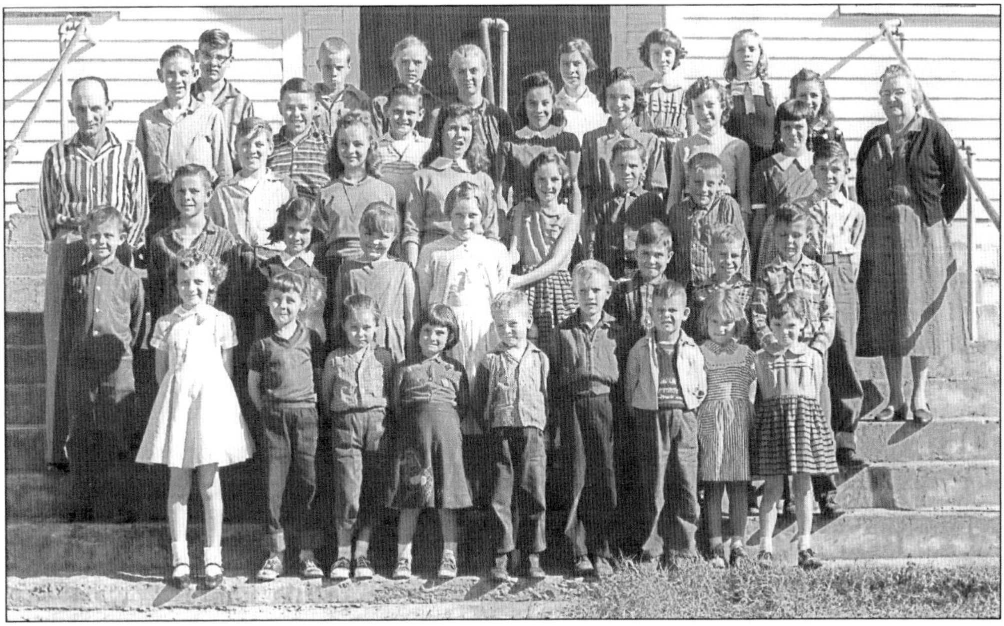

This Temperance Hall School group in 1959 includes, from left to right, (first row) Sandra Gail Lamberson, Dianna Fish, Brenda Sue Fish, ? Watts, Lucien Nokes, J.C. Allen, Lee Hale, Georgia Fay Parkerson, and Barbara Fay Fitts; (second row) Billy Bates, Junior Bates, Ann Watts, Beverly Driver, Marie Bullard, ? Watts, ? Woodard, and Gaylon Fish; (third row) teacher Ray Burton, Riley Bullard, Deborah Duke, Linda Watts, Brenda Fitts, ? Woodard, Hoyte Duke, ? Watts, and teacher Lillie Trapp; (fourth row) Jimmy Judkins, Lynn Lamberson, Hooper Judkins, Betty Dunham, Patricia Fitts, Janice Webster, and Linda Duke; (fifth row) Royce Evans, Jerry Oliver, Johnnie Ruth Hunt, Mary Jane Hunt, Juanita Woodard, Mary Fitts, and Candy Woodard. (Courtesy of Grace Close.)

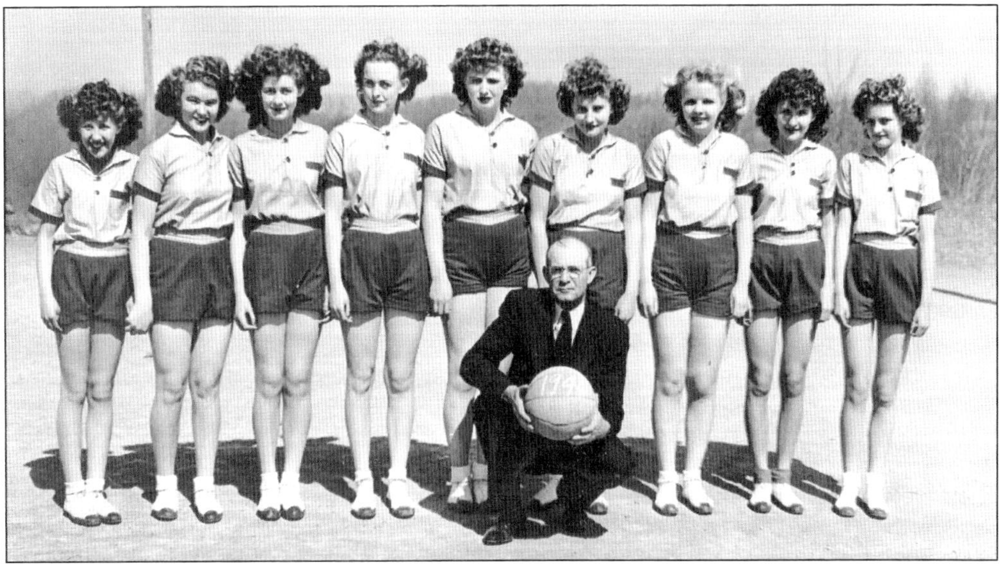

Walker's Chapel girls' basketball team in 1946 was coached by Floyce Vickers. From left to right are Marie Puckett, Juanita Foster, JoAnn Pack, Helen Ponder, Ruth Ann Cantrell, Jo Johnson, Alfidene Cantrell, Ruth Staley, and Edith Parsley. (Courtesy of Pat Barnes.)

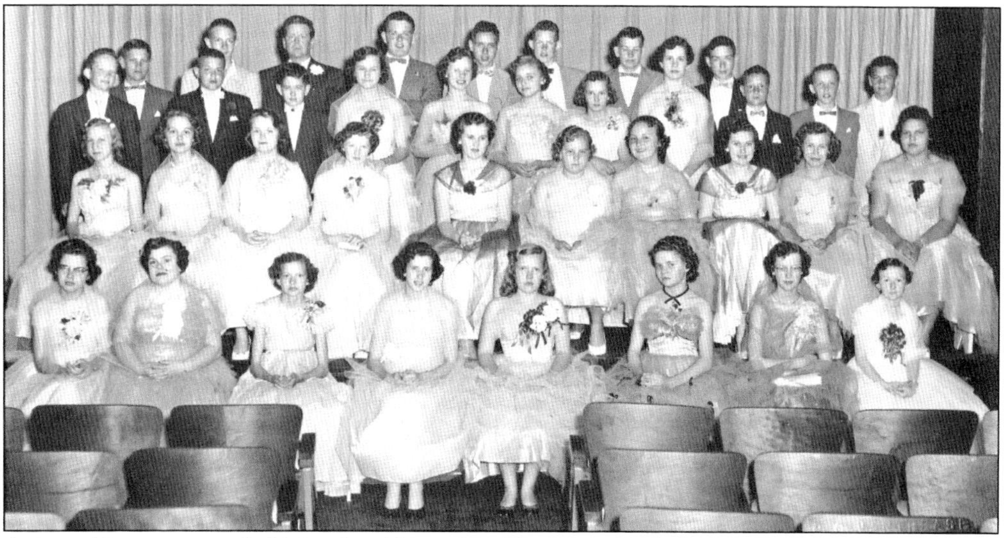

A formal banquet was held for the Alexandria Elementary School seventh and eighth graders each year. Taken in April 1956, this photograph shows the young people dressed for their night. From left to right are (first row) Betty Robinson, Virginia Foutch, Fay Nixon, Linda Lewis, Ruth Johnson, Marie Robinson, Helen Burton, and Judy Wright; (second row) Faye Turner, Hilda Ann Kelley, Elaine Crowder, Katherine Harvey, Madonna Corley, Barbara Kelley, Jean Parkerson, Carolyn Corley, Judy Clayborn, and Charlene Blew; (third row) Thomas Prichard, Don Malone, Willie B. Allen, Corkey Malone, Mackie Sandlin, Marlene Scott, Willie Jo Grandstaff, Gayle Rush, Buster Davis, Jimmy Williams, and Allen Mason; (fourth row) Johnny Williams, John C. Finney, Vesper Pistole (teacher), Jerry Pistole, William Davis, Larry Jones, Clifton Grandstaff, and Jack Brown. (Courtesy of Elaine Crowder Collins.)

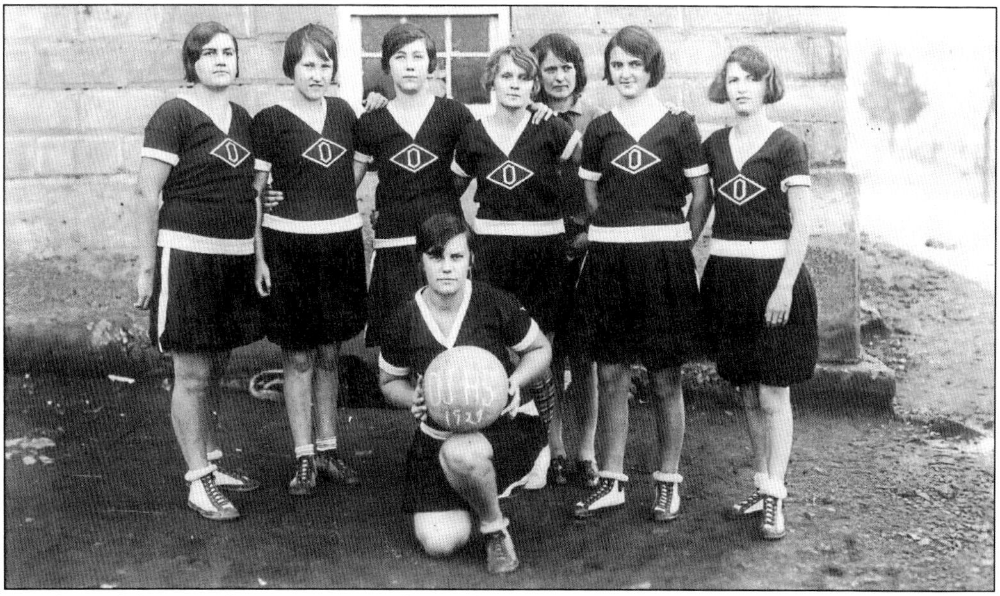

Members of the Dowelltown Junior High girls' basketball team look like winners in their uniforms in 1929. Standing from left to right are Lois Vandergriff, Pauline Malone, Floda McDowell, Sarah Fuson, Mala B. Vandergriff, and Lena Banks. Alene Gothard is holding the ball in front, and their teacher and coach Ruth Eubank is in the back. (Courtesy of Liberty Historic Group.)

Three

MAIN STREETS AND BACK ROADS

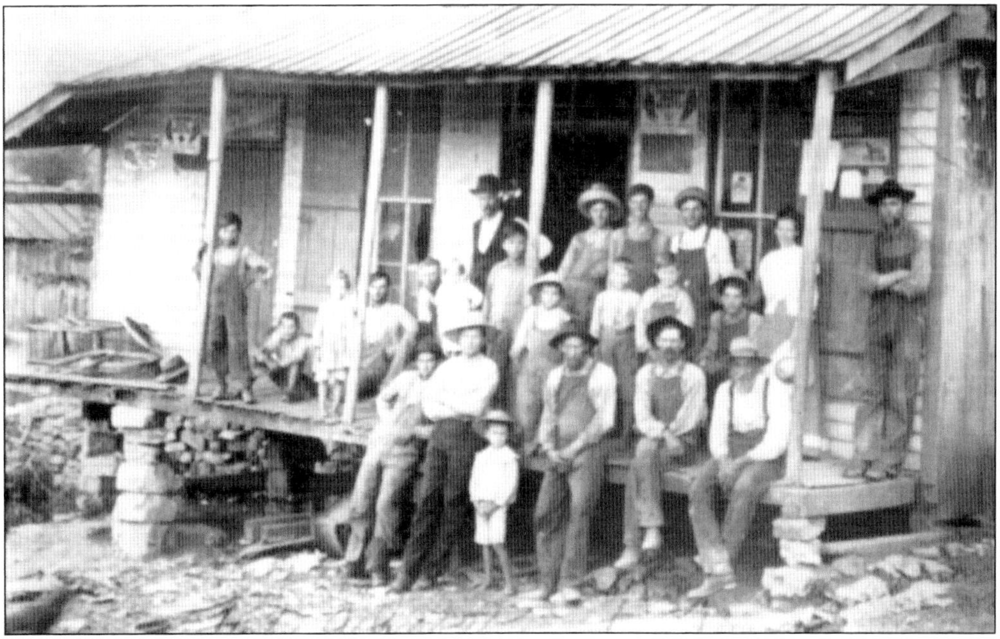

Lower Helton Store was located in the northwest end of the county. This picture taken in about 1914 shows some of the people of that time. Because travel was hard and work started at dawn and ended at dusk, these small businesses located every few miles along the roads thrived throughout the county. They provided the farm families with daily needs from groceries to overalls. (Courtesy of Justin Potter Library.)

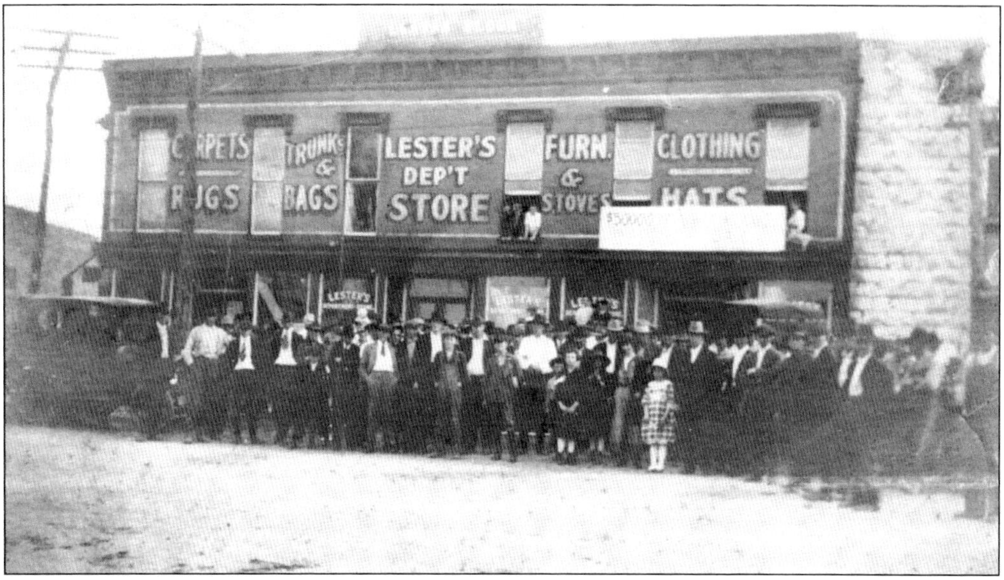

Lester's Dry Goods Store in Alexandria stood on the corner of High and West Main Streets on the south side of the public square. The business was open in the early 1900s, and this picture was taken about 1920. George Lester ran this store, which was later destroyed by fire. (Courtesy of Bill and Sue Corley.)

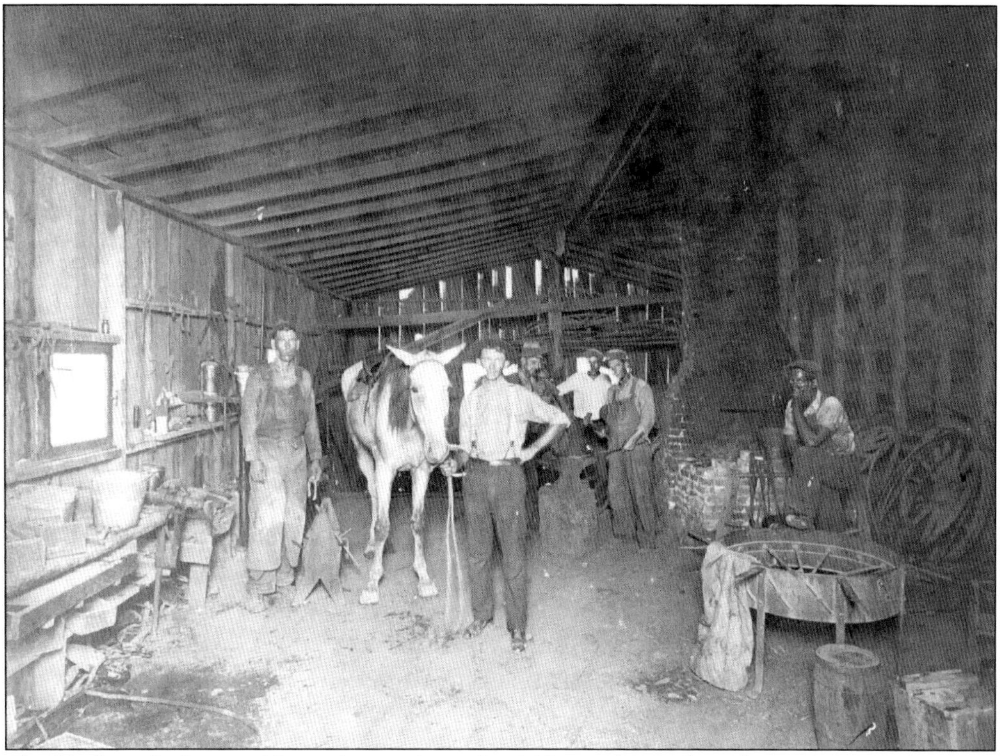

The blacksmith shop in Alexandria in the early 1900s was located on the upper west end of the square. Although most of the men in the photograph are unidentified, the young black man on the far right is believed to be Virgil Dowell. (Courtesy of Ria Baker.)

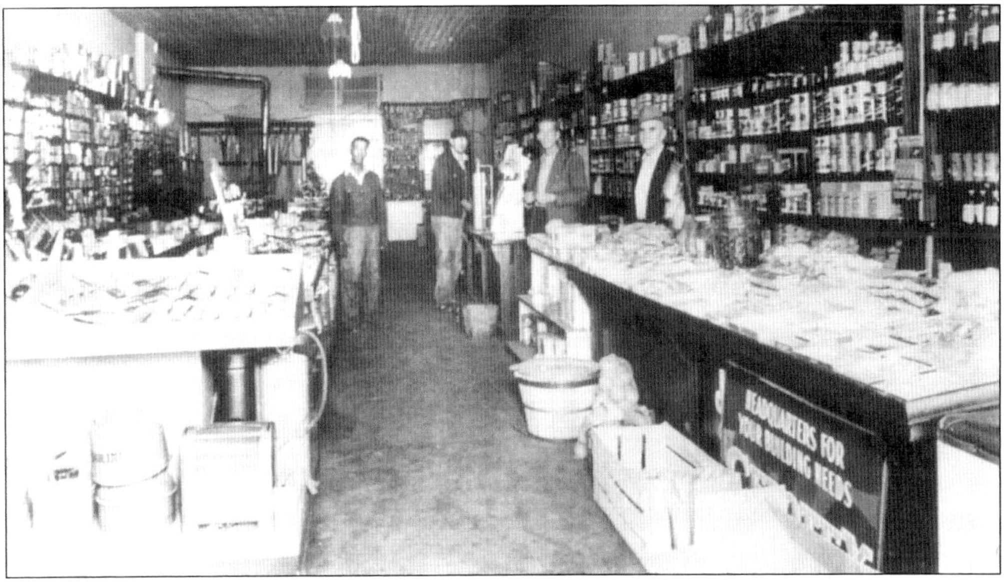

The Curtis Brother's Store in Alexandria was run by Will Curtis and sold building supplies and household merchandise. The store grew and added a furniture and appliance store in the building next door. The Alexandria store closed in the late 1960s and relocated to Smithville, where the fourth generation of Curtis brothers still owns and operates the business. (Courtesy of Ria Baker.)

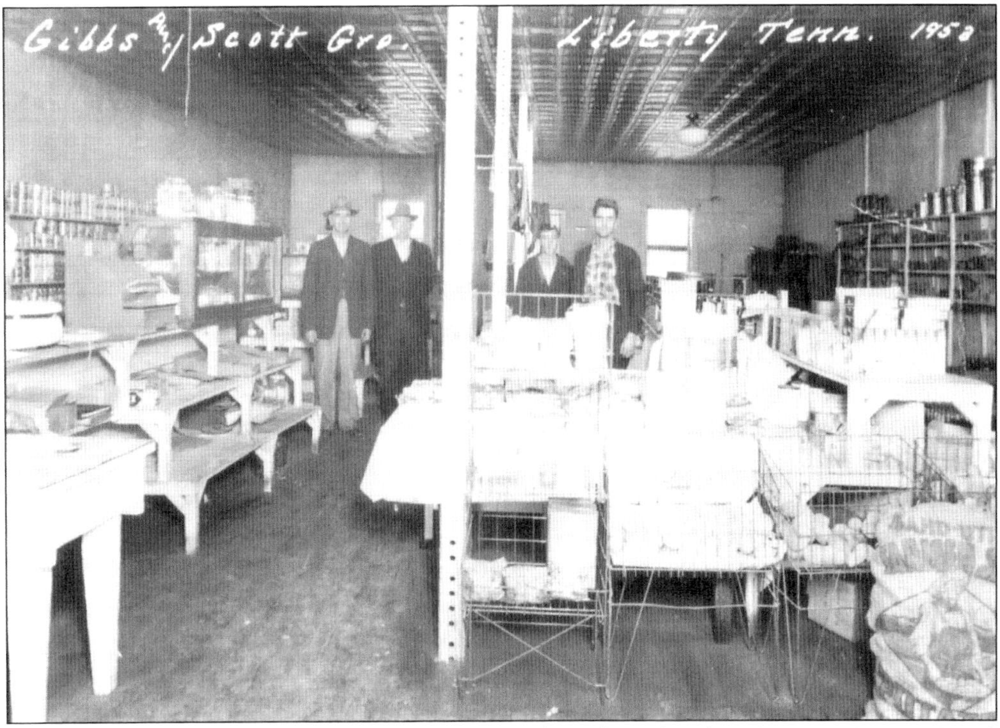

This picture of the Gibbs and Scott Grocery (located in Liberty beside Robinson's Grocery Store) was taken in 1953. Pictured from left to right are owners Clifford Gibbs and Livie Scott with Clifford's grandson Carl Gibbs Jr. and son Carl Gibbs. (Courtesy of Justin Potter Library.)

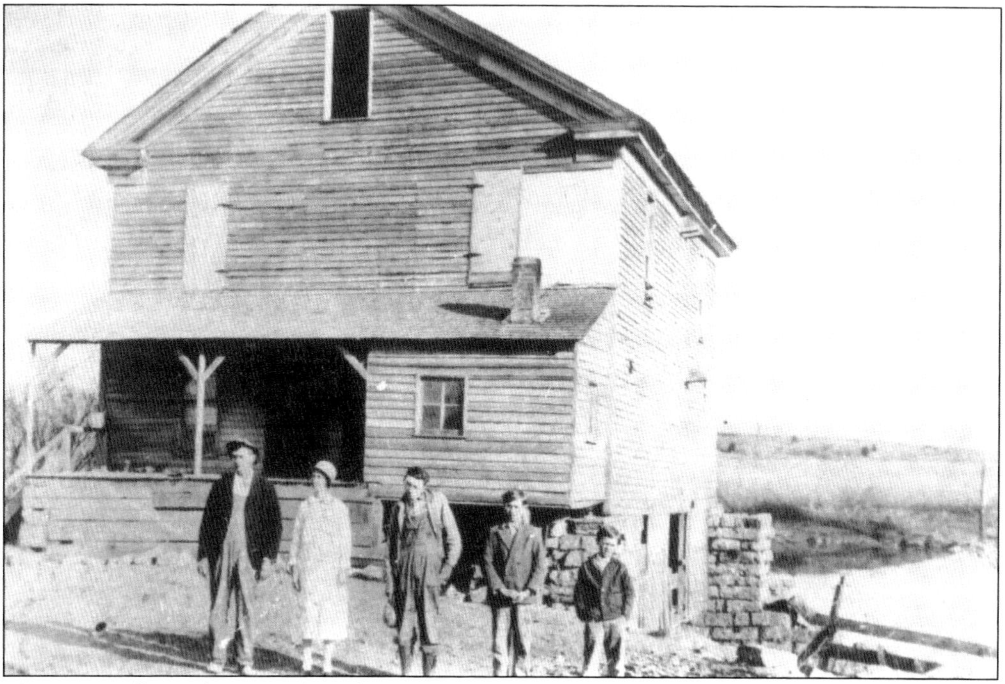

This gristmill stood on Smith Fork Creek just northwest of Temperance Hall in about 1920. It was built by Samuel Caplinger in 1821 and sold in 1842 to Nicholas Smith. However, at the time this picture was taken, the Midgett family was operating it. From left to right are Will and Bell Midgett, and their children Clarence, Odis, and James. (Courtesy of Lois Spencer.)

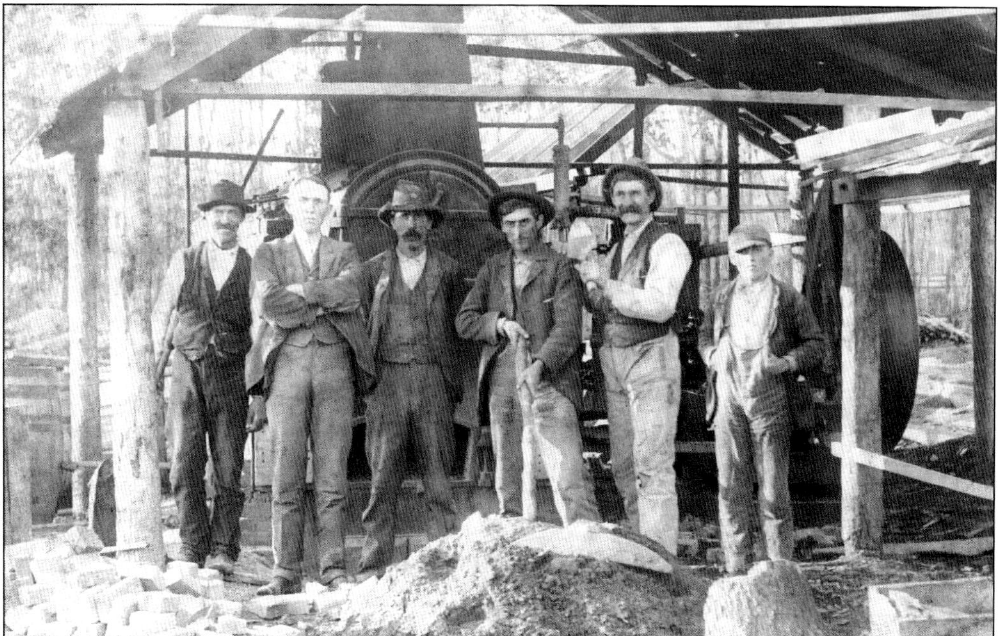

These brick makers in Smithville are, from left to right, J.E. Beckwith, Berry Childress, Sam Keith, Tom Walls, Tom Whaley, and Bob Keith. This picture was taken about three miles west of town in the early 1900s. (Courtesy of Judy Fuson.)

Cripps Mill on Moser Creek was in operation for many years and was run by the Cripps family for most of that time. The first mill was built on this site in 1813, but this picture was taken in August 1903. Gristmills powered by water were the earliest and most common industries of the county and were eventually established in many parts in the area. (Courtesy of Justin Potter Library.)

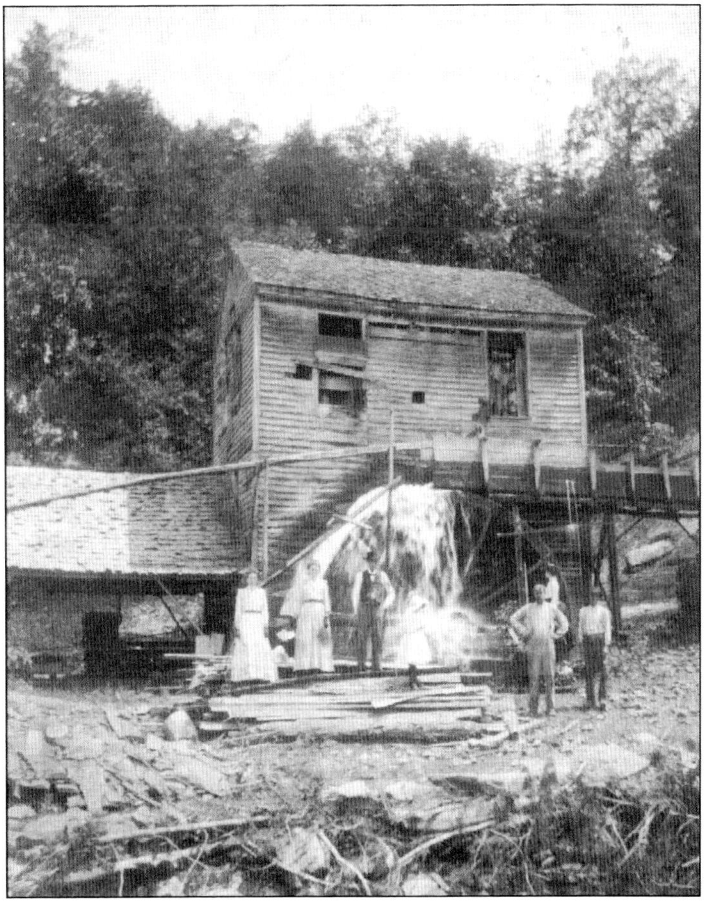

The livery stable and blacksmith shop in Liberty was located along Main Street just to the west of downtown in the early 1900s. (Courtesy of Liberty Historic Group.)

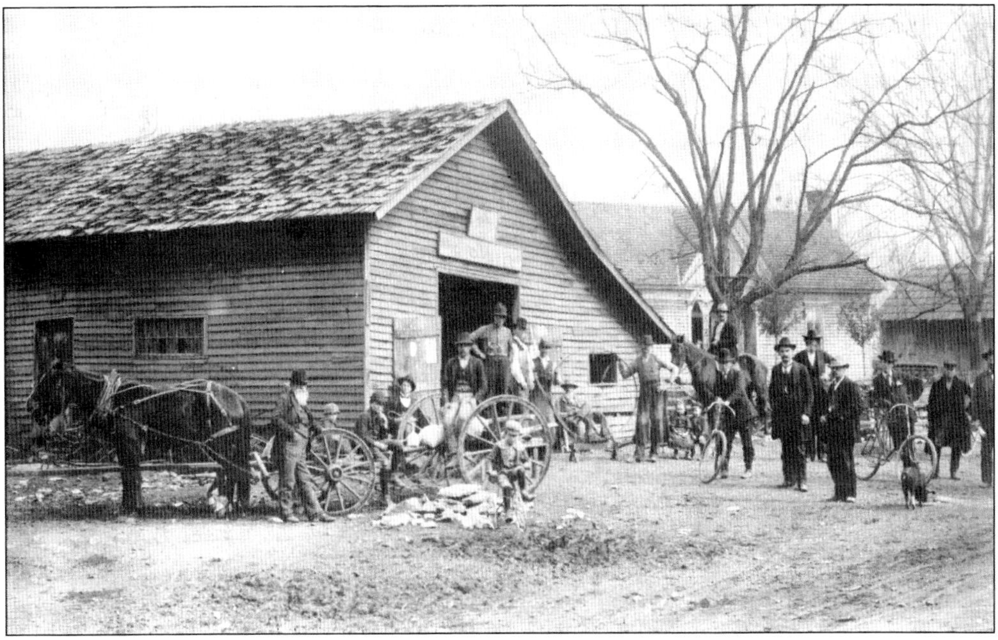

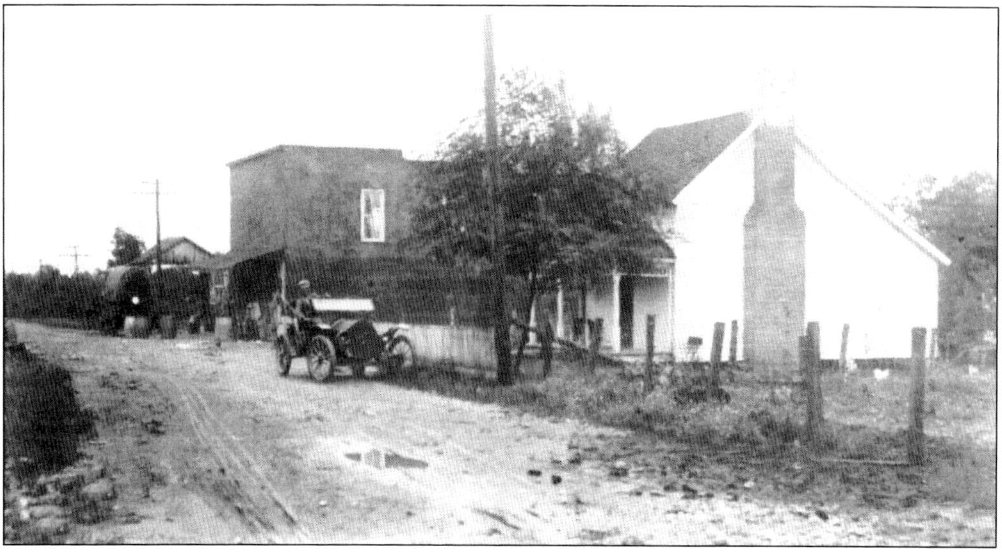

This is the Blend store in 1918, located at the Blend community on Snow's Hill. The store also served as a bus stop for several years and as a post office in the early 1900s, where John F. Hendrixson was appointed postmaster May 1, 1901. (Courtesy of Justin Potter Library.)

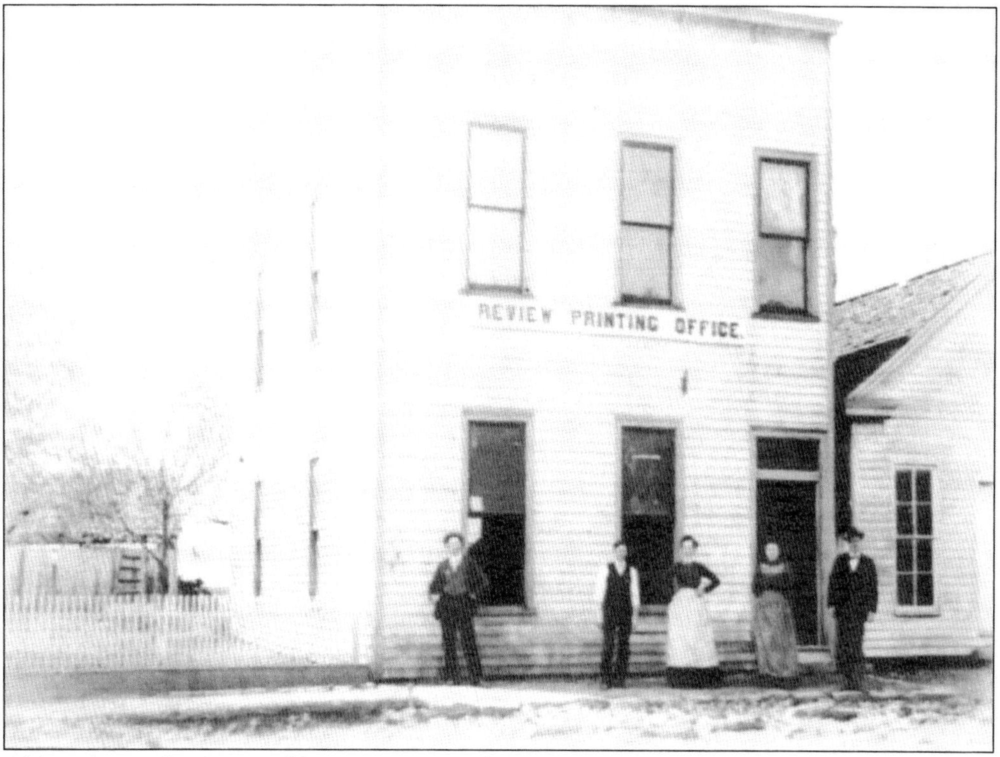

Although not the first weekly newspaper in the county, the *Smithville Review*, shown here in 1908, is still in operation. Percy Wallace started the paper in 1891, and three years later sold it to his brother Frank who built this building. Eugene Hendon (second from left), a native of Shelbyville, Tennessee, was the editor from 1905 until his death in 1946. (Courtesy of Justin Potter Liberty.)

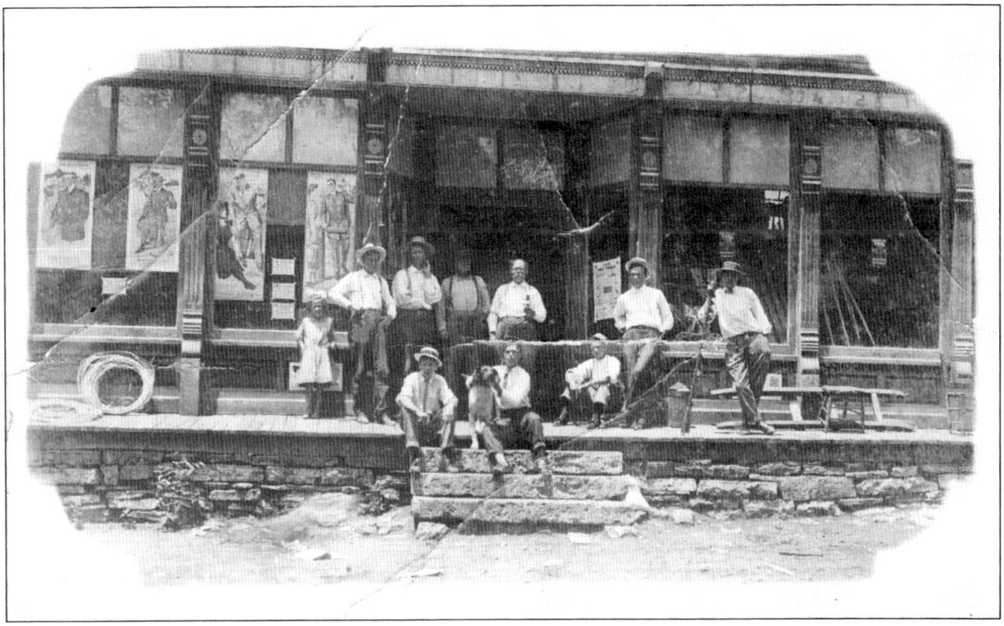

Vick's and Bright's General Store in Liberty was located on the corner of West Church and Main Streets. It burned and was never rebuilt. (Courtesy of Liberty Historic Group.)

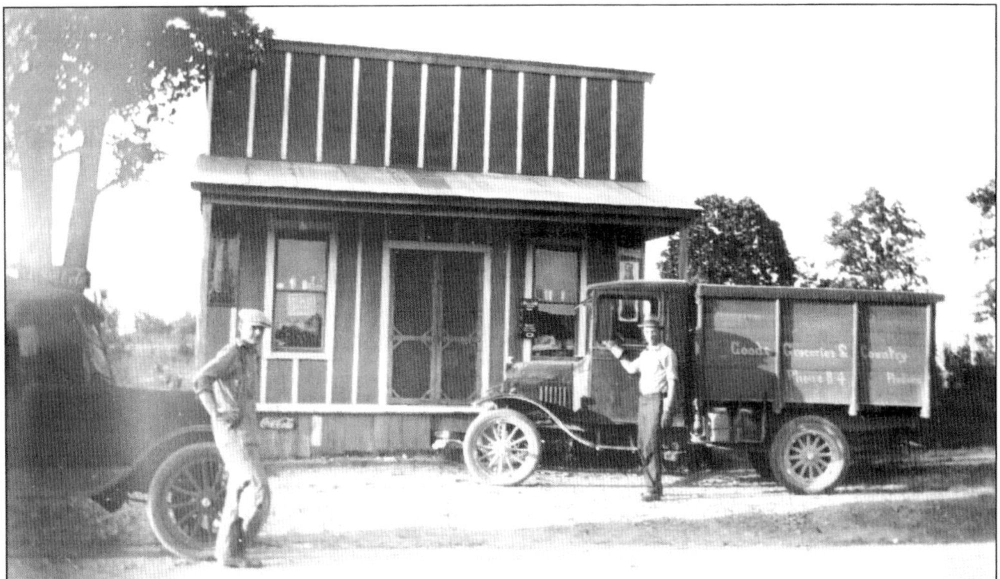

Willie Beckwith's Store stood on the Nashville Turnpike just west of Smithville. He also ran a peddling truck throughout the eastern part of the county. Seen here are Hershel Hoover at the truck on the left and Beckwith at his peddling truck in 1927. (Courtesy of Judy Fuson.)

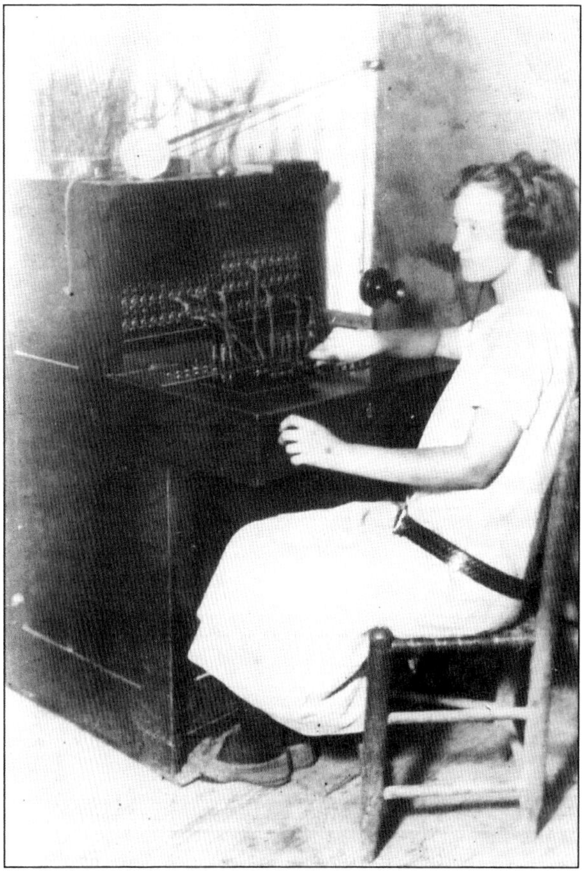

This is Willett Martin, the switchboard operator in Dowelltown. She later married Robert Anderson, and they opened a filling station and a funeral home together. Because they had no building to hold funerals in, they used their home for visitation and sometimes held funerals on the porch of the store downtown. They later moved to Alexandria and owned a funeral home there. (Courtesy of the Paschal family.)

In the early 1900s, James Edgar Evins traveled around selling coffee and spices. This picture shows his sons William Jackson (W.J.) Evins, standing, and Joseph Landon (Joe L.) Evins, seated. Joe L. grew up to become a US congressman, serving from 1946 until 1976 and working tirelessly for his beloved state and county. (Courtesy of Justin Potter Library.)

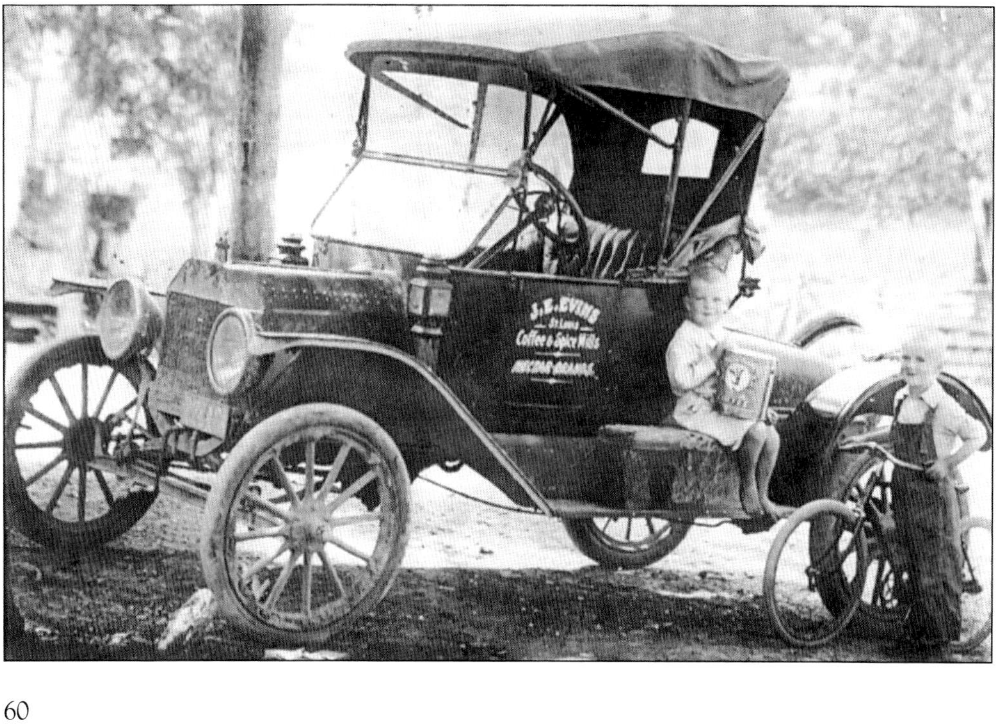

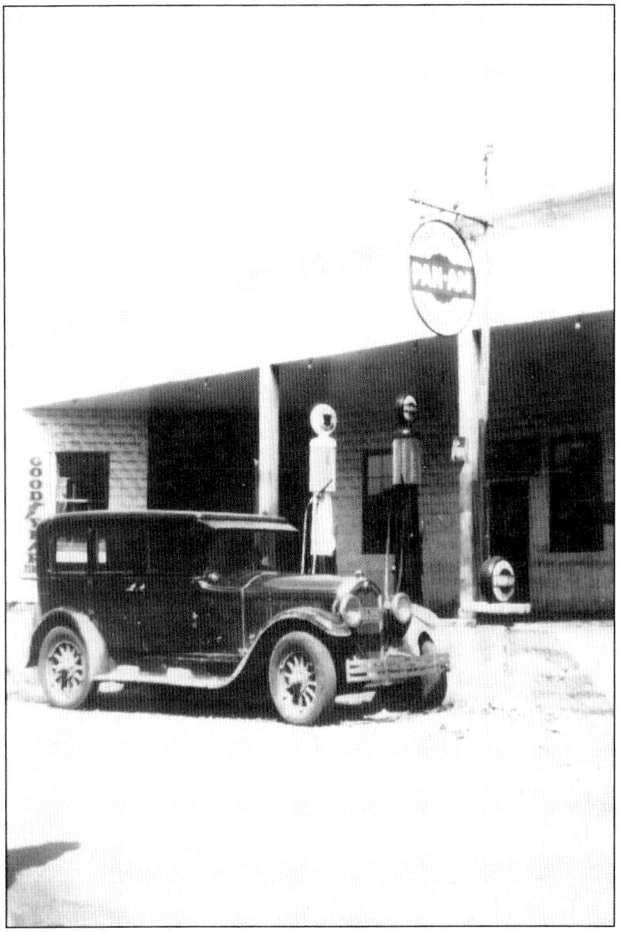

Anderson's Service Station was located on the corner of West Main and Mill Streets in Dowelltown and was owned and operated by Robert and Willett in the 1930s. The building was once Turner's Dry Goods Store and was owned by J.T. Turner of Dowelltown. The building was destroyed by the 1974 tornado. (Courtesy of the Paschal family.)

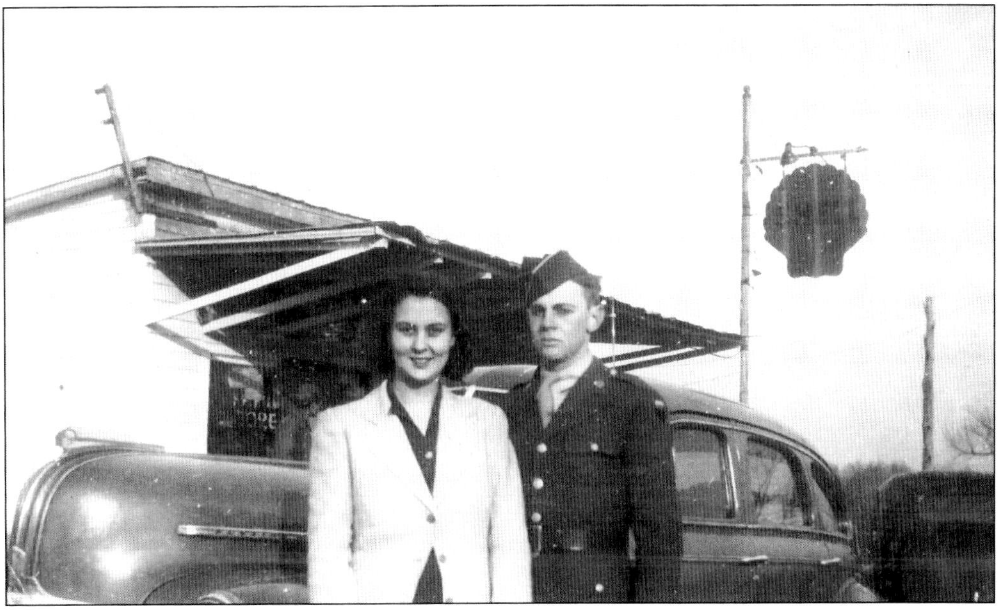

Eudene and Inez McDowell Driver are waiting for the bus at Fally Hill's store at the top of Old Snow Hill Road in 1943. Eudene was killed the next June during the D-Day invasion in Normandy. He was brought back home and is buried at Whorton Springs Cemetery. (Courtesy of David McDowell.)

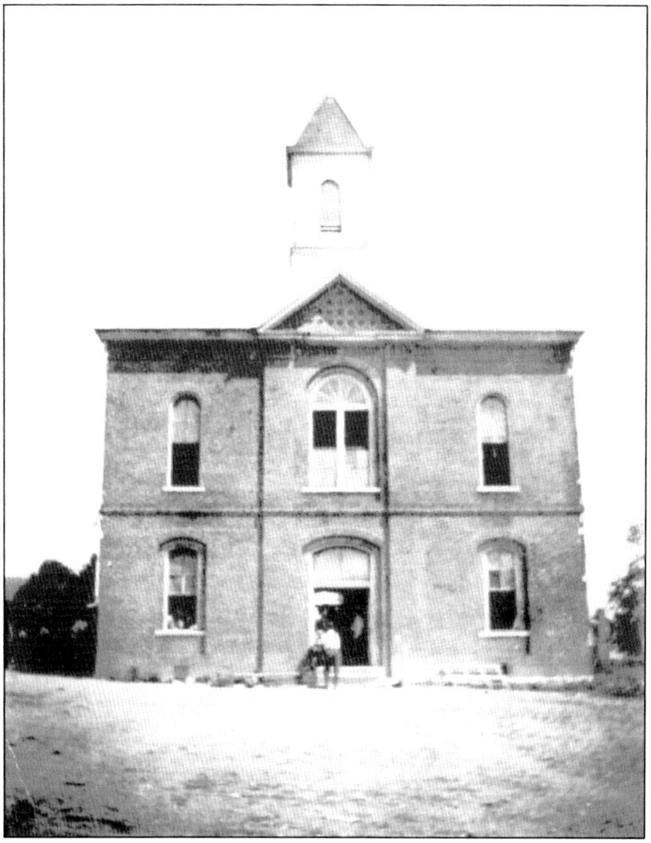

This is the second courthouse that was built in DeKalb County in 1890 in the center of the square. This picture was taken in 1912; the courthouse was destroyed by fire in 1925. (Courtesy of Justin Potter Library.)

This picture of the Smithville Square was taken in 1917 and shows the day that the boys were sent to fight in World War I. It was taken from a courthouse window looking northeast. (Courtesy of Justin Potter Library.)

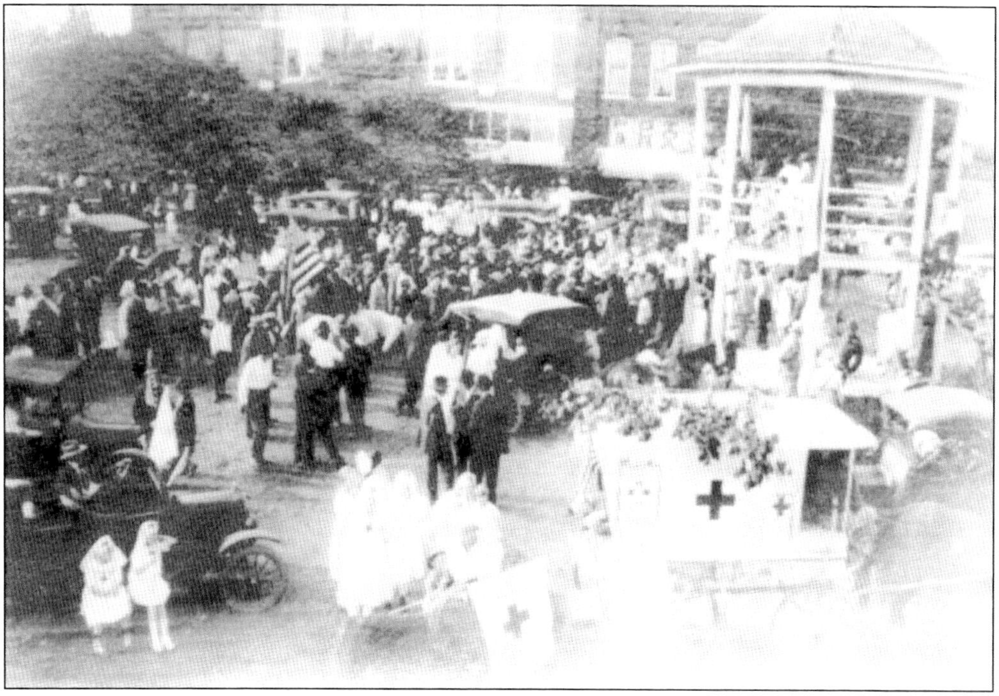

Winket Tramel is standing at the hand gas pump in front of his little country store just west of Smithville on the Nashville Turnpike in the 1930s. He was a Methodist minister and was named after Wingate T. Robinson, his grandfather's commanding officer in the Civil War. When his grandfather said the name with a Southern hill accent it sounded like "Winket," which is why he was not named Wingate. (Courtesy of Annie Ruth Greer.)

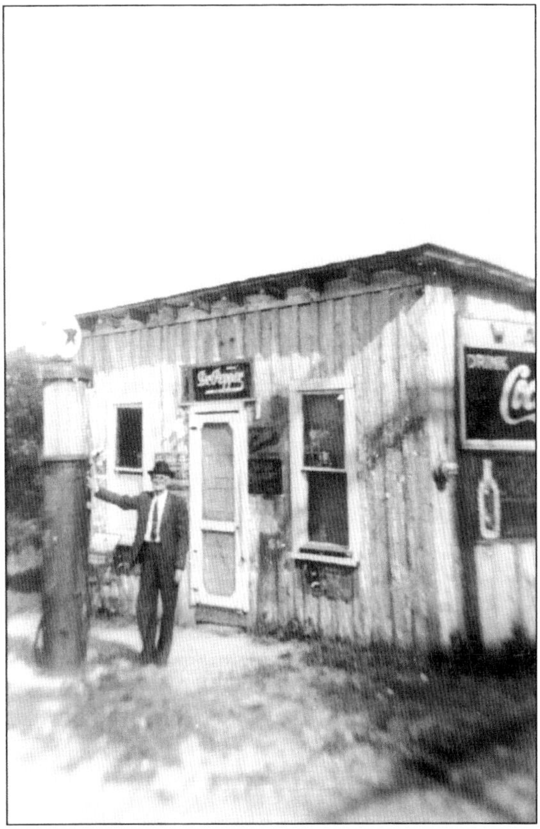

Erby Oakley's Service Station was located on High Street in Alexandria. This picture was taken around 1920. Erby and his wife, Ida, owned and operated the station until the mid-1970s. (Courtesy of Ria Baker.)

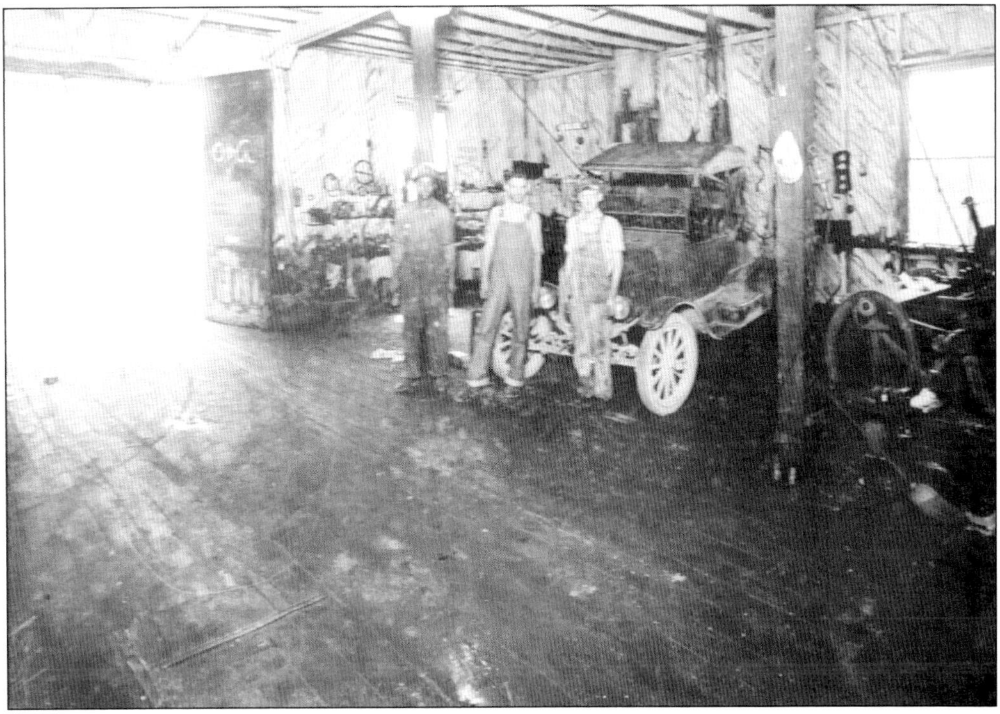

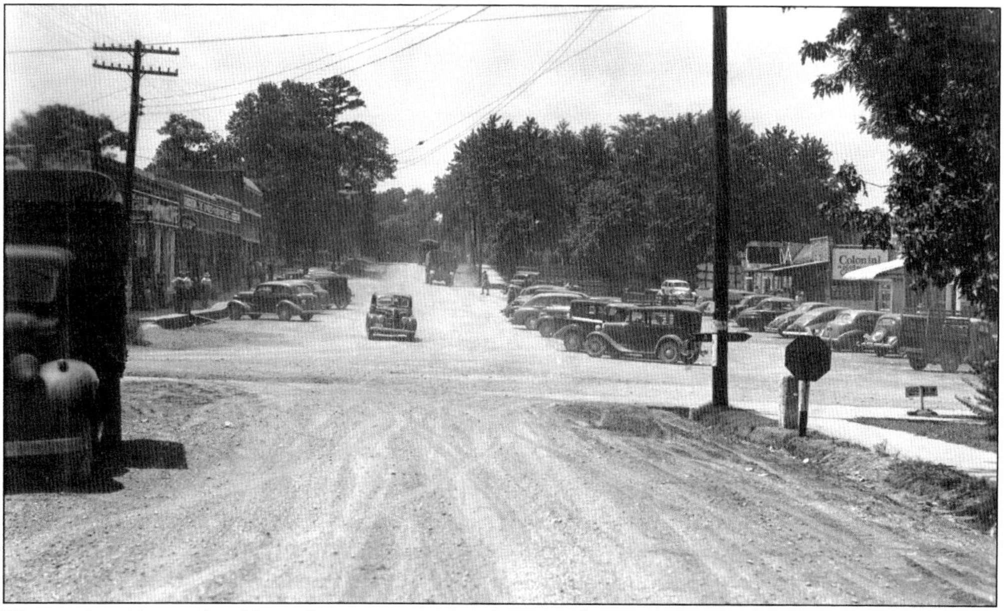

This is the Alexandria Town Square in 1942. This was the summer the World War II maneuvers took place in the county, as evidenced by the Army trucks traveling down West Main Street in the background. (Courtesy of Ria Baker.)

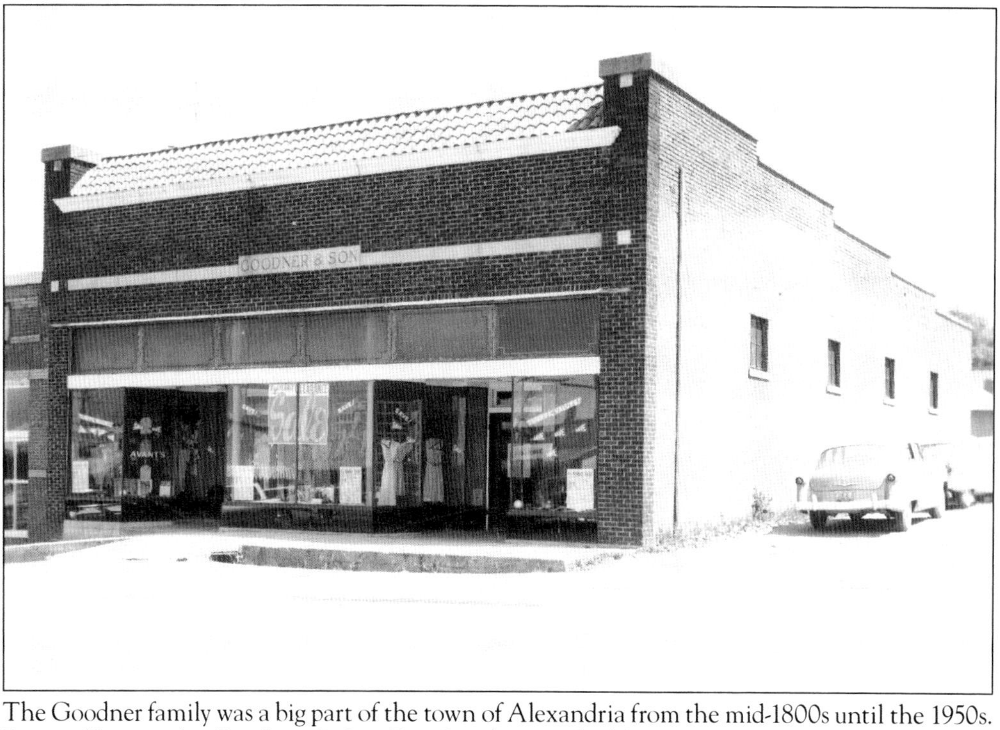

The Goodner family was a big part of the town of Alexandria from the mid-1800s until the 1950s. Pictured here is the Goodner & Son Dry Goods Store building on the southwest corner of the square. Their store was established in 1856, and the first building burned in 1929. Clay Avant was the owner and operator of the store when this picture was taken in the 1960s. (Courtesy of Ria Baker.)

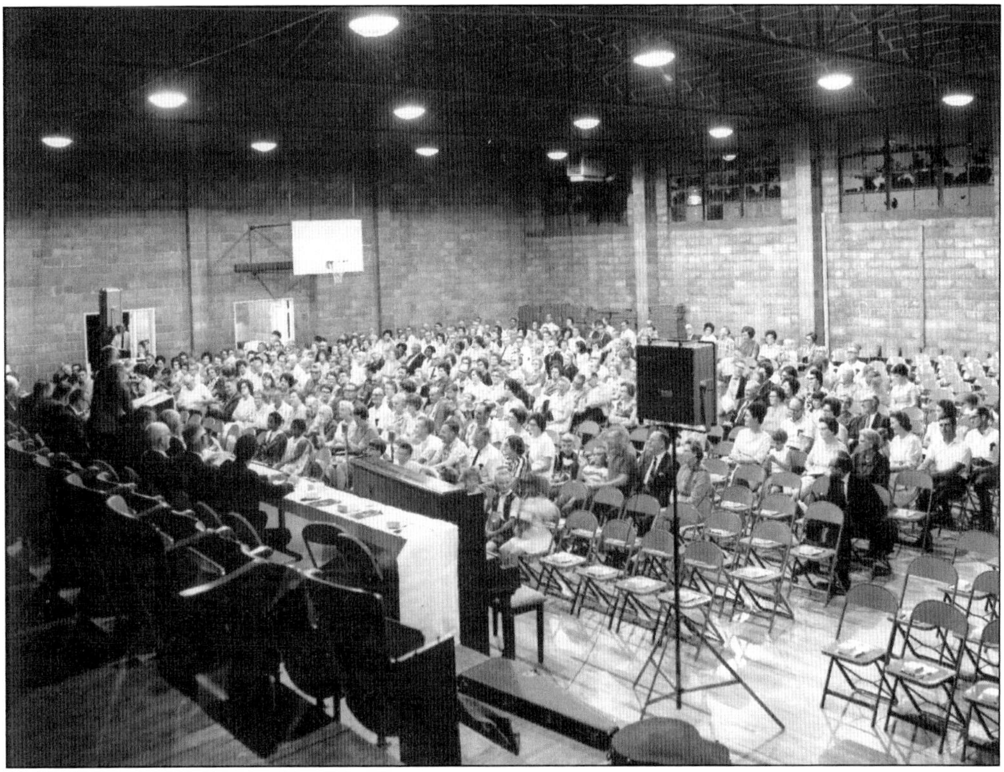

DeKalb Telephone Co-op was established in 1951 and opened for business in 1953. This picture taken inside the Alexandria Elementary School gymnasium shows an annual membership meeting in the mid-1960s. (Courtesy of Ria Baker.)

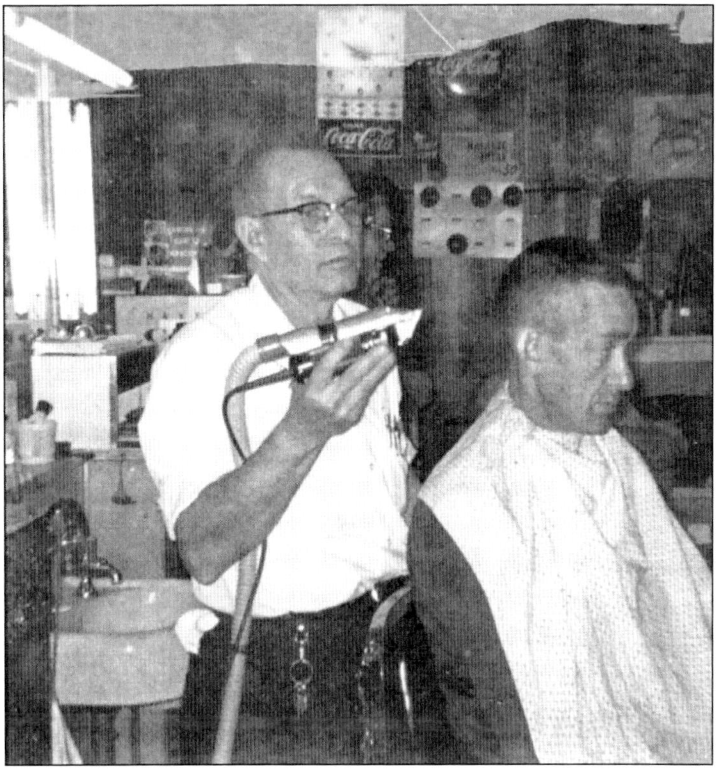

In Alexandria, Jennings Barbershop was the hub of information. James Jennings cut hair in Alexandria from the 1930s until his death in 1973. Pictured are barber James Jennings and Jimmy Reasonover getting a haircut in the late 1950s. (Courtesy of Ria Baker.)

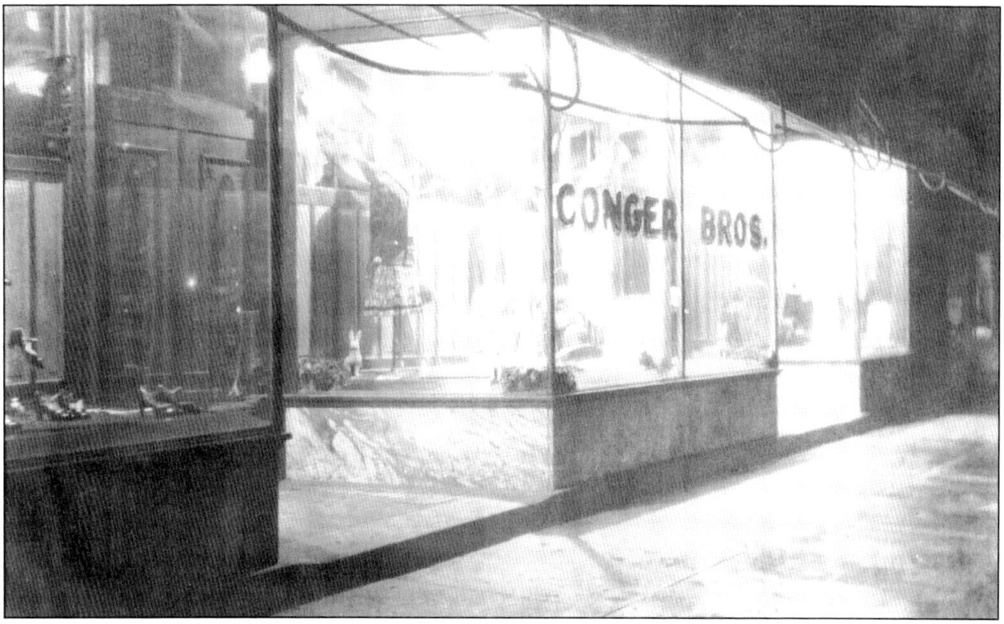

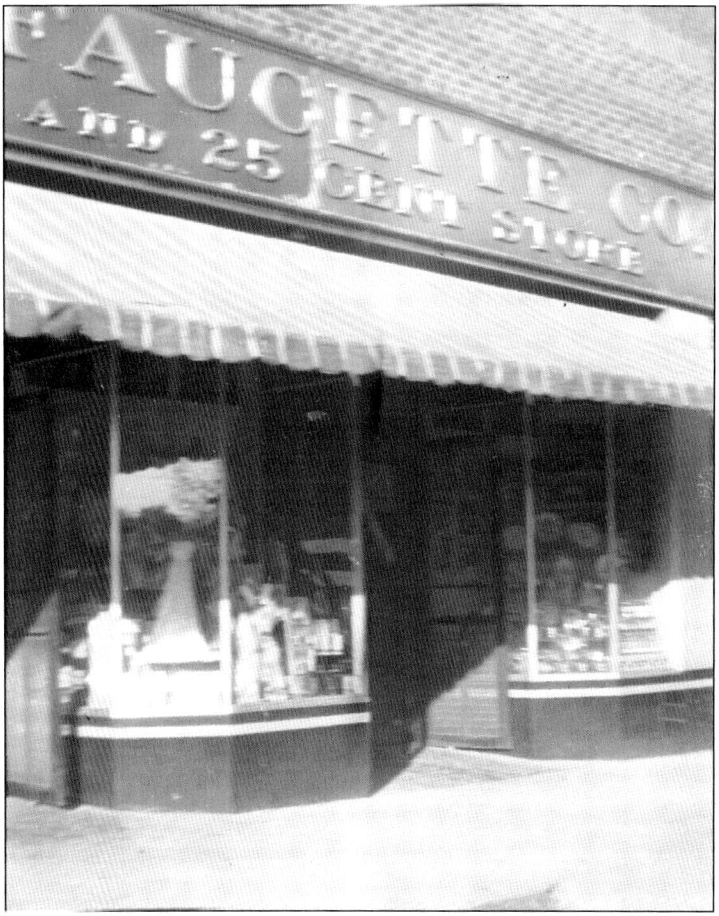

Pictured in 1928, the Conger Brother's Store was located on the north side of the square in Smithville where the 303 Building is now. A fire destroyed the entire block where this store was located in 1931. (Courtesy of Justin Potter Library.)

The Faucette Co. 5, 10, and 25 Cent Store was in Smithville around 1940 where the Fuston's 5 and 10 Cent Store was later located. This is now the location of Fluty's Shoe Store on West Main Street. (Courtesy of Annie Ruth Greer.)

Charles Mauldin, seen here at work around 1940 in Whaley's Drugstore in Liberty, lived at 384 Main Street with his mother, Mandy. Percy and Exum Whaley, owners and operators of the store, boasted hot sandwiches and a nickel slot machine. The building was formerly a saloon with one wall of mirrors and a soda fountain still remaining. (Courtesy of Liberty Historic Group.)

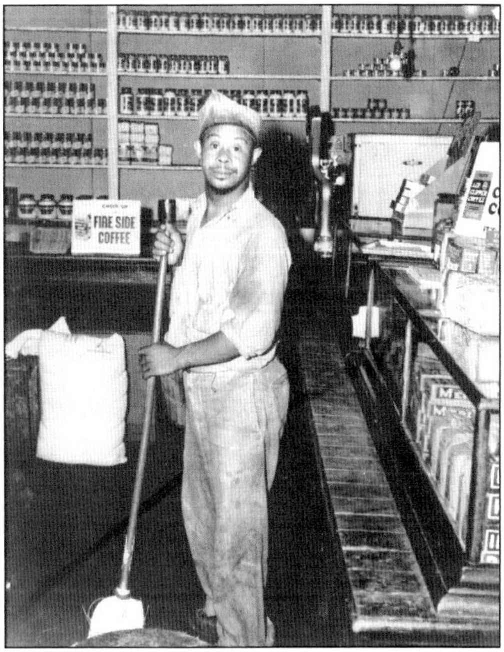

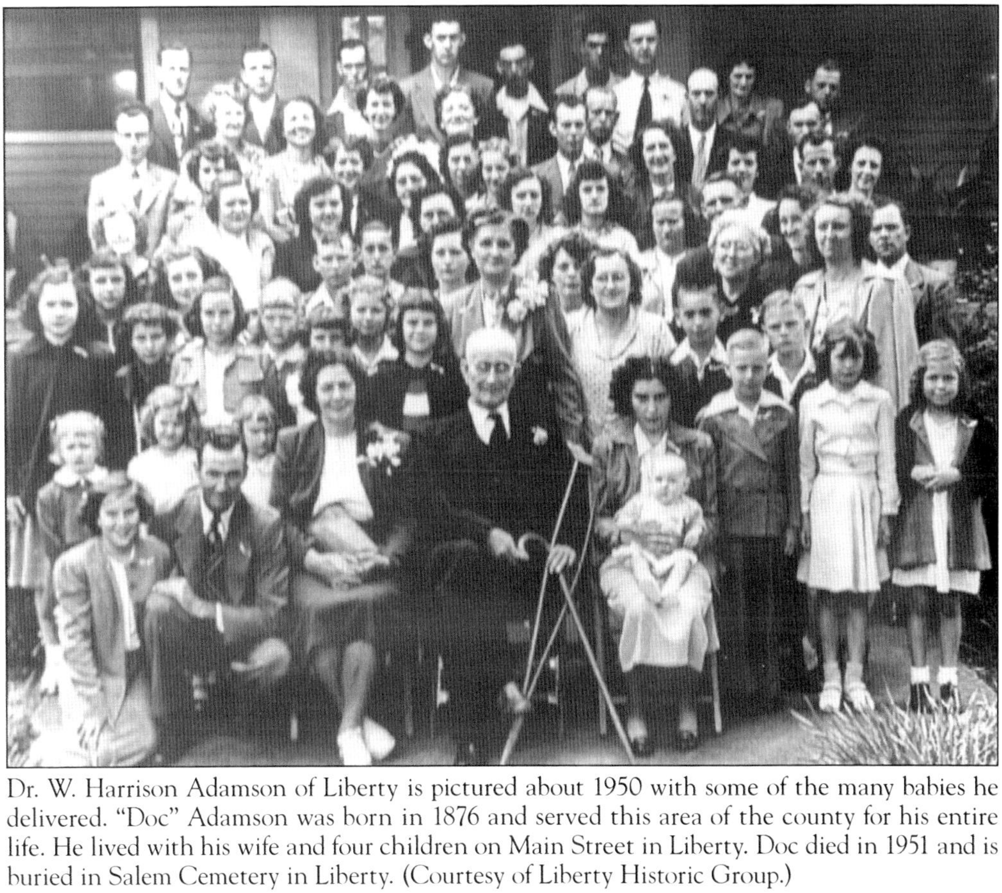

Dr. W. Harrison Adamson of Liberty is pictured about 1950 with some of the many babies he delivered. "Doc" Adamson was born in 1876 and served this area of the county for his entire life. He lived with his wife and four children on Main Street in Liberty. Doc died in 1951 and is buried in Salem Cemetery in Liberty. (Courtesy of Liberty Historic Group.)

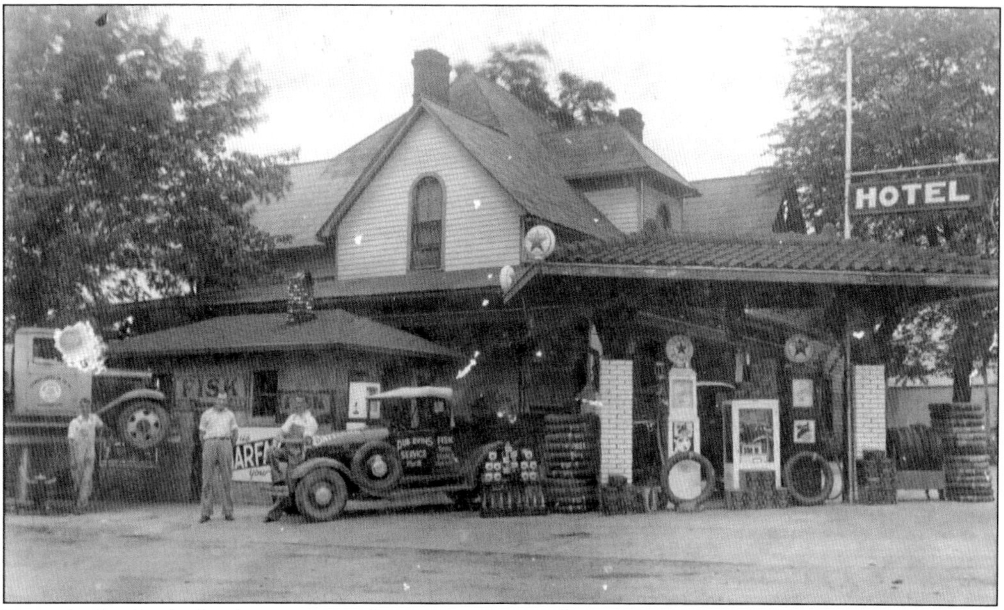

Ewen Staley built this house around 1899 on the southwest corner of College and Main Streets in Smithville. Around 1930 it was bought by Edgar and Myrtie Evins, who converted it into a hotel, which was run by Paul and Mary Claire Willoughby. Edgar's son, W.J. (Dub), leaning on the front of the truck, then built and operated Smithville's first service station on the corner of the lot. (Courtesy of Tommy Webb.)

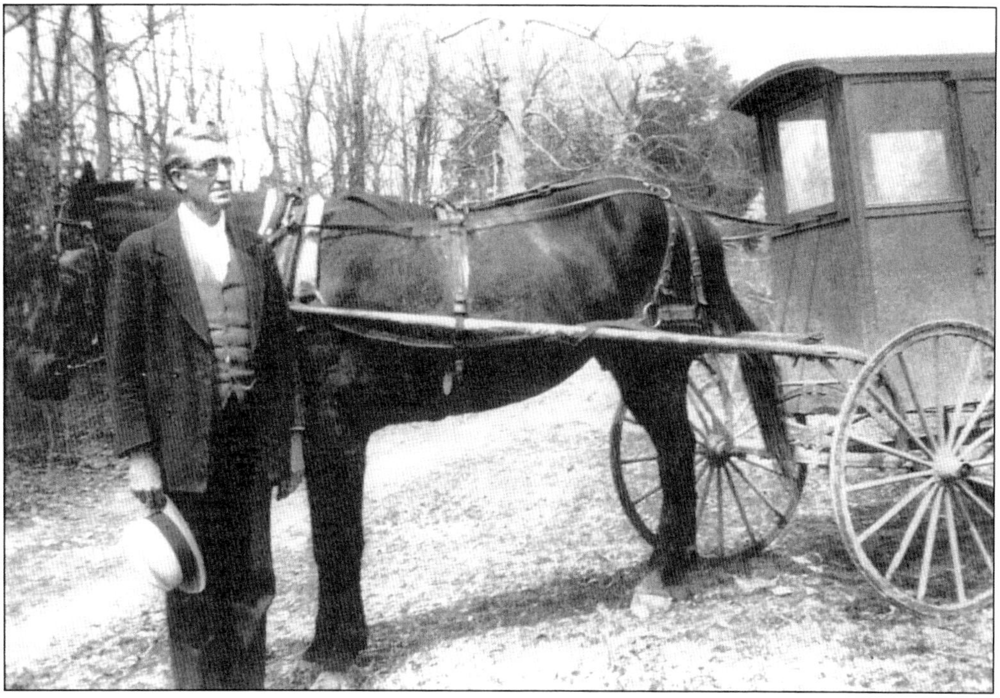

In 1920, John J. Tramel was a farmer living on Indian Creek. He later moved to Liberty, near Salem Baptist Church, and became a Rural Free Delivery mail carrier. This picture of Tramel with his horse and mail cart was taken in about 1925. (Courtesy of Liberty Historic Group.)

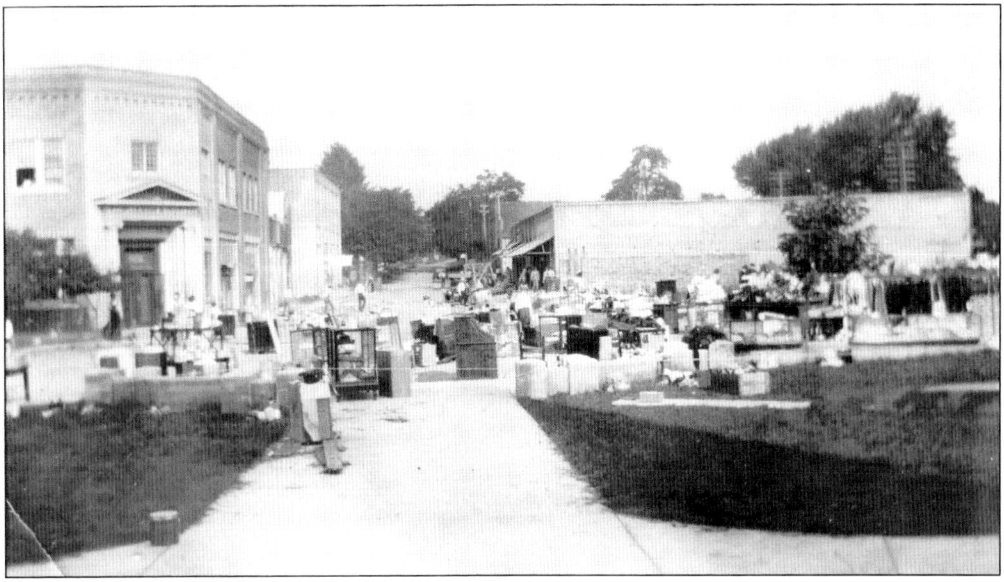

This photograph was taken the morning after the fire on June 18, 1923, that burned the Staley and Evans Store. This is a view from the county courthouse on the Smithville Square and shows the things saved from the fire. Notable is the building on the left, which was the First National Bank and later Cantrell's Jewelry Store. (Courtesy of Peggy Huffstetler.)

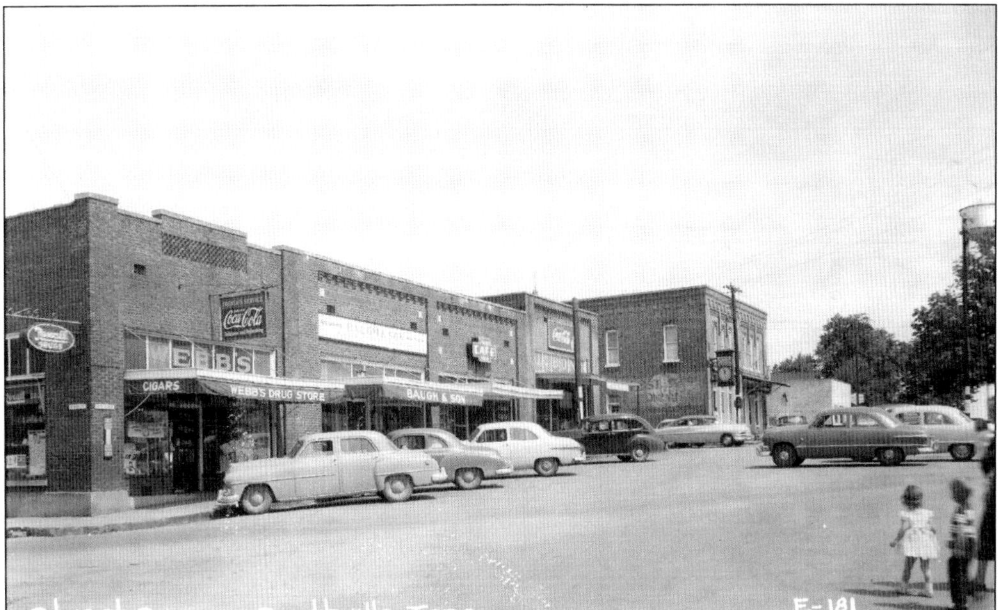

Located on the corner of West Main Street at the public square in Smithville, F.Z. Webb's Drugstore is the oldest continually run store in the county. It was established by Webb in 1881 and is where he met his true love, Amanda Smith, when she came in to shop. It is still owned and operated by the Webb family. This photograph was taken in the mid-1950s. Also pictured on this block are the Baugh and Son Clothing Store, Trapp's Cafe, and J.C. Bond's Grocery Store. The Farmers and Traders Bank on the next block was built in 1894 and is the oldest building still standing on the square. (Courtesy of Carol Williams.)

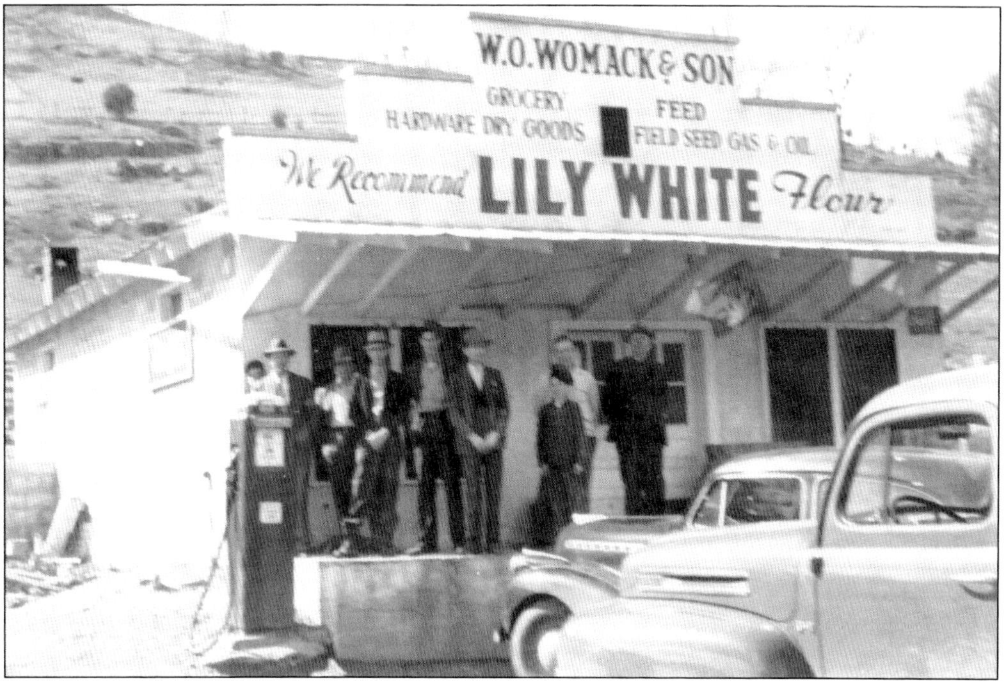

Located on Dry Creek in 1947, W.O. Womack & Son Grocery carried farmers' bills from one crop to another. Pictured in front of the store are, from left to right, Will Allen Cathcart, John A. Stephens, Edwin Owens, Odell Johnson, Dave Stephens, Jimmy Womack, Robert Fuston Jr., and W.O. Womack. (Courtesy of Louise Frazier.)

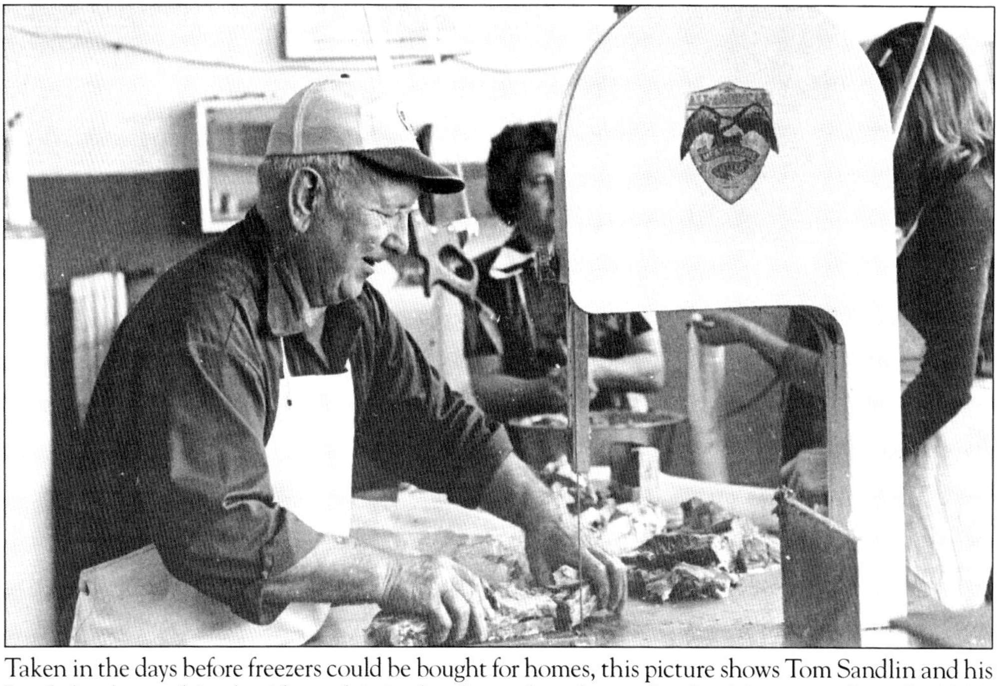

Taken in the days before freezers could be bought for homes, this picture shows Tom Sandlin and his family hard at work in the Alexandria Locker, located on the south side of the square from the 1940s through the 1970s. They also rented freezer space to customers. (Courtesy of Genrose Davis.)

Four

GOOD TIMES FOR ALL

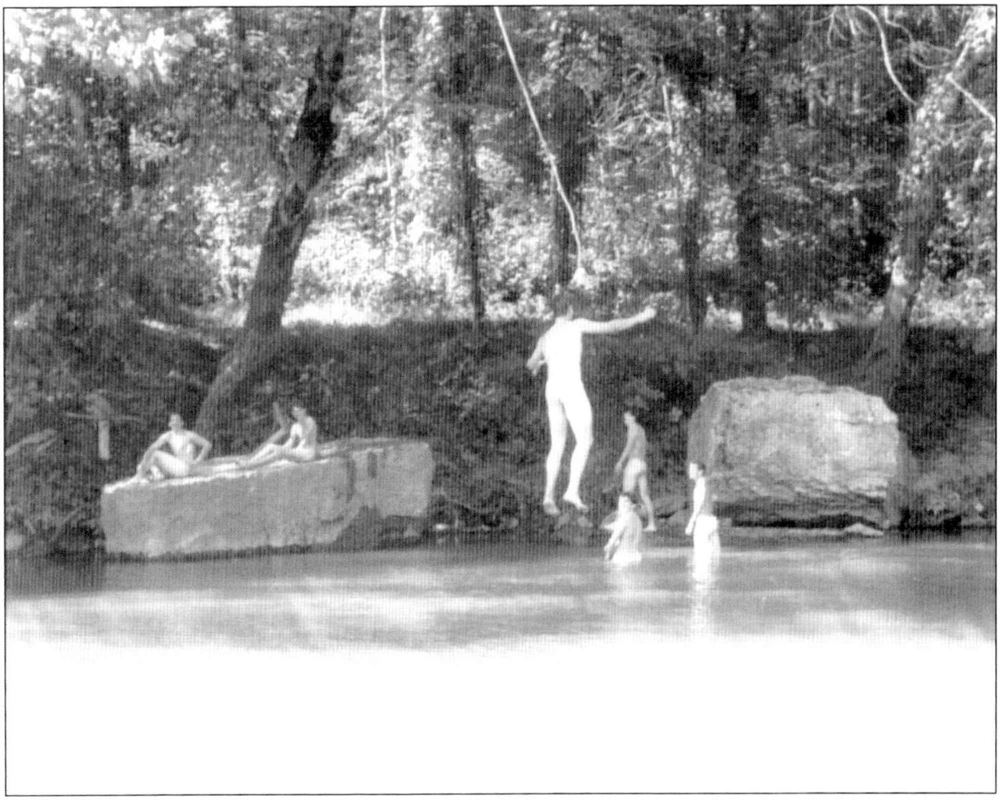

On a hot summer day was anything better than a cool dip in the creek or lake? This picture shows a bunch of teenage boys cooling off and having fun at the Gin Bluff swimming hole on the Smith Fork Creek between Liberty and Dowelltown. (Courtesy of Justin Potter Library.)

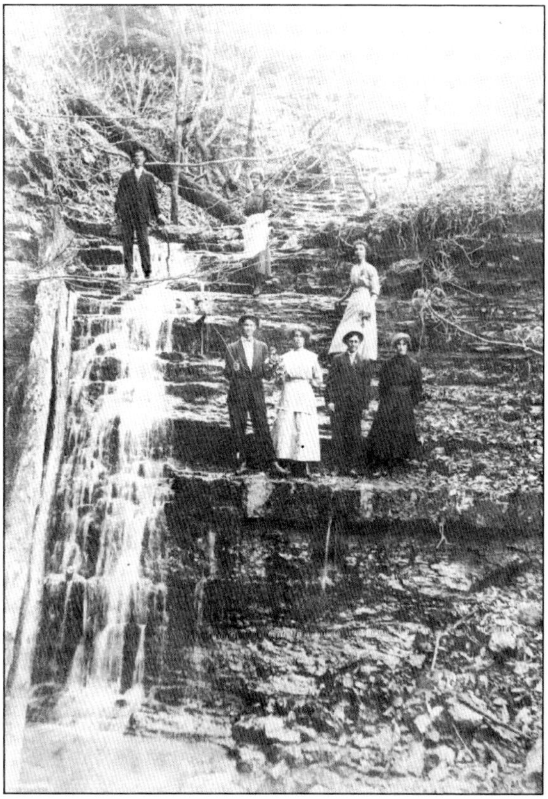

On April 5, 1913, a spring fling was held at the falls in Egypt Hollow on Dry Creek. Young people usually congregated at places like this every spring after a winter inside. The people in this picture are, from left to right, (first row) Billie Parker, Mae Hayes, Troy Vandergriff, and Lizzie Mullican; (second row) Emily Beckwith; (third row) Fate Mullican and Ola Parker. (Courtesy of Judy Fuson.)

Dowelltown ladies (from left to right) Ocie Oakley, Mary Etta Oakley, Martha Ella Vandergriff, and Maude Oakley had a musical group in the late 1800s. Individuals offered music lessons to groups at this time, which resulted in the formation of many bands throughout the county. (Courtesy of Ron Paschal.)

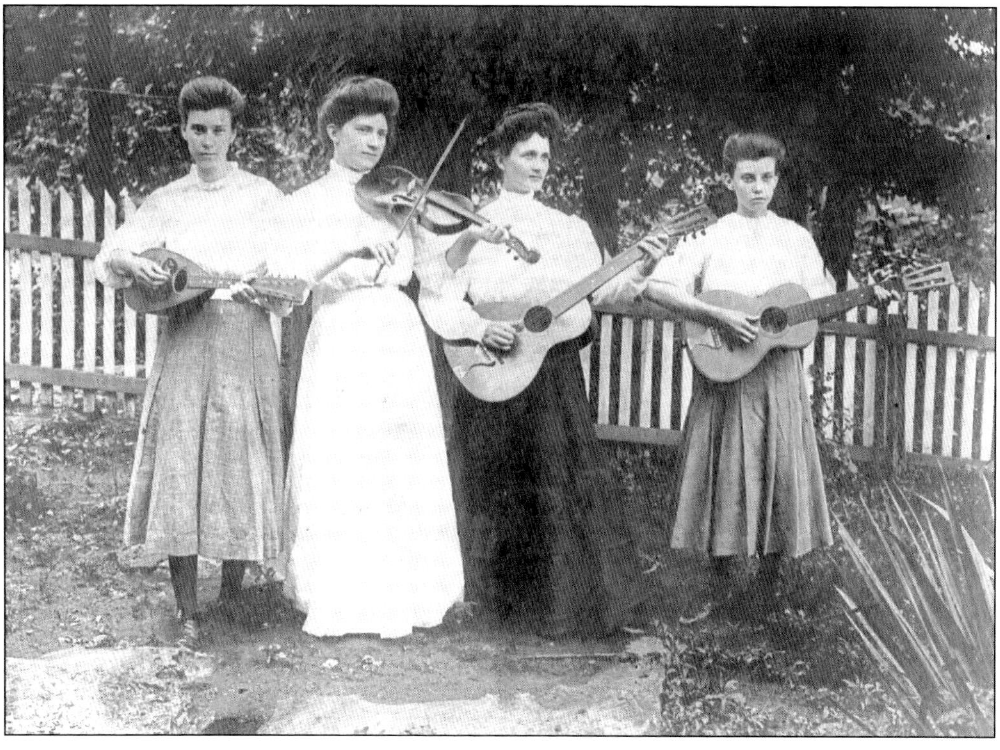

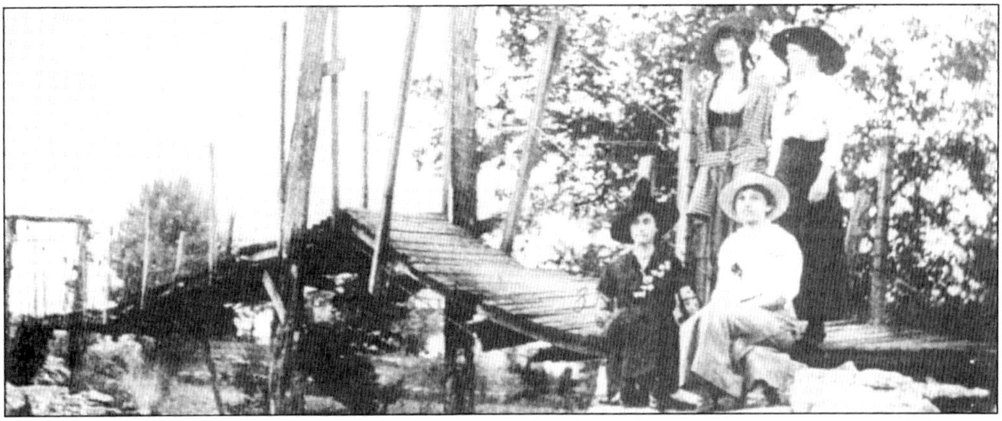

From left to right, Myrtle Smith, Betty Joe Dinges, Eula Butterbaugh, and Emma Dinges are shown in about 1907 on the Swinging Bridge over Hickman Creek that led to the DeKalb County Fairgrounds in Alexandria. (Courtesy of Ria Baker.)

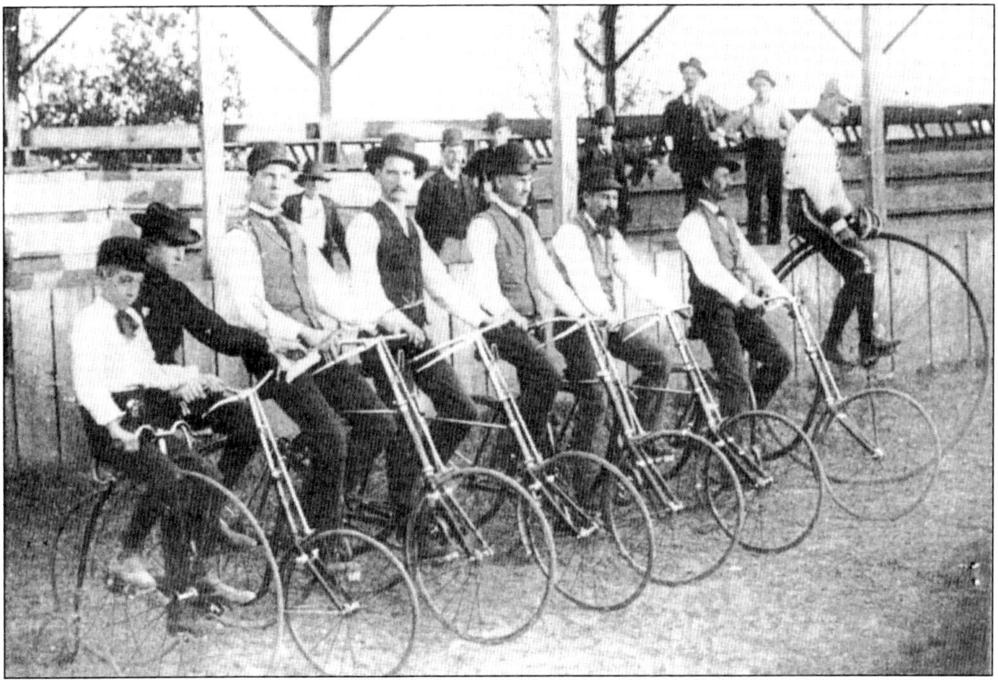

A bicycle club photographed at the DeKalb County Fair in Alexandria in the early 1890s includes, from left to right, Frank Roy, Rob Roy, Will Odom, Bob Bruce, Miller Schuer, J.F. Roy, John Rutland, and Lavader Woodard. (Courtesy of Ria Baker.)

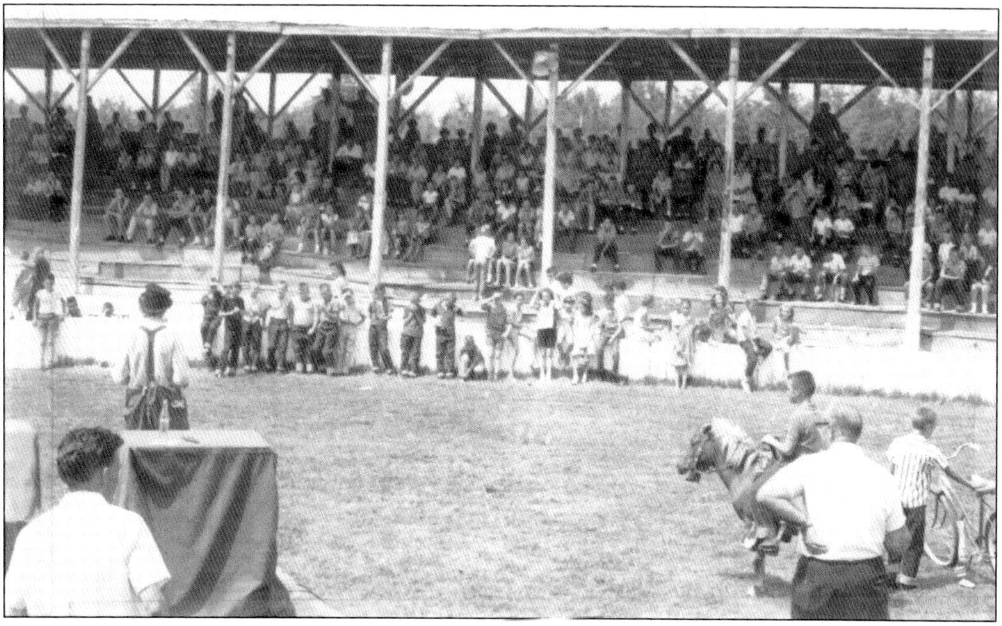

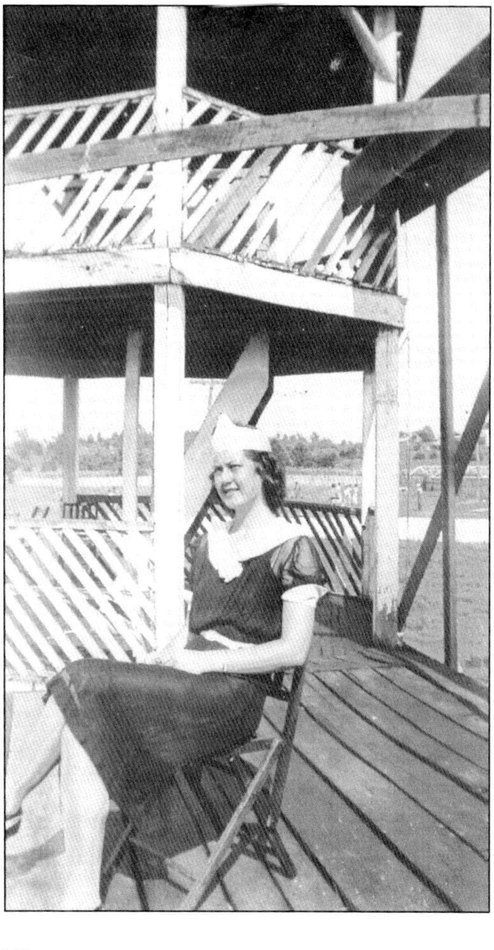

This mid-1950s photograph of the DeKalb County Fair's Children Day boasts clowns, cheap rides, and both a bike and a pony to be given away. Located in Alexandria, this fair is in the National Register of Historic Places. Known as the "Grandpa Fair of the South," it has been in operation since April 15, 1856. The grandstand seen here is one of the only ones still in use in the United States. (Courtesy of Ria Baker.)

This young lady, Gaynell Brown, won Most Beautiful Girl at the fair in 1938. Unlike pageants today, the lady was chosen from the crowd on the first day of the fair. Gaynell was born and raised and lived and died in DeKalb County. Both a wife and mother, Gaynell was also the Alexandria postmistress in later years. (Courtesy of Mac Willoughby.)

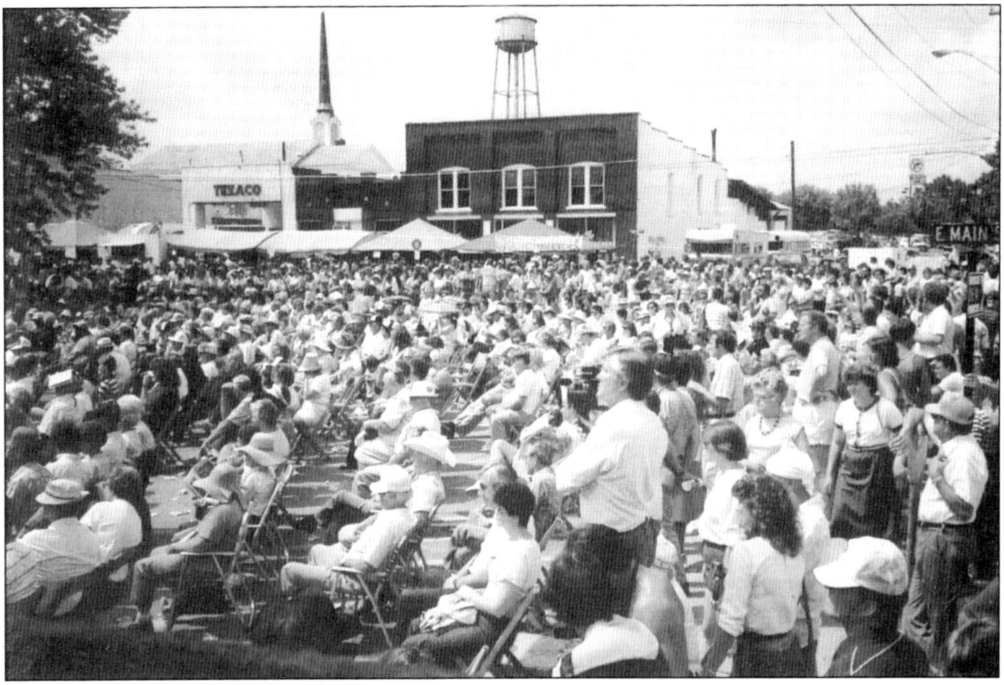

The Smithville Fiddler's Jamboree started in 1971 and was first held on the west side of the courthouse with 714 musicians and an estimated 8,000 people to enjoy the music. It is always hot on the first weekend of July, but many people sit out in the sun to watch those wonderful musicians. This is when the Fiddlers Jamboree was moved to the east side of the square and shows a larger crowd of spectators enjoying the music. (Courtesy of Annette Greek.)

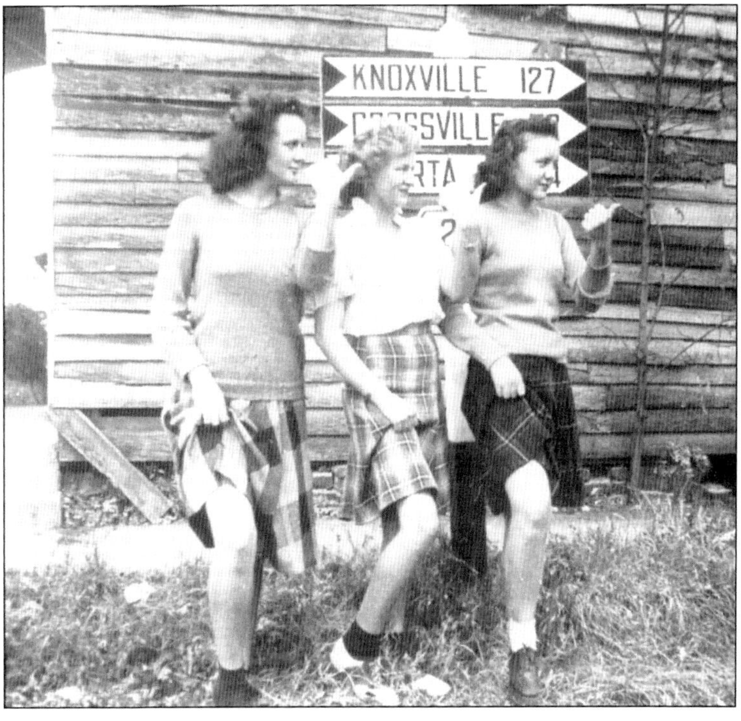

From left to right, Clarene Hendrixson, Christeen Tramel, and Emojene Cantrell are standing at the side of the old Webb House on the corner of East Main Street thumbing for a ride in 1945. Although many young men traveled using their thumb, these young ladies are only having fun for the picture. (Courtesy of Ruth Taylor.)

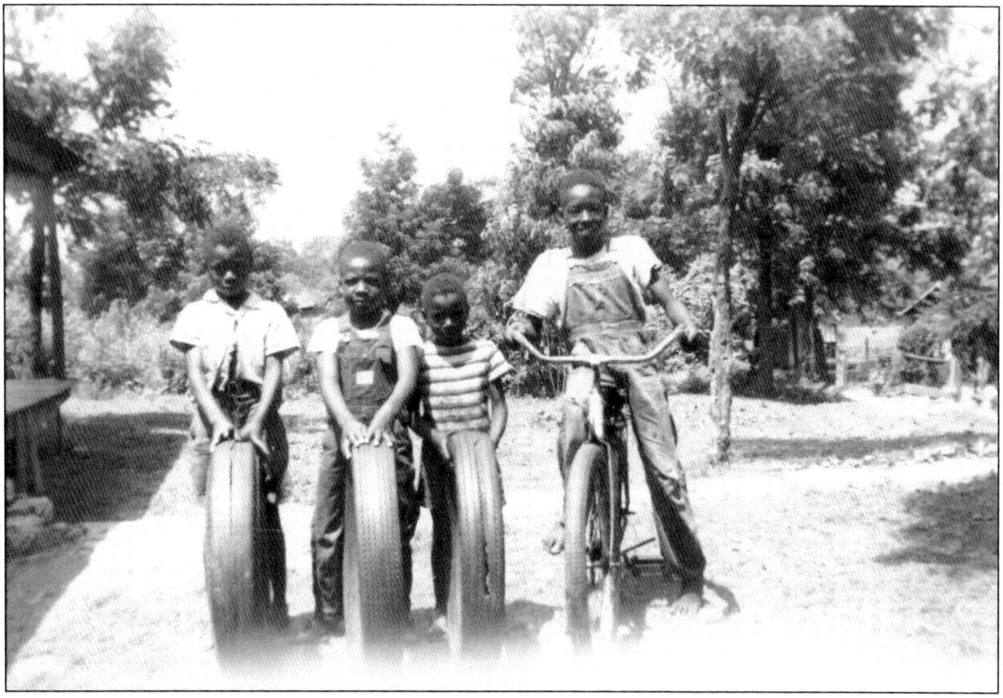

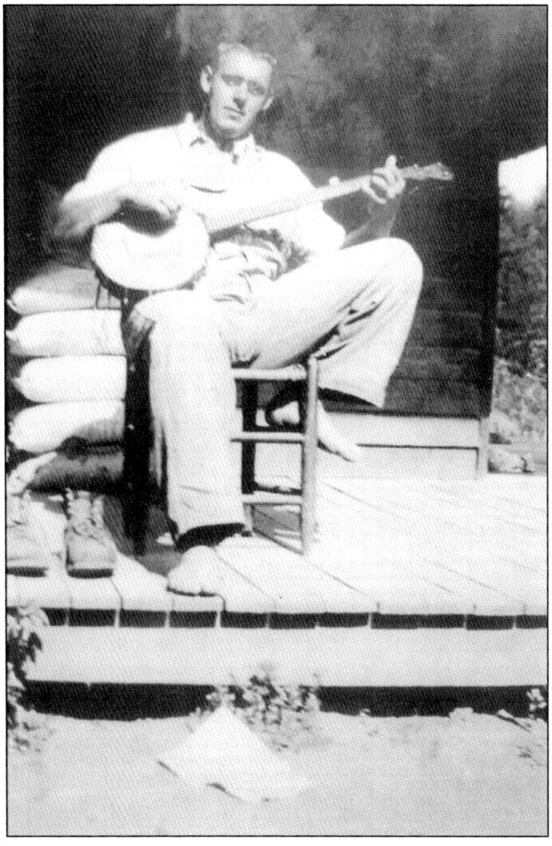

In the 1950s, this group of boys in Alexandria still used old tires and of course their bikes to have fun. With no electric games to play, children were left to use their imagination to fill the long summer days. (Courtesy of Inez Bass.)

Shown with his old-time banjo, Resen Page has pulled off his dusty brogans and picked while resting from a long day's work on the farm in Poison Hollow, which is now under the lake. This picture was taken around 1930. (Courtesy of Ophel Page.)

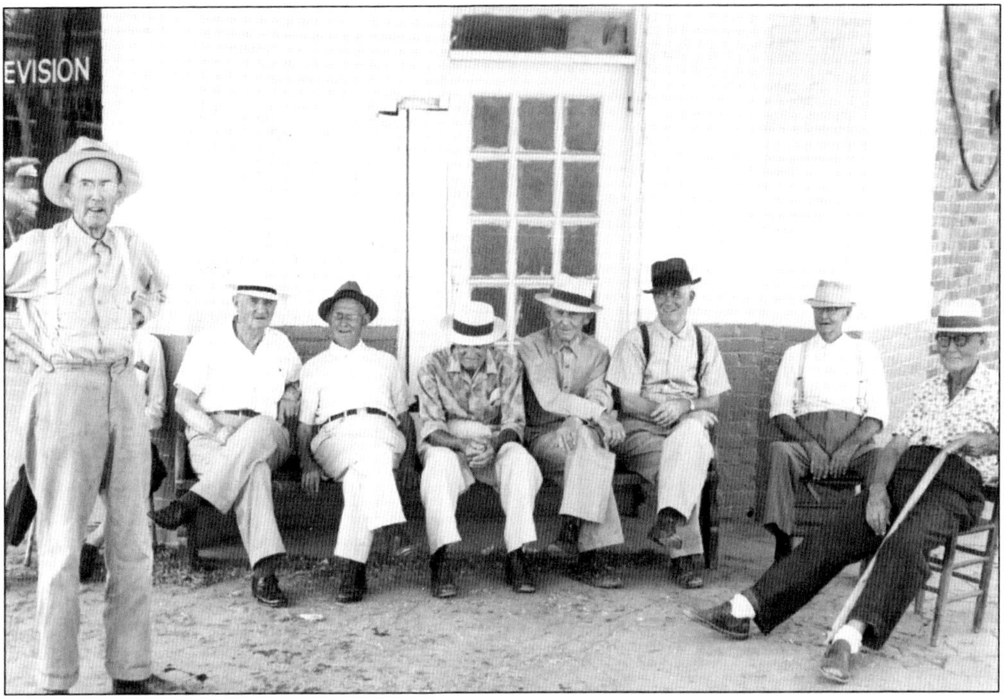

These men are whittling away the day in front of Curtis Brothers Store in Alexandria. This was a local pastime in most every town in the county. The only thing that changed was the men who were whittling. Standing is John Lee Willoughby. Seated from left to right are Albert Davenport, Ed Nixon, Tommy Malone, Andrew Foutch, Bob Oakley, Liv Malone, and Jeff Sandlin. (Courtesy of Mac Willoughby.)

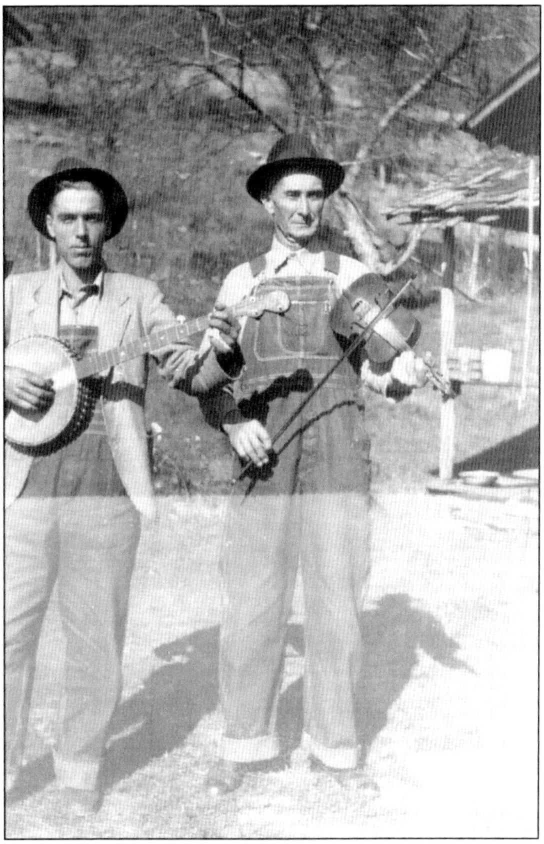

Boots Carter (playing the banjo) and Will Taylor (fiddling) are passing time on the farm around 1930. Before radio and television, friends and neighbors often gathered to entertain themselves. (Courtesy of Allie Fuson.)

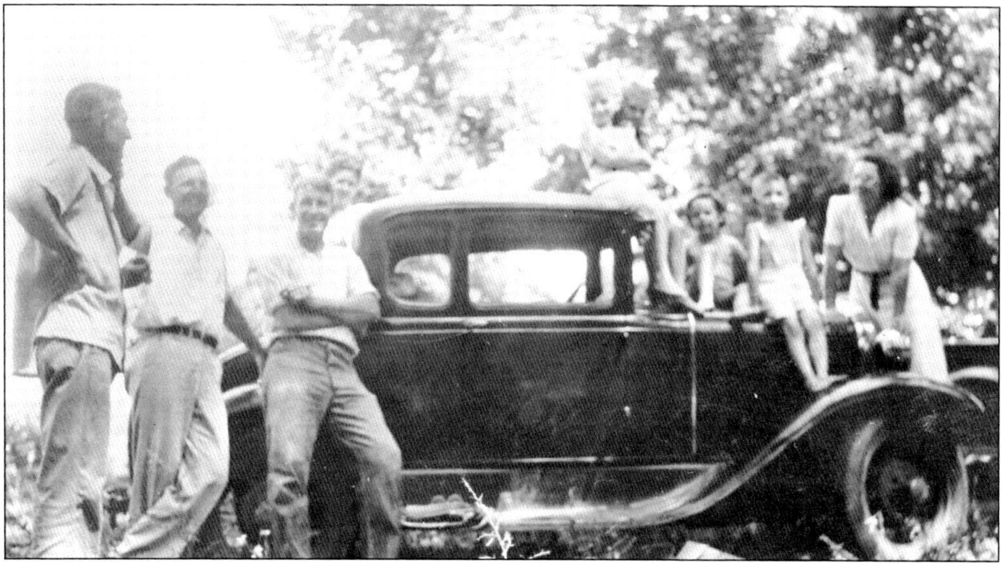

A Sunday afternoon drive to visit with friends was always a great way to spend the day. Pictured from left to right are Marvin Christian, Alvie Foutch, Charles Jennings, Betty Mayfield, Sandra Hooper, Lynn Foutch, Daris Jennings, Bobby Christian, and Mai Foutch. (Courtesy of Beulah Jennings.)

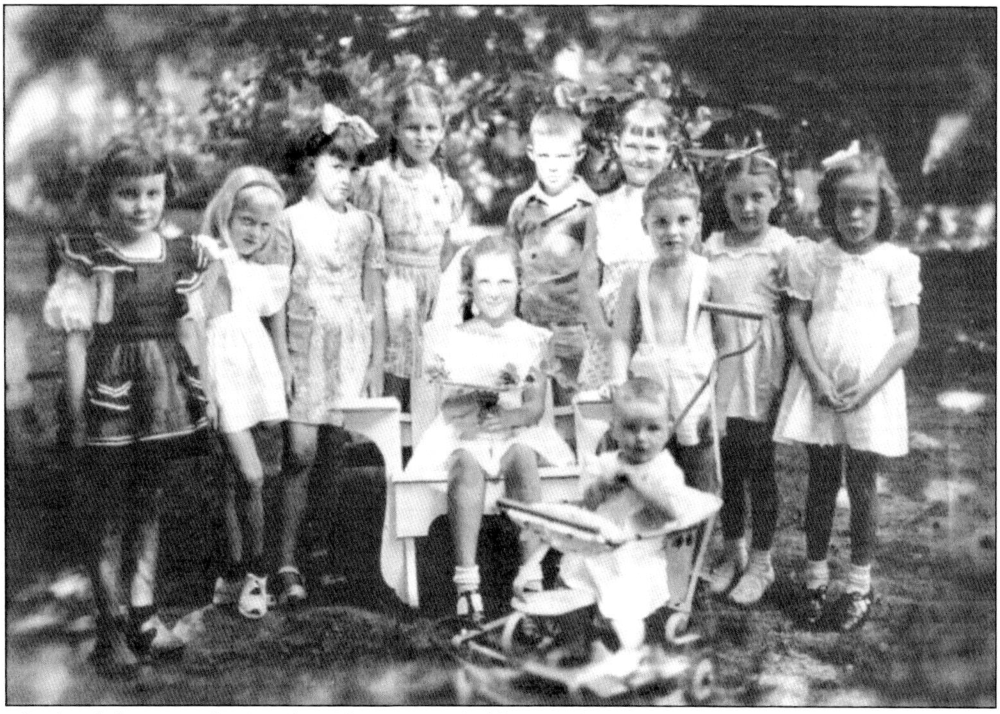

This birthday party for Carolyn Thomas was held around 1945 in Smithville. Pictured from left to right are Peggy Beckwith, Joanna Evins, unidentified, Rosemary Twilla, Carolyn Thomas, James Ed Rice, Mary Jane Rice, Bethel Thomas Jr., Delma Vanhooser, and unidentified. The baby is probably Doreta Vanhooser. (Courtesy of Peggy Huffstetler.)

Five

Down on the Farm

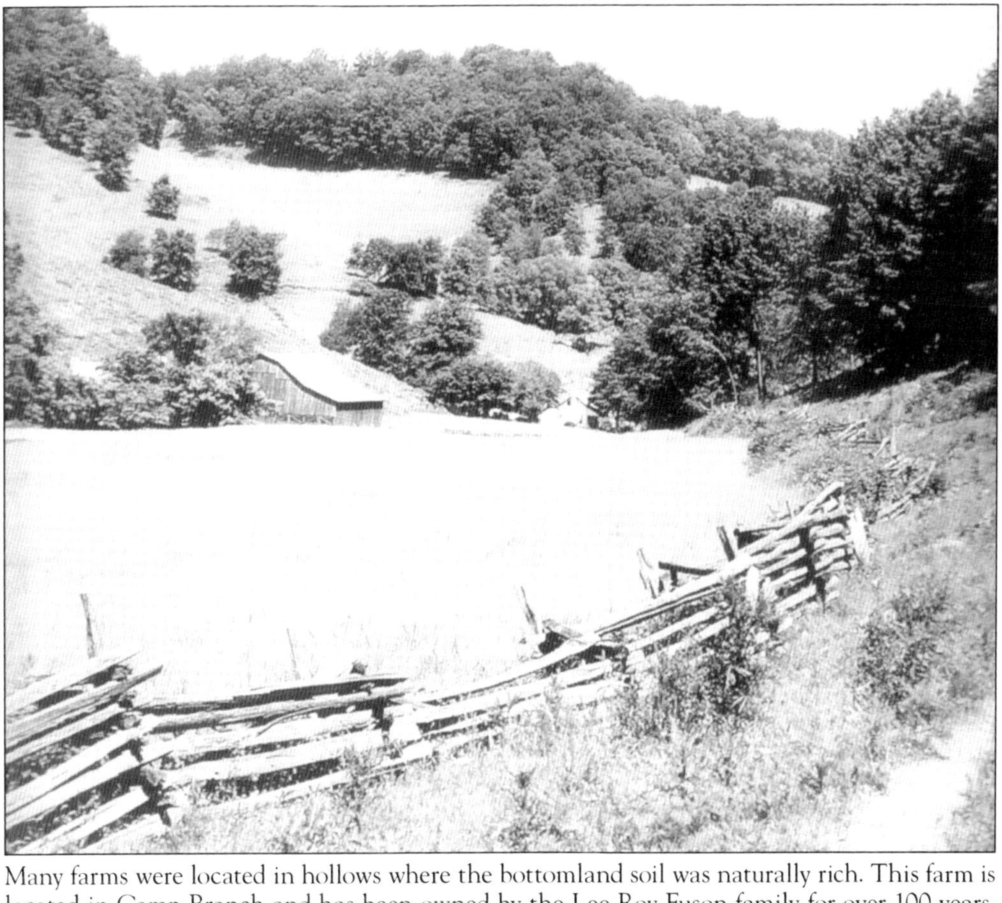

Many farms were located in hollows where the bottomland soil was naturally rich. This farm is located in Camp Branch and has been owned by the Lee Roy Fuson family for over 100 years. The rail fence shown in this picture was common on farms in times past. (Courtesy of Thomas G. Webb.)

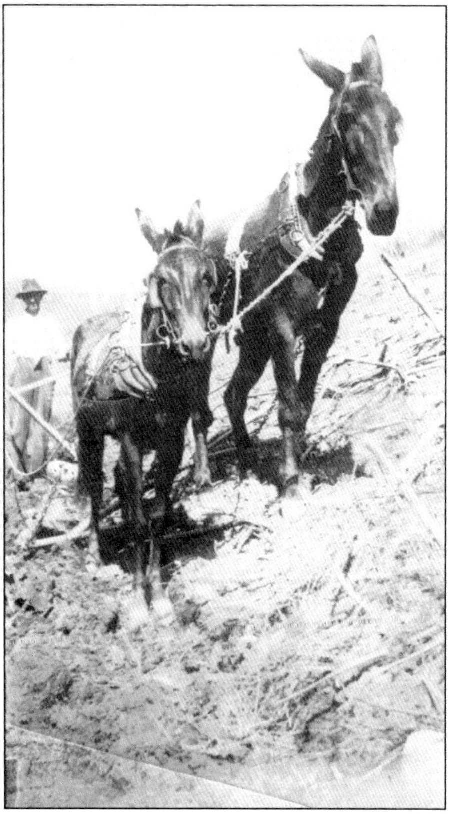

Mules were just right for the hill farms, but if the two mules did not walk at the same speed, the faster mule would be tied to the slower one farther back, as seen here. This prevented the fast mule from getting too far ahead. Riley Page is turning ground here for corn with a hillside plow on a farm on Camp Branch in the 1940s. (Courtesy of Geraldine Cook.)

Much corn was grown on the hillsides in the past, and the mules were the plow pullers for that. Roy Fuson is getting his mules together to do some farming on Camp Branch in the 1940s. This farm has been in his family for over 100 years, and the house in the background is where Roy was raised from 1909; he lived in that hollow all his life. (Courtesy of Junior Fuson.)

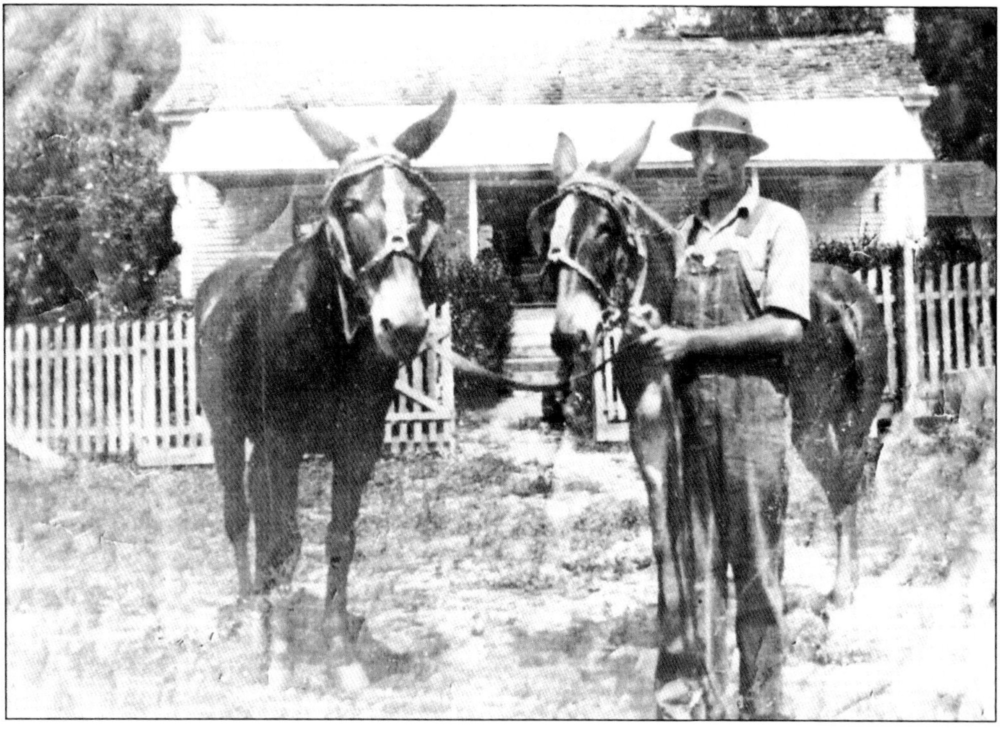

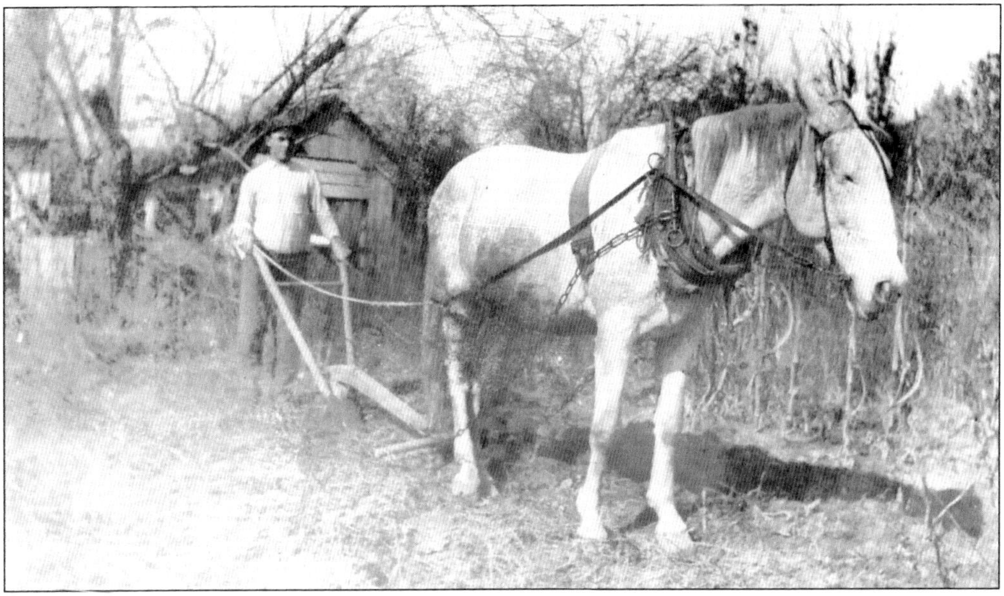

Anson Beckwith is plowing in his garden west of Smithville with a bull-tongue plow pulled by Ole Joe in the early 1920s. Mules were used for preparing land for crops, tending the crops, digging potatoes, riding around, and pulling wagons and buggies. This old mule looks as though it had a hard life. (Courtesy of Judy Fuson.)

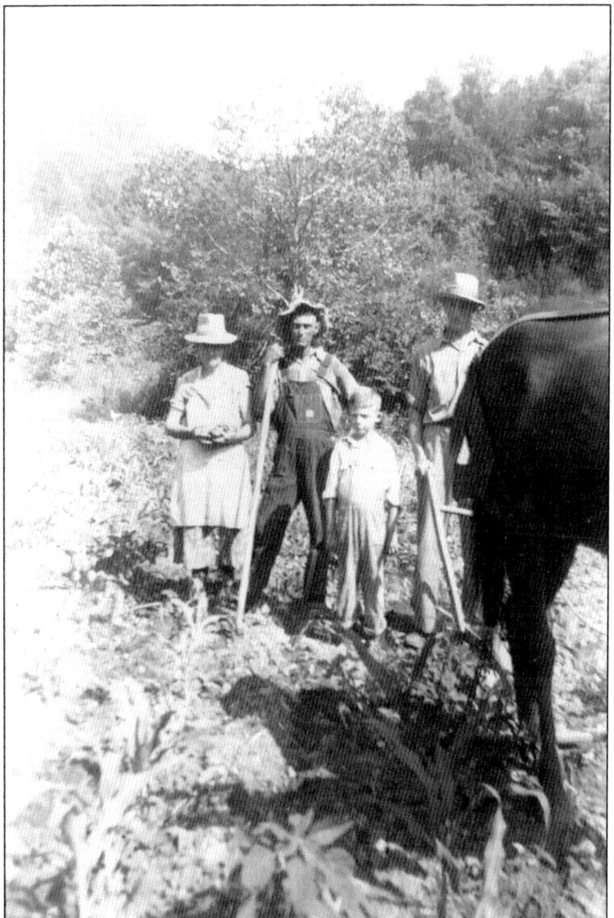

Working in gardens during the summer resulted in having food during the winter months. Nola and Horace Taylor and Jim Fuson (right) with his son James are doing some plowing and hoeing in this garden around 1945. (Courtesy of Debbie Nixon.)

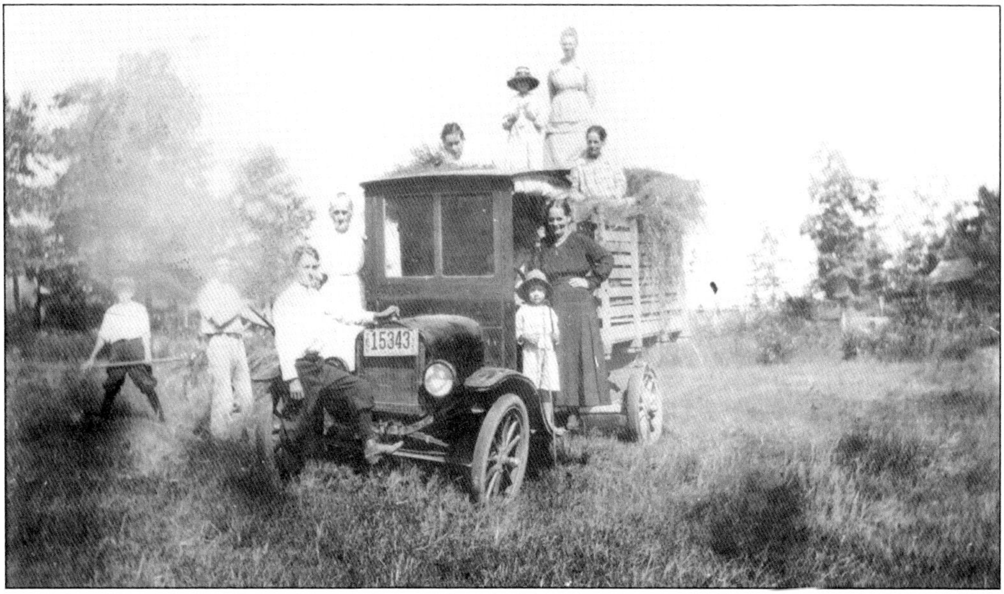

This family is hauling loose hay out in Willie Beckwith's truck around 1920. The women appear to be having a nice hayride. Ocie Beckwith is standing on the top and Mary Elizabeth Martin is on the left side of the truck. (Courtesy of Judy Fuson.)

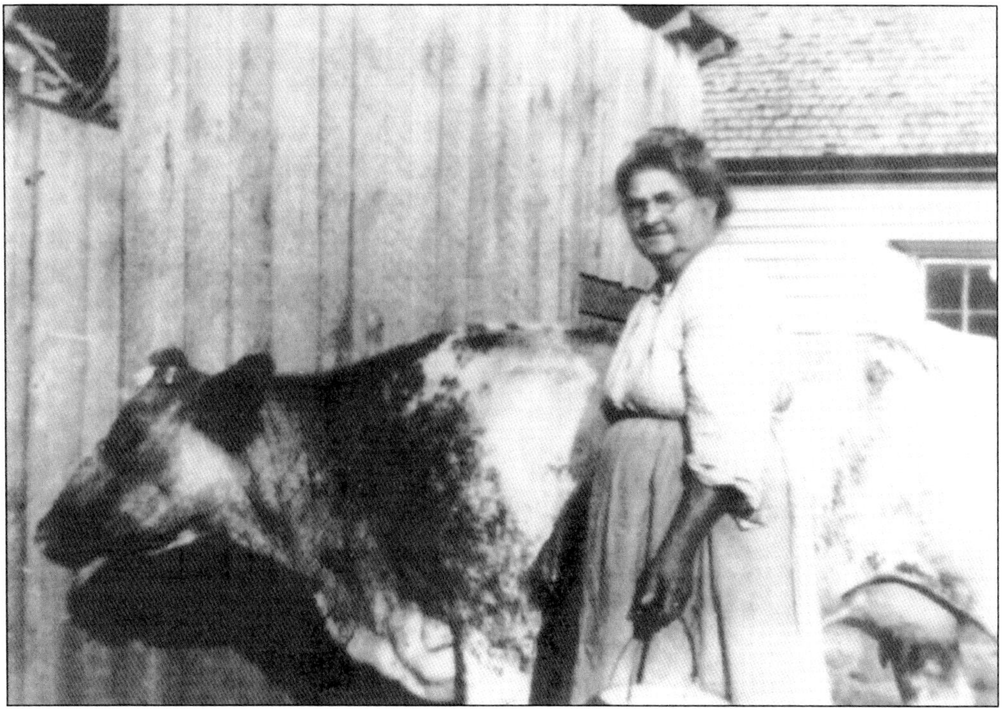

Hatton Mason milked her cow in Temperance Hall in 1925. Milking was a daily task no matter how the weather was or how one was feeling. The milk was also usually stored in a nearby spring to keep it cool when the owners had no icebox or refrigerator. (Courtesy of Justin Potter Library.)

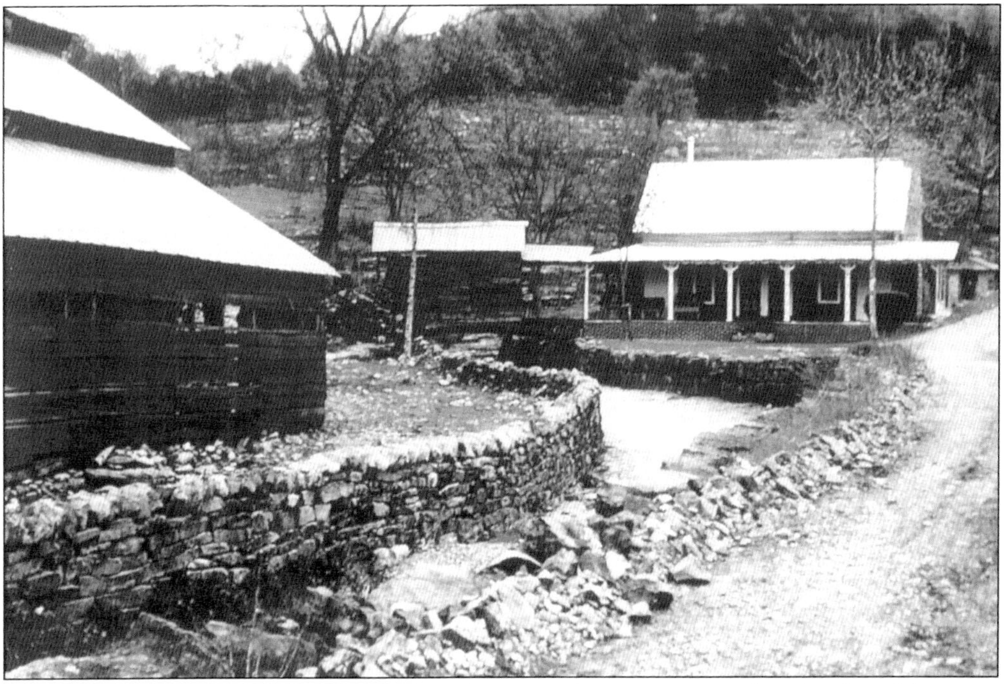

Rock walls and fences on farms required much time and energy to erect, but they lasted for many years, helped retain livestock, and were a means to clear pastures and fields. In this farm on Hannah's Branch at Will Caplinger's home, the rock wall also helped prevent erosion from the creek. This picture was taken in 1956. (Courtesy Justin Potter Library.)

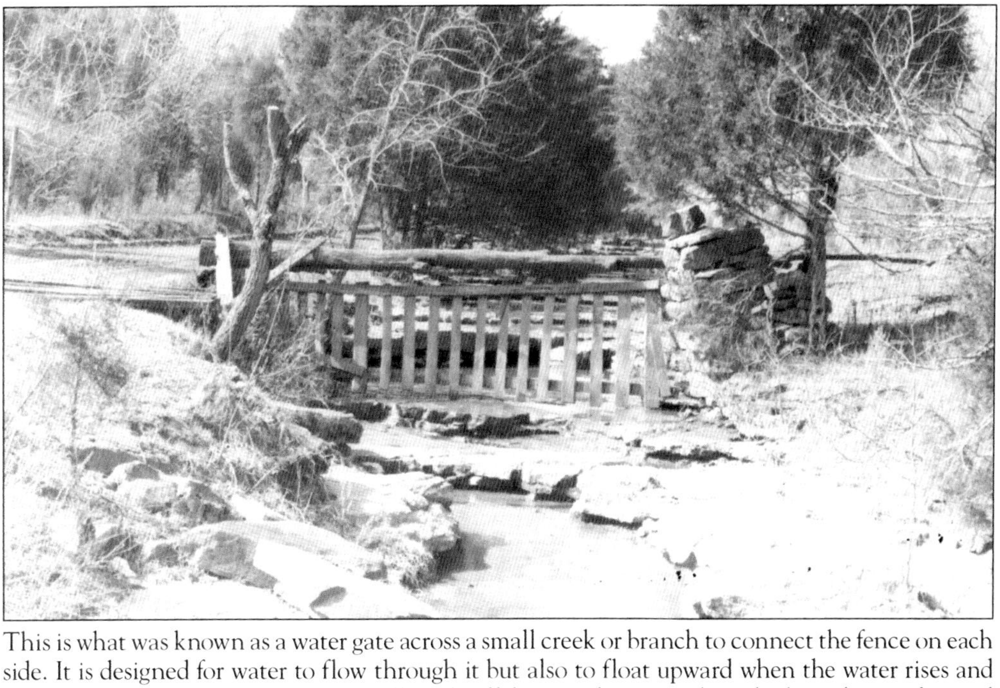

This is what was known as a water gate across a small creek or branch to connect the fence on each side. It is designed for water to flow through it but also to float upward when the water rises and flows faster. However, sometimes it will wash off during a big rain when the branch rises fast and high. This water gate was on a farm on Dismal Creek in 1976. (Courtesy of Thomas G. Webb.)

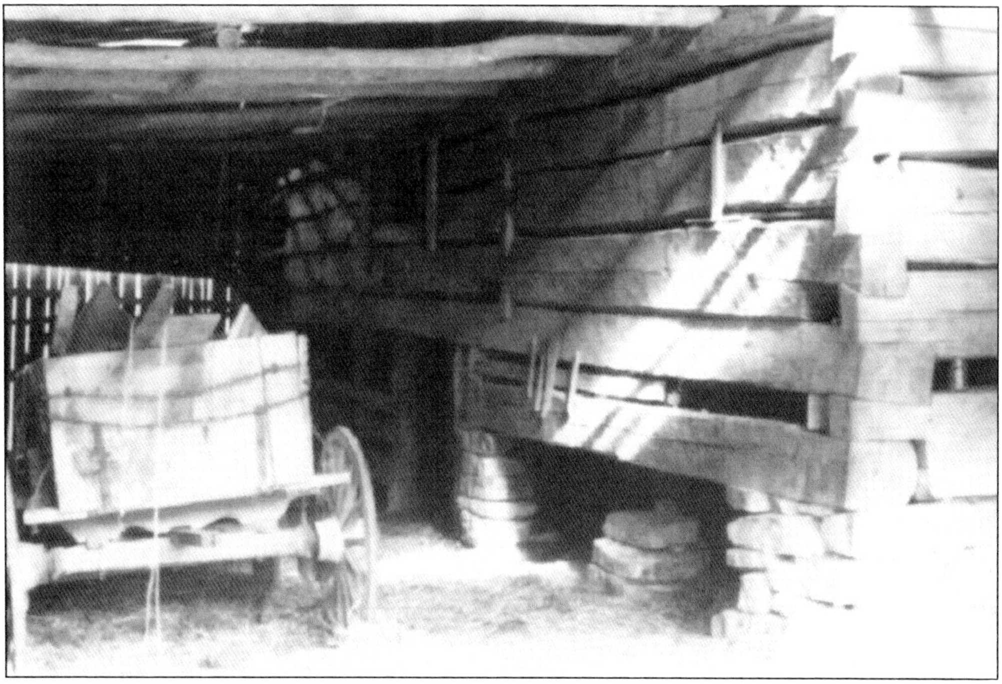

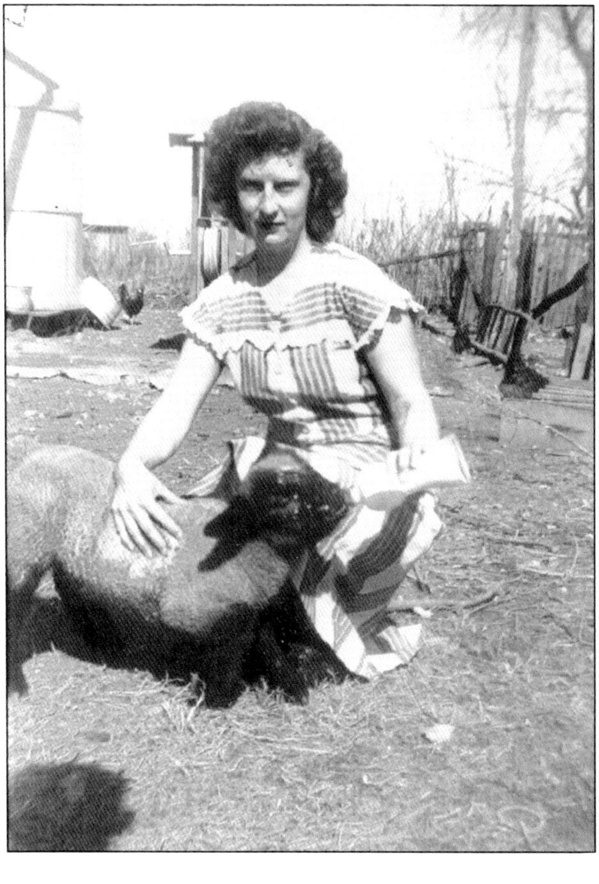

Barns were usually built on a farm before the house. It was the most important part of every farm. This log barn is on the old Jonathon Griffith farm on Dismal Creek. Louis and Reba Fuson now own and live on this farm in the house that is over 100 years old. This area is called the gangway of the barn; the wagon used for many different things is stored here. (Courtesy of Thomas G. Webb.)

Ruth Taylor is feeding her pet lamb, which had been taken from the herd on their farm on Hurricane Ridge in the late 1940s. Notable is the water tank in the background. Many homes at that time accumulated rainwater to use in addition to water from wells and springs. (Courtesy of Ruth Taylor.)

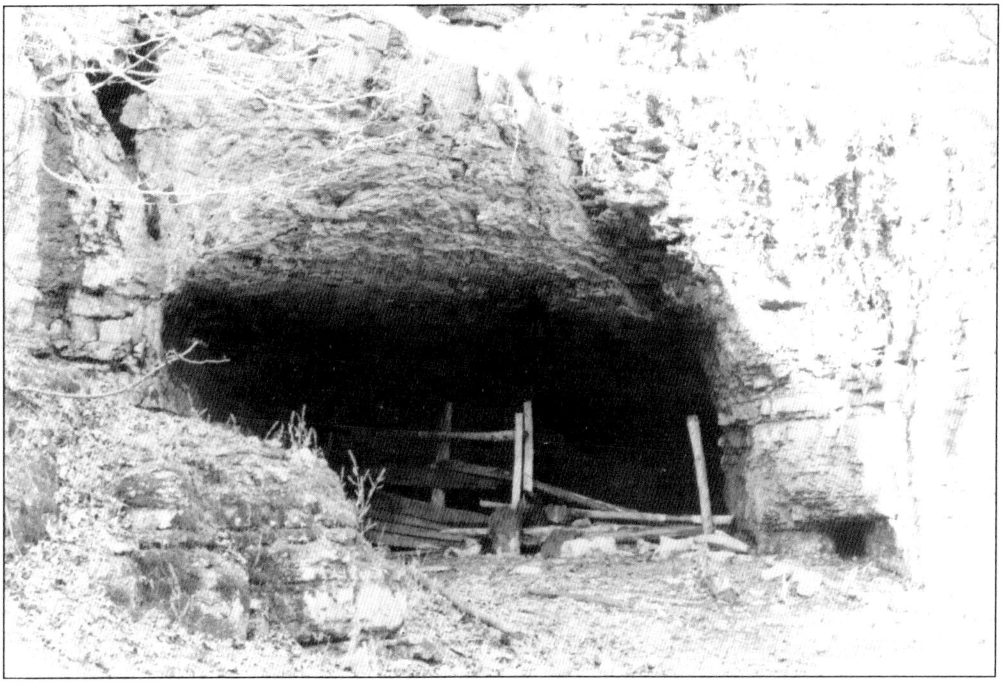

Ebenezer Snow settled in the upper part of Dry Creek in 1806 and did not even have to build a barn. He just placed a few poles across the entrance of two caves and stabled his horses there. Frosty Tramel owned the cave when this picture was taken in 1976. (Courtesy of Thomas G. Webb.)

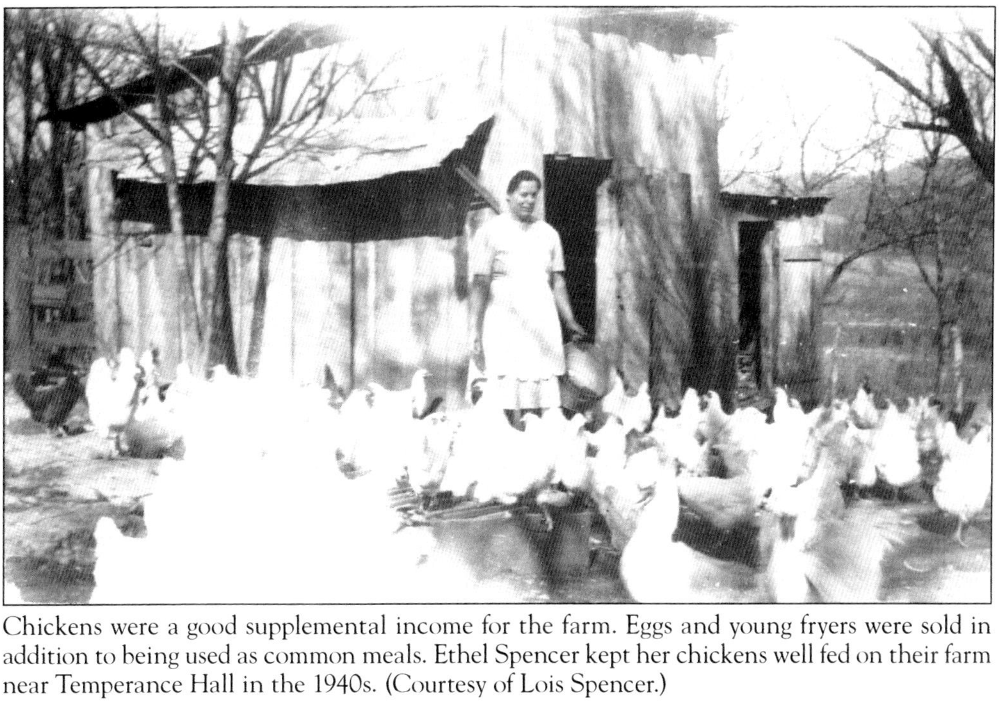

Chickens were a good supplemental income for the farm. Eggs and young fryers were sold in addition to being used as common meals. Ethel Spencer kept her chickens well fed on their farm near Temperance Hall in the 1940s. (Courtesy of Lois Spencer.)

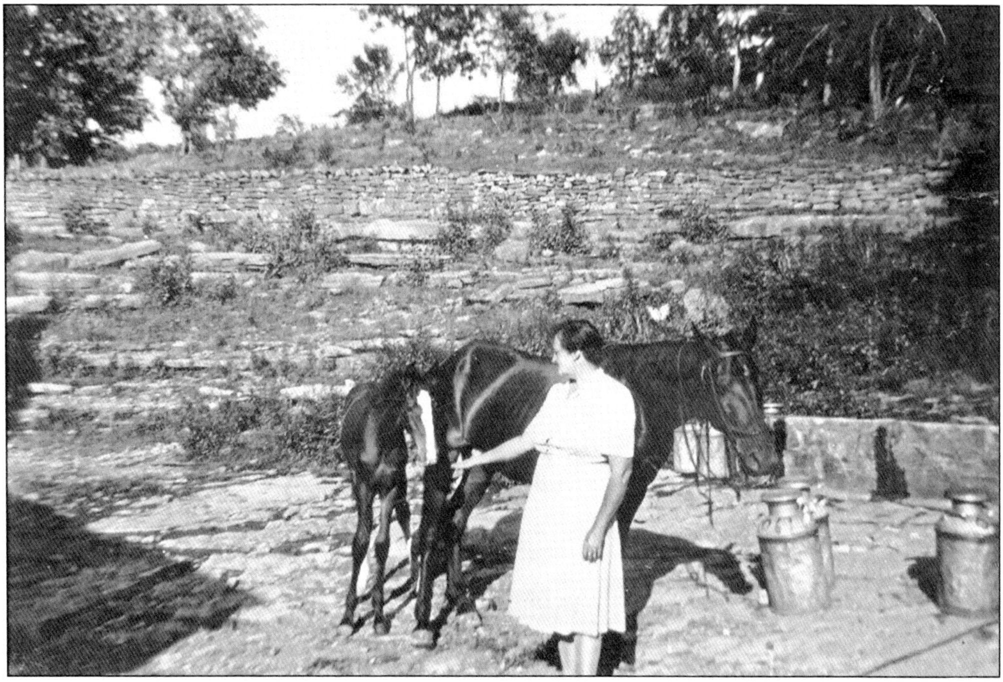

On a farm in Temperance Hall, Ocie Carter is admiring a young colt alongside milk cans near the barn. She has been called a grand lady. Born on April 27, 1899, to Dr. Robert Wiley Mason and Mary Hatton Mason, Ocie was one of eight children. She wrote a community article for the *Smithville Review* for many years, keeping the day-to-day life of her area recorded. (Courtesy of Ria Baker.)

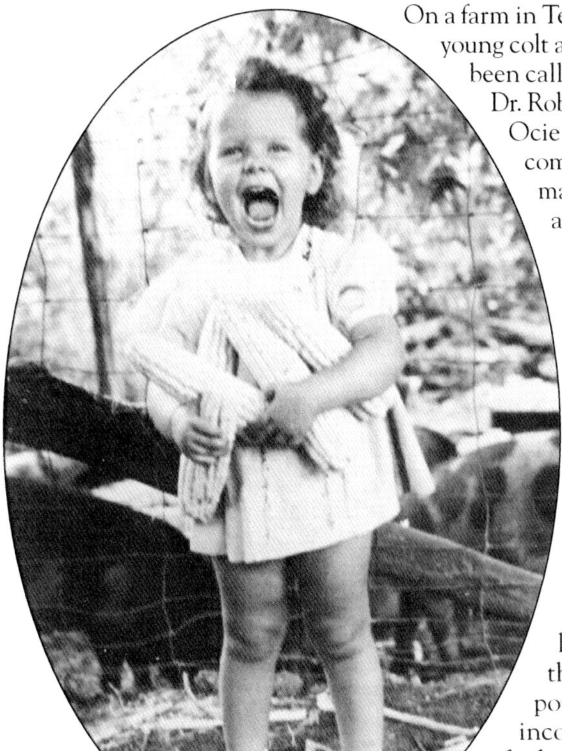

Although city folks could raise many farm animals in town, swine were prohibited by law in the city limits. Therefore, everyone in the country kept pigs both to use for putting pork on their table and to sell in town for income. Daris Jennings is pictured in 1943 feeding the pigs on their farm located on what was then called Mockingbird Hill between Alexandria and Liberty. (Photograph by Beulah Jennings, courtesy of Daris Mullinax.)

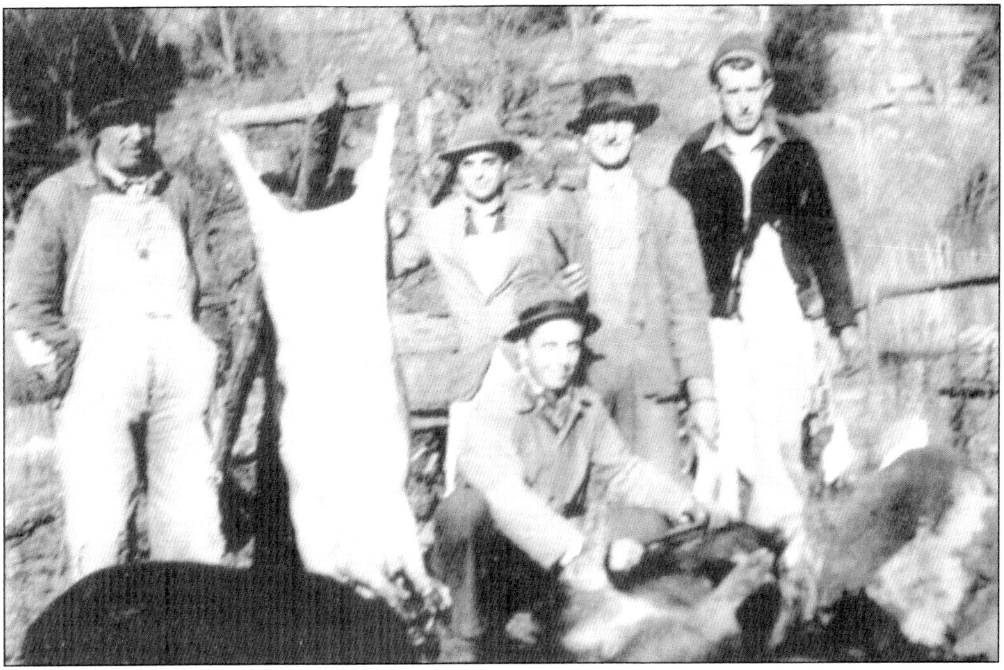

Hog killing usually took place as community events any time in the winter months from November through January. The meat was cured and stored in a smokehouse, and the cooks would only have to walk out and cut off what they wanted. That was easier than traveling to a grocery store. This hog killing was in Possum Hollow around 1940. Pictured from left to right are Delton Tramel, Gloston Mullican, Fate Mulican, and Alvie Mullican. In front is Austin Mullican scraping a hog. (Courtesy of Justin Potter Library.)

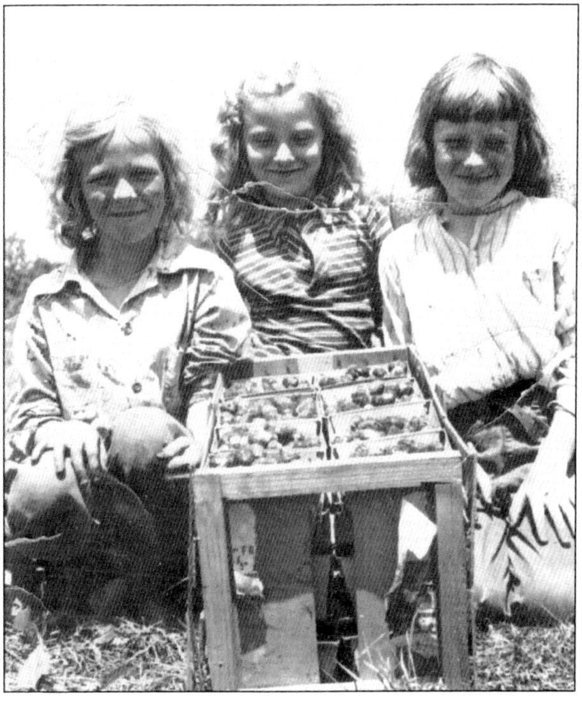

Picking strawberries was a good job for young people on the farm. Marguerite Tramel and Frankie and Johnnie Hendrixson had been hired by Algie Lee Vanderpool, who grew the strawberries for the public. These girls may have eaten a few strawberries while doing their job here in 1950. (Courtesy of Marguerite Jones.)

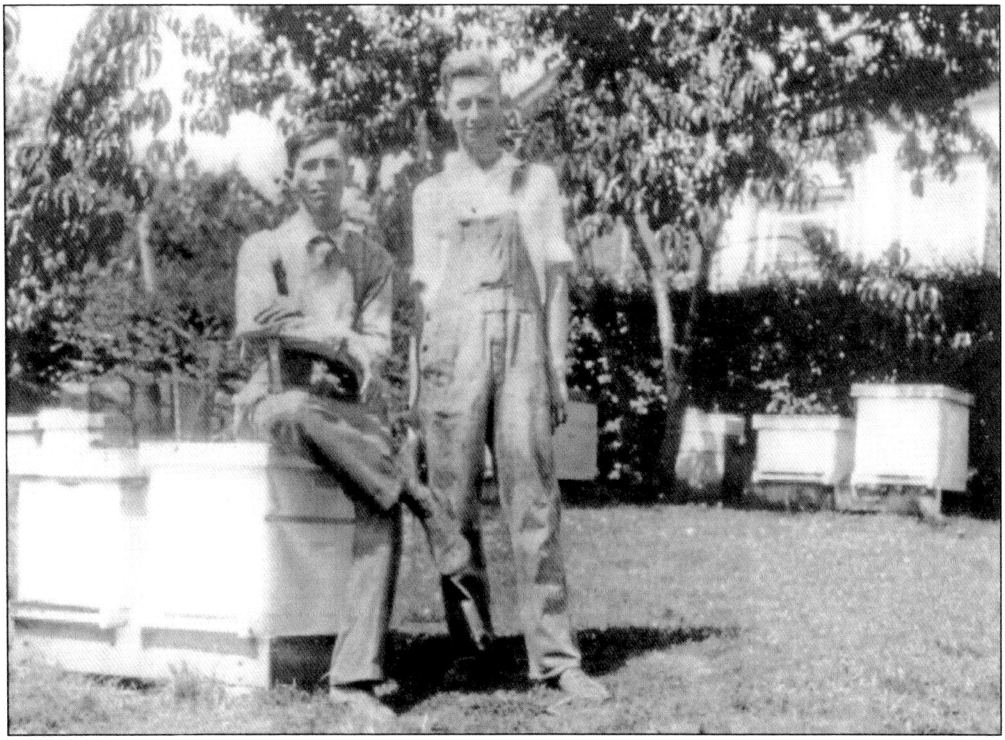

This is John Ivan Banks, sitting on one of his beehives, and his son Carl Boyd Banks. According to Will T. Hale's *History of DeKalb County* published in 1915, "J.I. Banks, of Dry Creek, is regarded as one of the best beekeepers of the State. He makes a specialty of queens and has patrons throughout the Union." (Courtesy of Tom Simpson.)

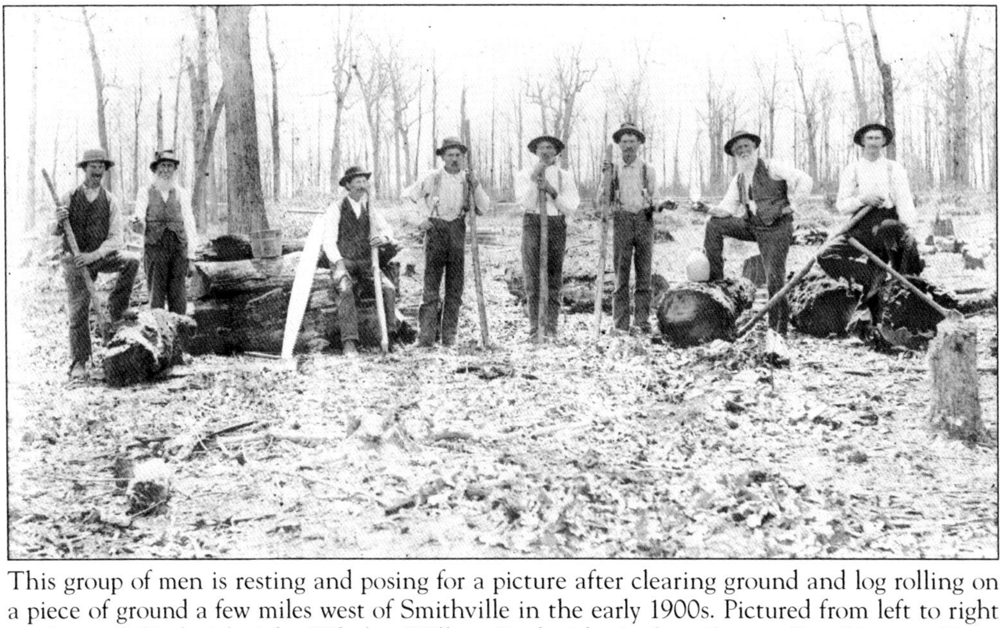

This group of men is resting and posing for a picture after clearing ground and log rolling on a piece of ground a few miles west of Smithville in the early 1900s. Pictured from left to right are James E. Beckwith, John Whaley, William Beckwith, Andrew Patton, Sam Vanatta, Berry Cantrell, James R. Beckwith, and Tom Whaley. (Courtesy of Judy Fuson.)

William Henry and Lucy Frances Curtis Farler are standing in front of a log building with wooden shingles on their farm on Capling Ridge around 1900. (Courtesy of Peggy Huffstetler.)

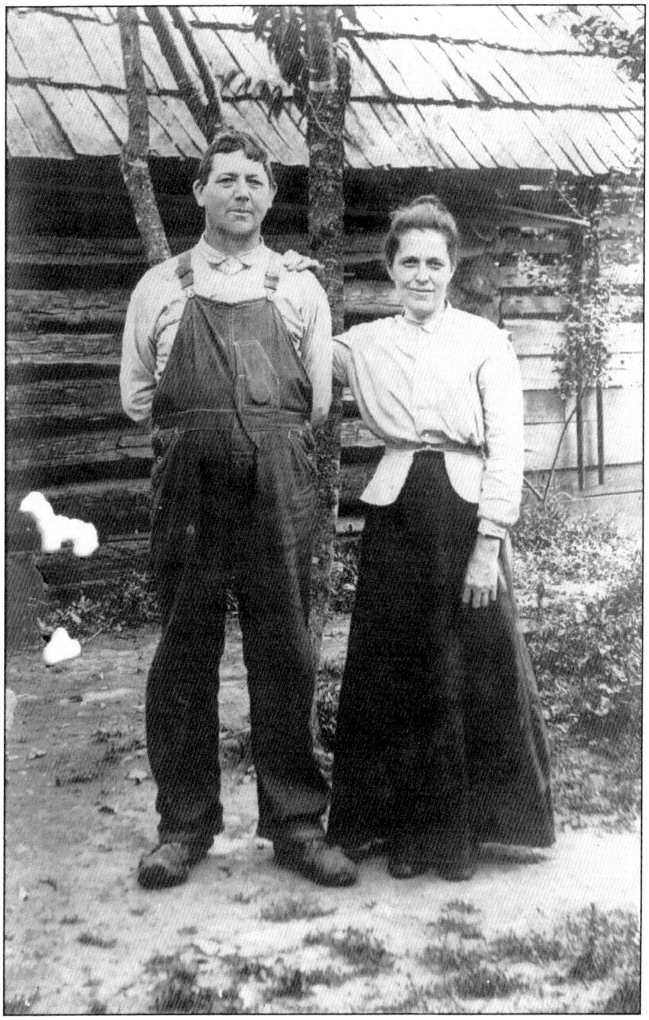

John Ivan Banks is riding on the back of a wagon of hand-picked corn. He raised hybrid seed corn for the market in the 1950s. Jim Banks is driving the 1942 Allis-Chalmers tractor pulling the corn wagon, and Will Keaton is sitting on the front of the wagon. (Courtesy of Tom Simpson.)

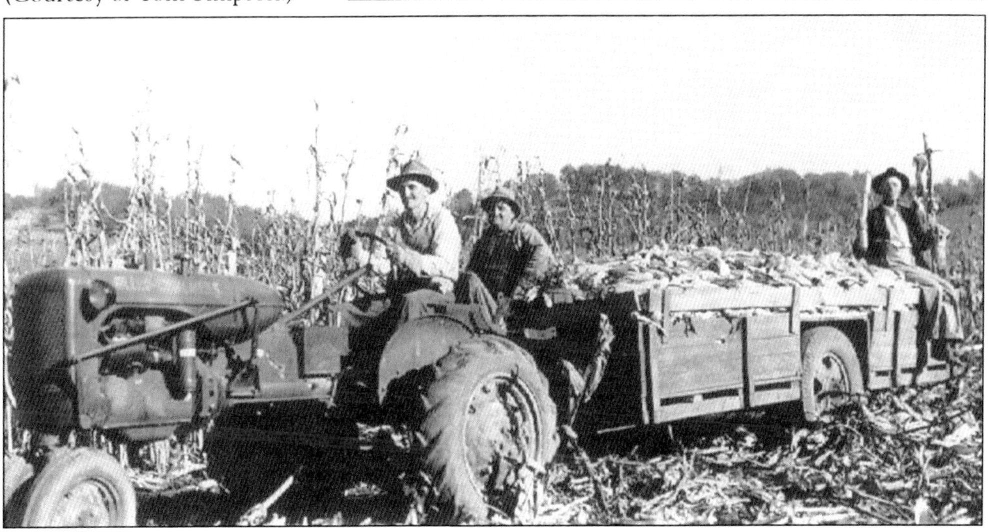

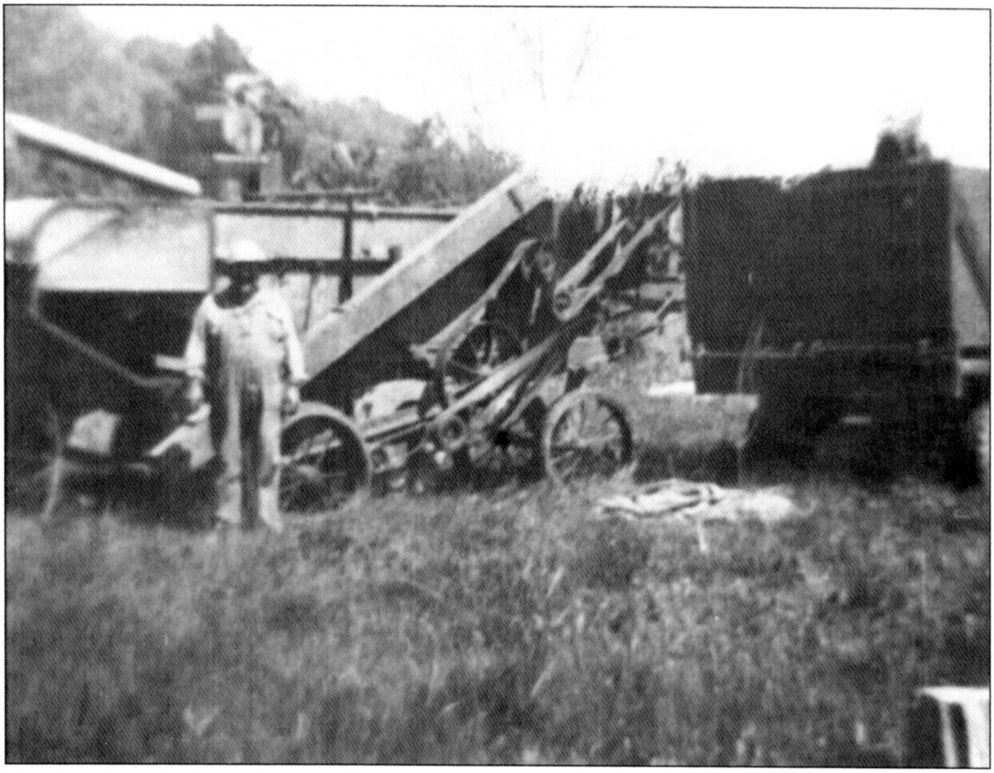

Tom Sandlin, of Alexandria, traveled from farm to farm thrashing wheat in the 1940s. The shocks of dried wheat were loaded into the gasoline-powered thrashing machine to separate the wheat kernels from the stalks. The straw comes out one end, and the grain was sifted and dumped out on the other end and sacked for transportation to the market. (Courtesy of Genrose Davis.)

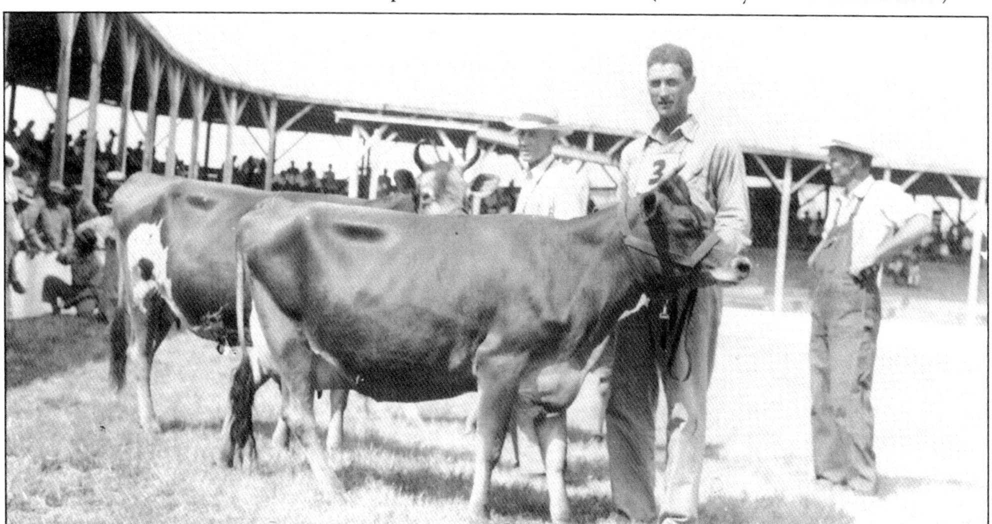

Walter Brown, who owned and lived on a farm on New Hope Road in Alexandria, is showing his Jersey milk cow at the annual DeKalb County Fair in the early 1940s. Selling milk was a common source of income on many farms here at that time. (Courtesy of Virginia Brown.)

Six

UNDER THE LAKE

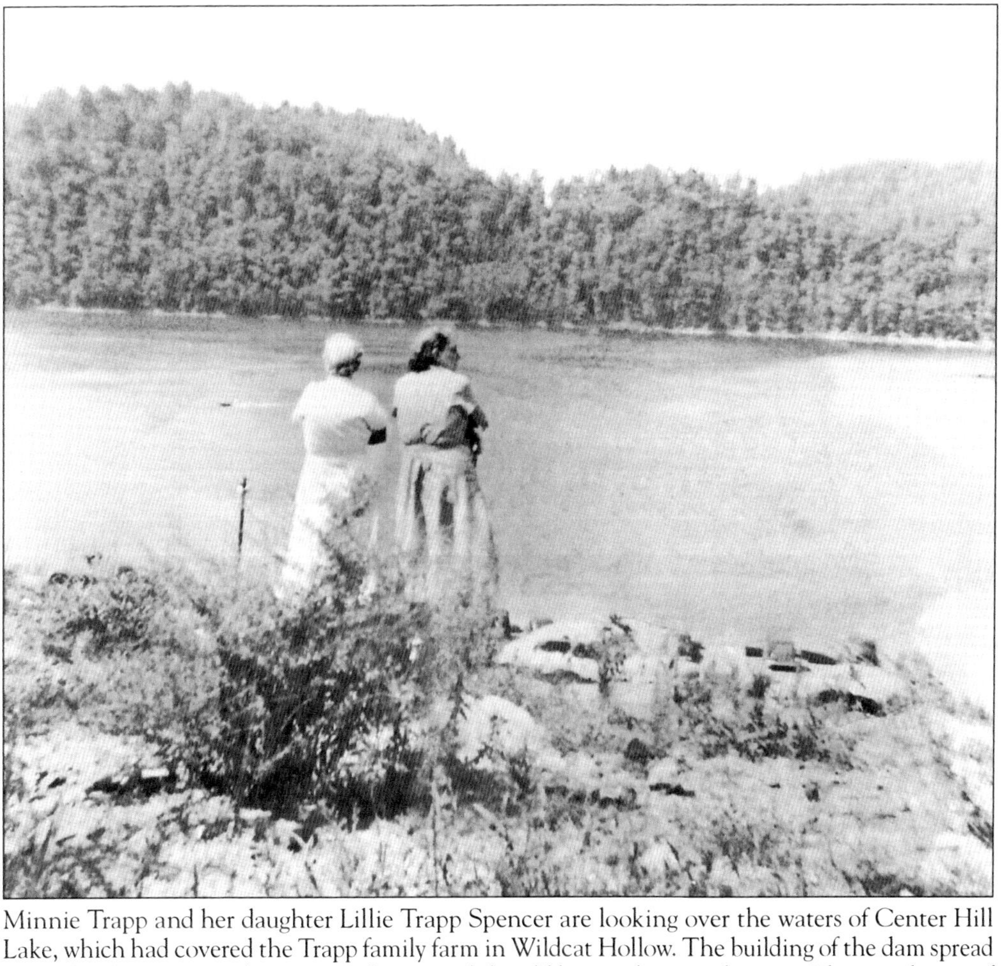

Minnie Trapp and her daughter Lillie Trapp Spencer are looking over the waters of Center Hill Lake, which had covered the Trapp family farm in Wildcat Hollow. The building of the dam spread many families apart and permanently covered the old home places with water. The population of DeKalb was about 4,000 less in 1950 than in 1940. (Courtesy of Leota Mac Bennett.)

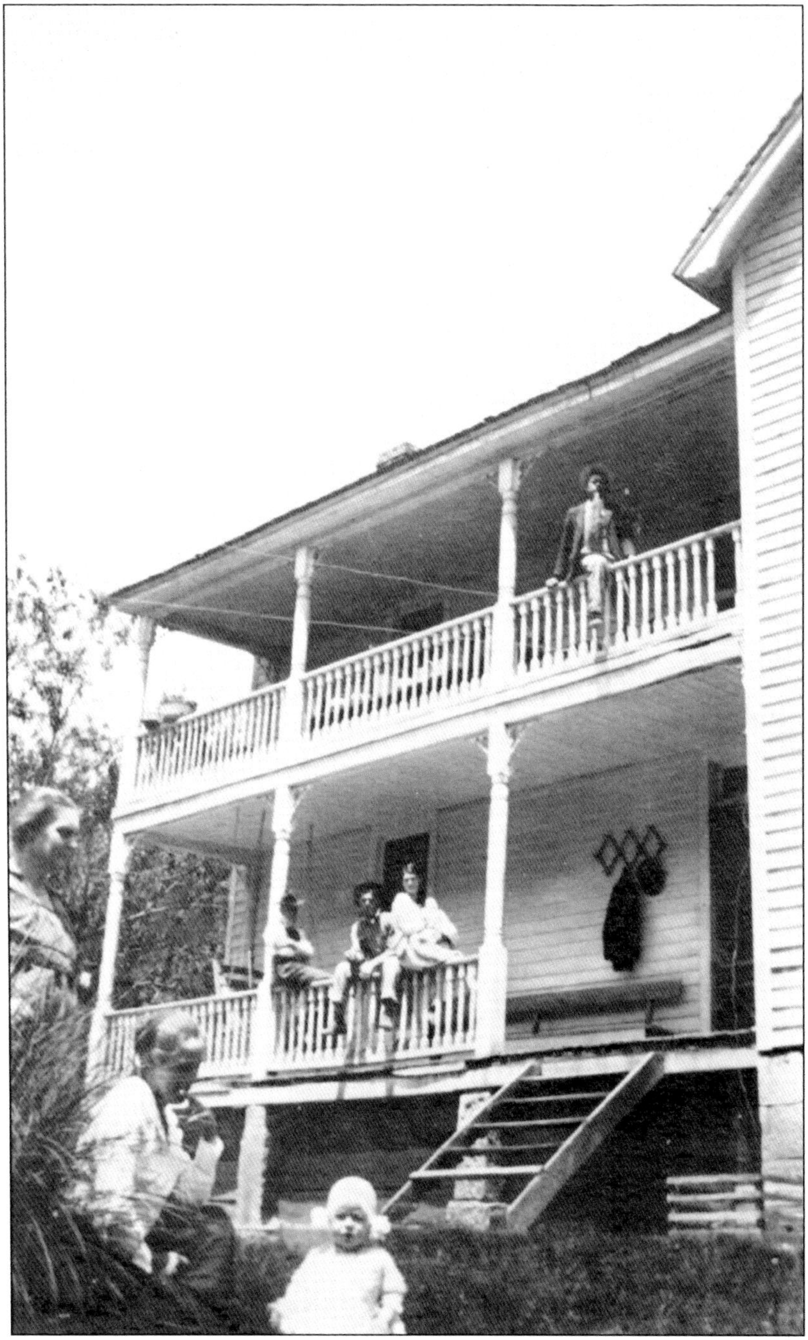

This large two-story house in Buckeye Hollow was the home of Rozias and Evaline Page and their seven children. Their daughter Vennie and her husband, Barney Taylor, bought the house after both her parents had died by 1936. There was a large spring flowing from the hill higher than the house, and the water was piped to the kitchen in the house and to the barn to a watering trough. A house with running water was not a common thing at this time. Some members of the family are sitting on the porch rails and playing in the yard in this picture. This home place is now under the lake. (Courtesy of Ophel Page.)

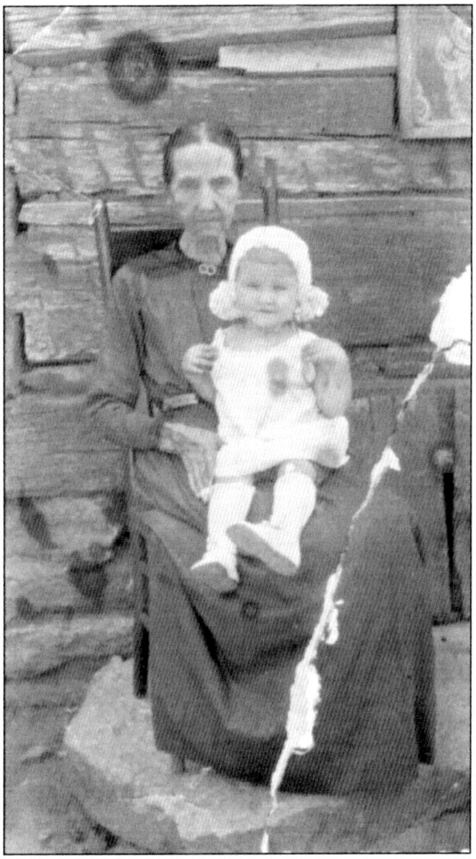

Hannah Taylor, the eighth of ten children of John B. "Bully John" Taylor and Drucilla Turner, was born in 1851 and lived on Indian Creek her entire life. The Taylors were abundant in that area. Hannah married another Taylor, Isaiah W. "Zade," a son of Ezelkial Wilder Taylor Sr. They had only one child, Riley, who died young. The little girl sitting in Hannah's lap around 1928 is great-niece Maxine Clark. (Courtesy of Debbie Nixon.)

Claude Walker and his family lived on Indian Creek about a mile from Caney Fork River before Center Hill Dam formed the lake and covered his farm. He is showing off his new year-old colt in this picture in the early 1940s. (Courtesy of Cindy Hatton Taylor.)

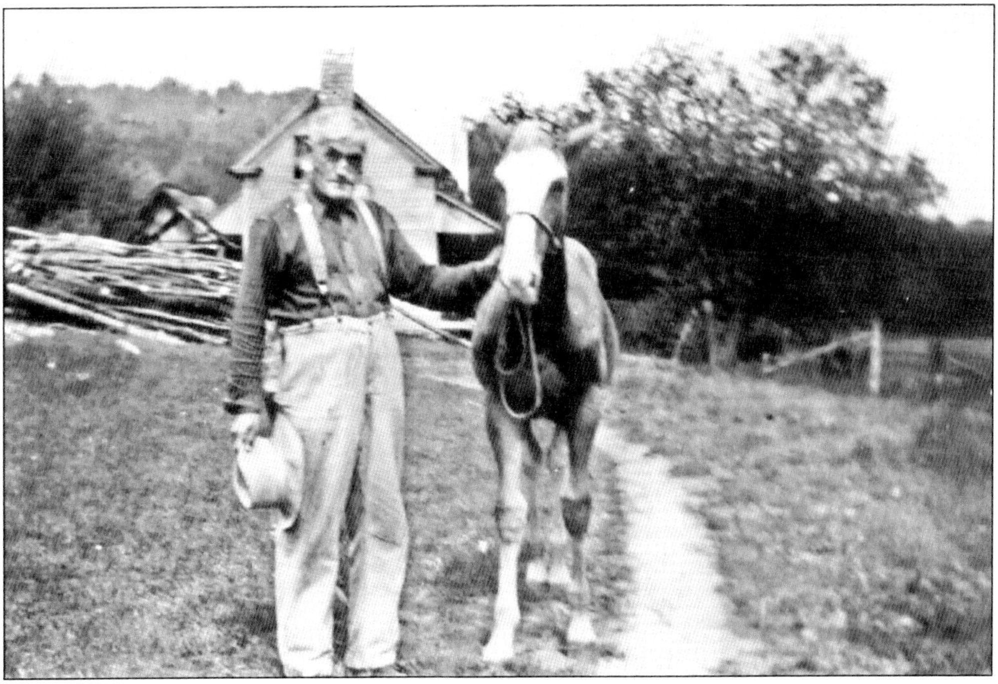

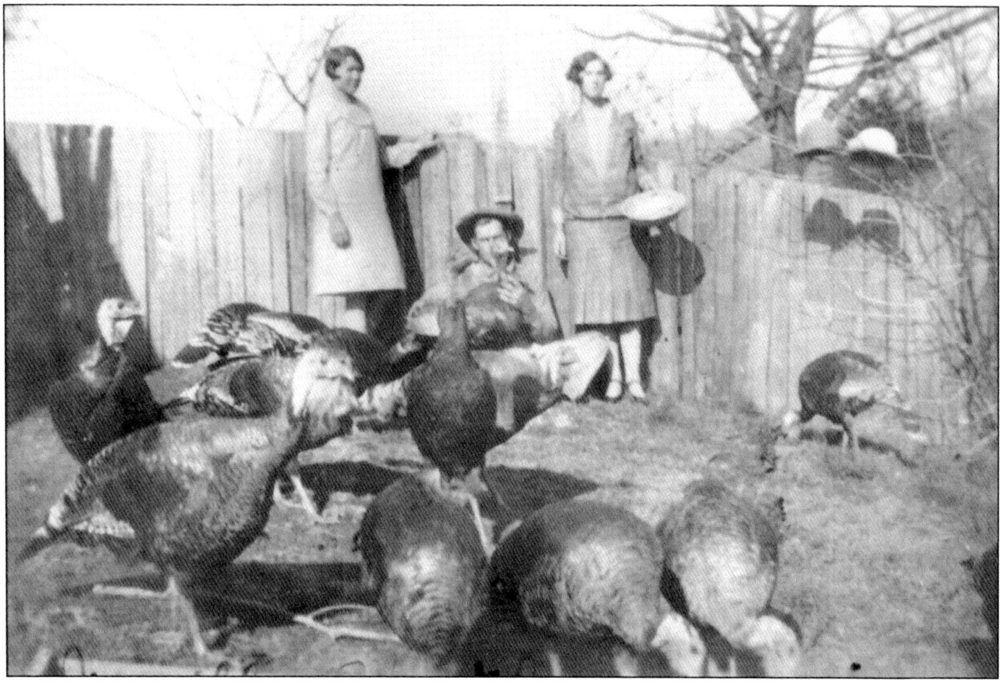

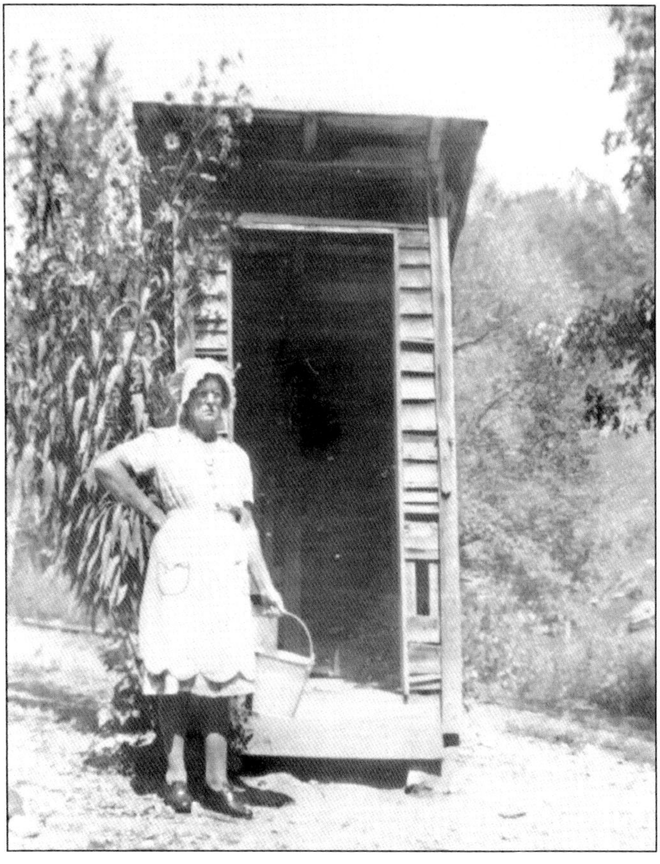

Haskel Page and his wife, Winnie, along with his sister-in-law Jewel Page are feeding the turkey flock on their farm on Indian Creek. He raised these turkeys for the market, and they are just about ready for sale. Happy Thanksgiving! (Courtesy of Ophel Page.)

Vinnie Page Taylor is taking her bucket to the well. She is standing in front of the well house in Buckeye Hollow in the late 1930s. Not every well had a house built over it, but this one was constructed to protect the people while drawing water by hand. (Courtesy of Ophel Page.)

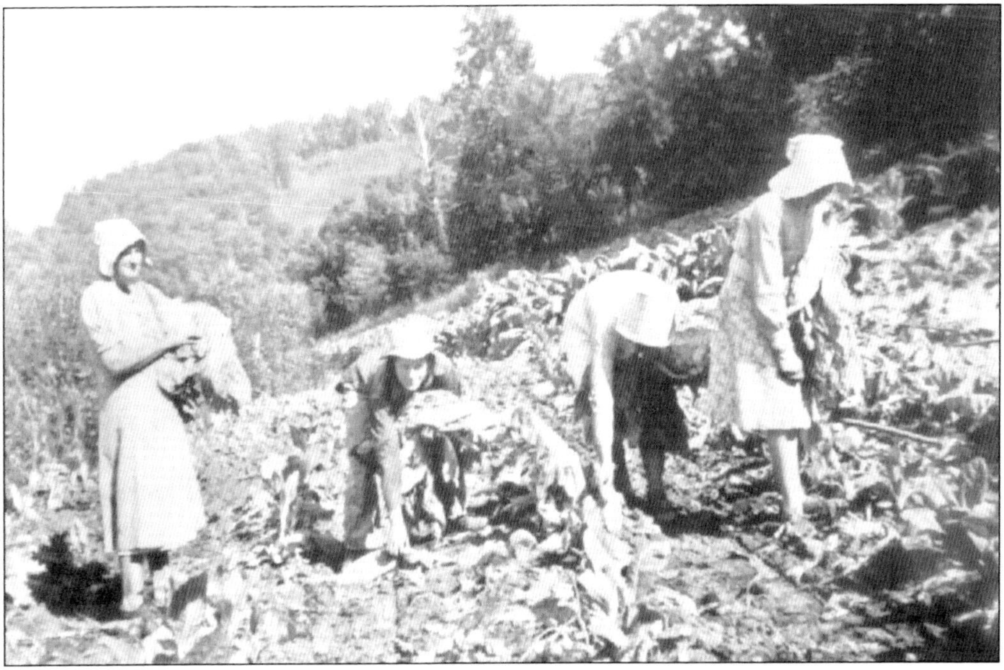

Ladies wearing their bonnets went out to help the men in the tobacco patch by picking up the leaves that had fallen off the tobacco stalks while cutting. Pictured are, from left to right, Cumiller Walker, Cindy Hatton Taylor, Dora Taylor, and Winnie Page on Haskell Page's farm on Indian Creek. (Courtesy of Cindy Hatton Taylor.)

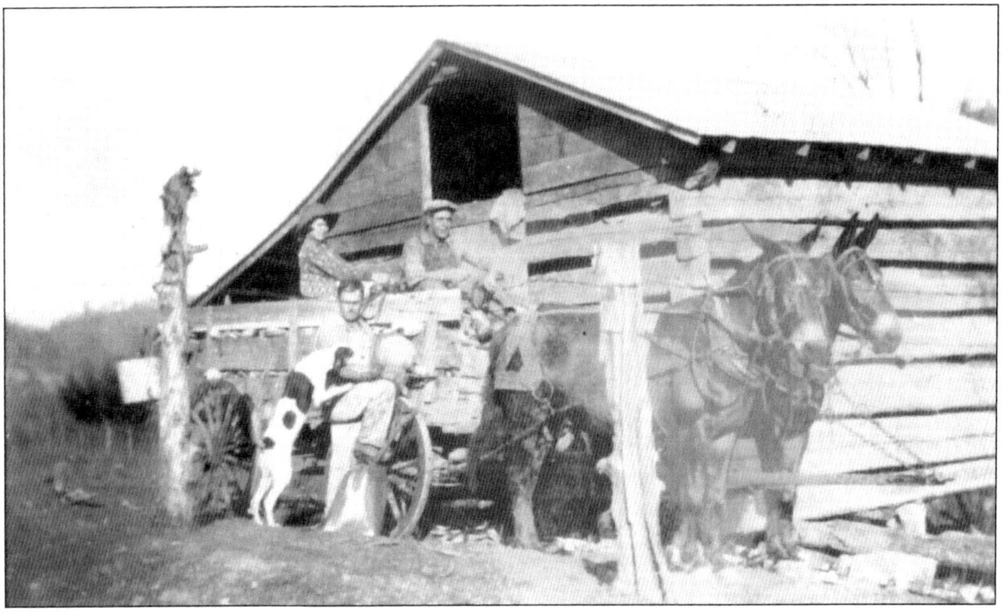

Resen Page and his wife, Jewel, are in the wagon in which they had been gathering corn with Resen's brother Haskell on Haskell's farm at the mouth of Indian Creek. They are sitting in front of the corncrib around 1930. They may have had pumpkins in the corn field also, for Haskell is holding one with his dog at his side. Planting double crops in the same field was common at that time. (Courtesy of Ophel Page.)

Orvin Pack stands in front of his home near the Narrows of Caney Fork River. This house was washed away during the great flood of 1929. The house was tied down with cables to hold it, and Orvin's mother, Jenny Parker Pack, was moving things from the first floor to the second floor. Orvin went by boat to get his mother; he went inside and rescued her just before the house was washed down the river. (Courtesy of Frances Caplinger.)

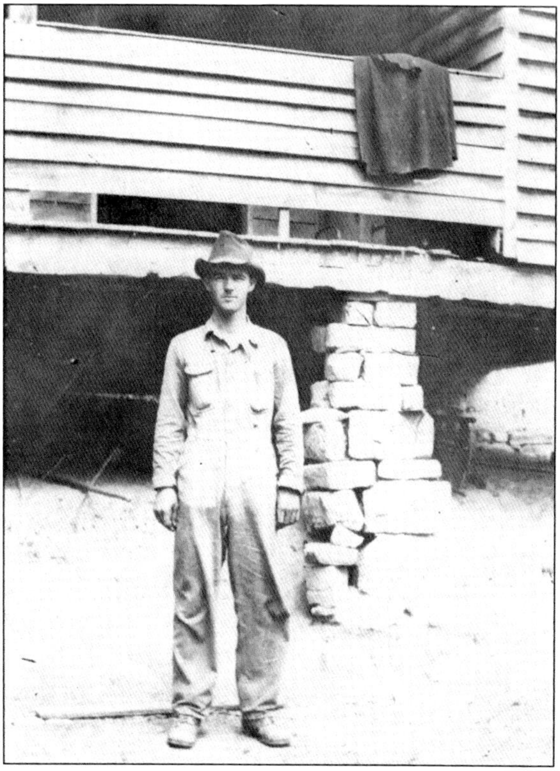

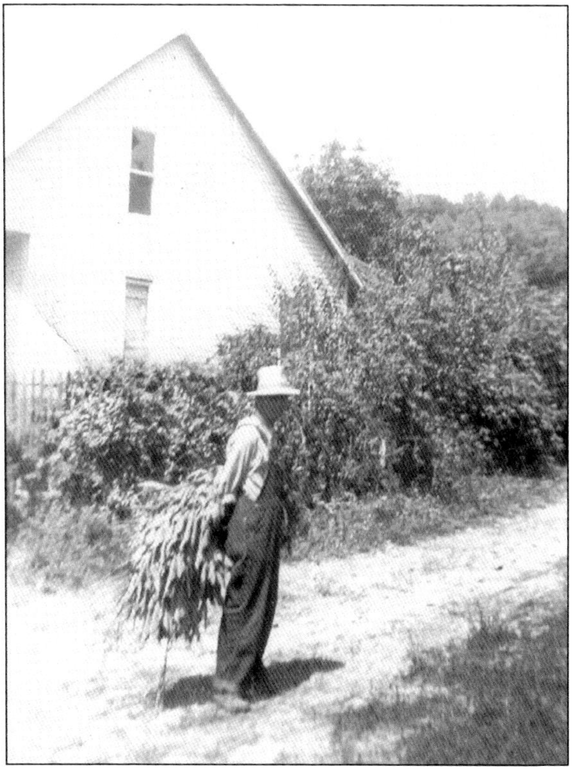

Horace Taylor and his wife, Nola, had a farm on Indian Creek with eight children. He is carrying a bundle of horse weeds to feed to his mules. This was a common wild crop that grew around the creek and river and was used as a feed supplement when the corn crop got low or eventually ran out. (Courtesy of Debbie Nixon.)

The people who lived near water were anxious to have purple martins around to help reduce the number of mosquitoes. The Page family in Poison Hollow is putting up a martin house here in the 1940s. Resen is pictured at the top receiving some help from his children, Gene (below him), and, standing from left to right, Erma Dell, Barbara C., and Ophel. (Courtesy of Ophel Page.)

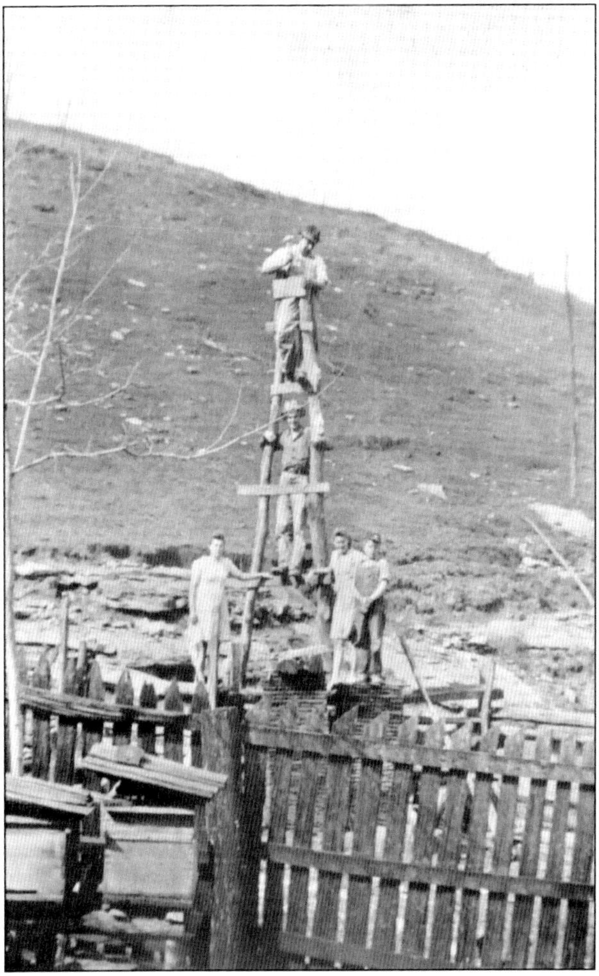

This was a prayer group on Indian Creek in the 1940s. They met at Haskel and Eliza Nixon's home for special prayers. From left to right are (first row) Ira Nixon, Lockie Nixon, Doyle Allen Taylor, Haudie Evans, and Venson Evans; (second row) Dora Waller Taylor, Lula Waller Greer, Eliza Nixon, Hobert Taylor, Dorla Nixon, Nola Taylor, Willie Taylor, and Haskel Nixon; (third row) Willie Herman Taylor, Eliza Waller Taylor, Robbie Dean Greer Walker, Audrey Taylor Snyder, Jess Evans, Willie Cowan, Cumiller Walker, Riley Page, and Isaac Taylor. (Courtesy of Ruth Taylor.)

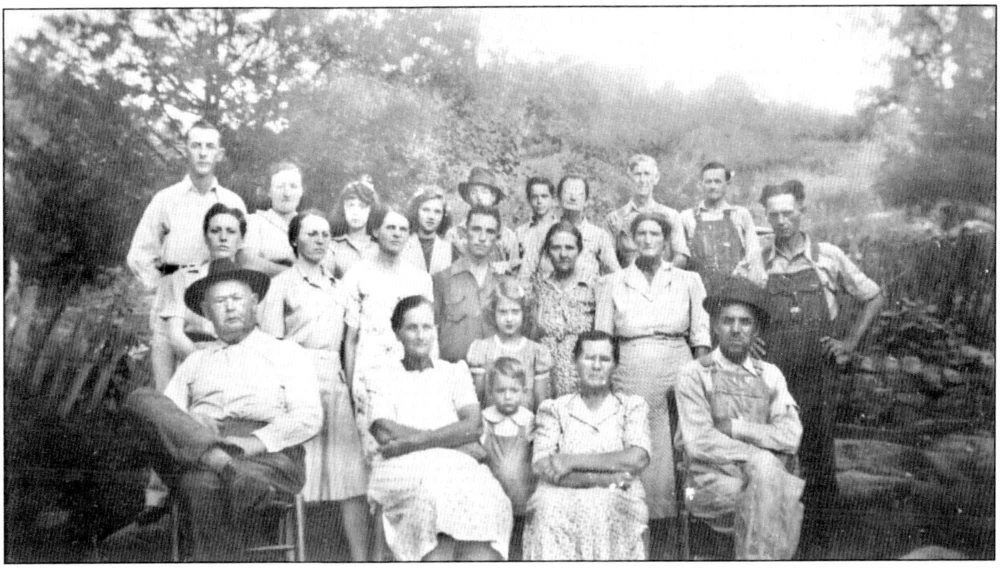

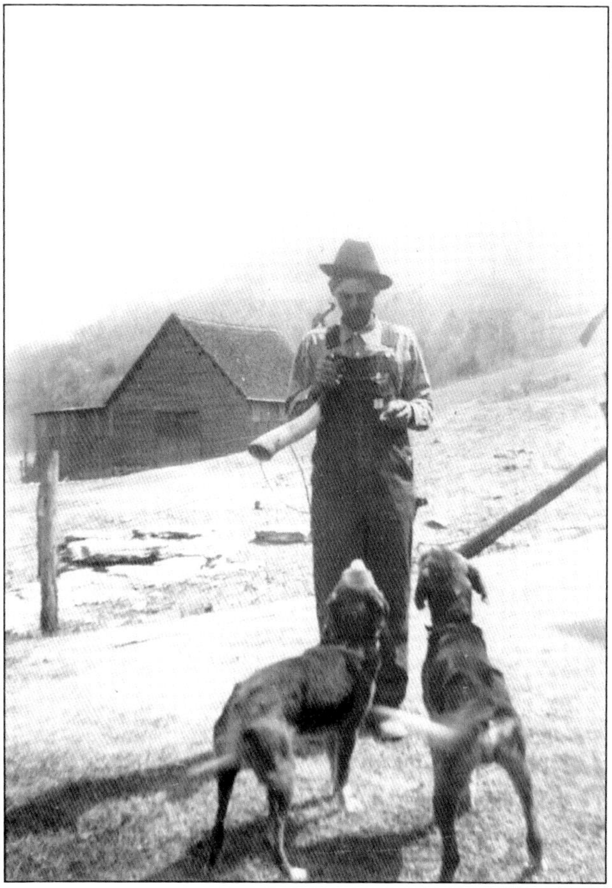

Fox hunting was a favorite pastime in the early 20th century. Shown on his farm on Indian Creek around 1945, Chess Taylor is using his fox horn to call his hounds and get them prepared for hunting that night. (Courtesy of J.B. Taylor.)

Barbara Cee Page is doing the washing in Poison Hollow in the 1940s with a rub board in a zinc tub filled with water and a hand-turned wringer. She is standing in front of the large concrete water tank at the back of the house while her sister Erma Dell watches from on top. (Courtesy of Ophel Page.)

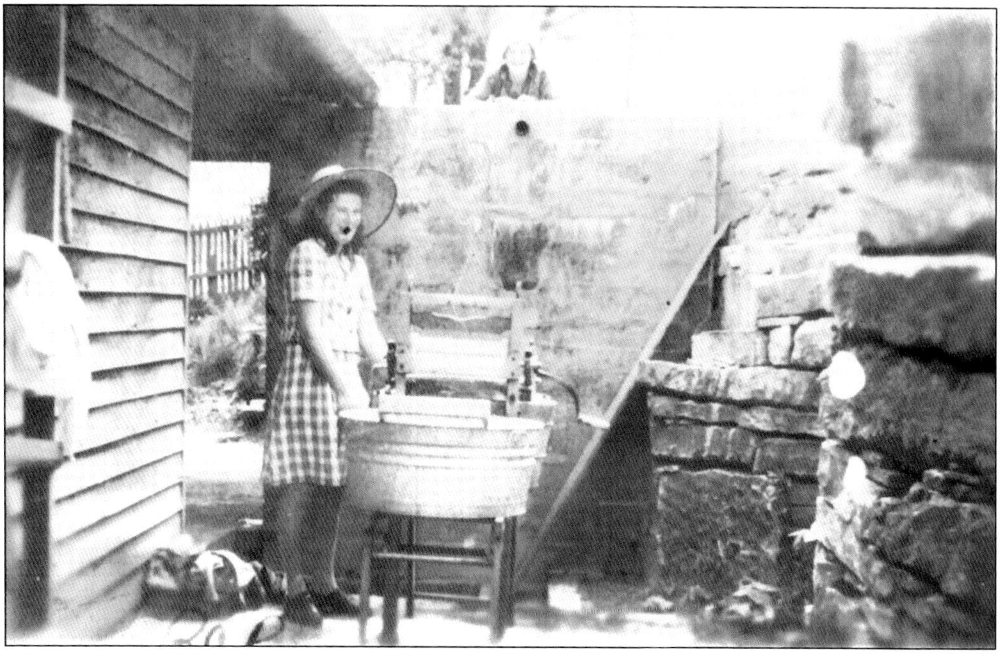

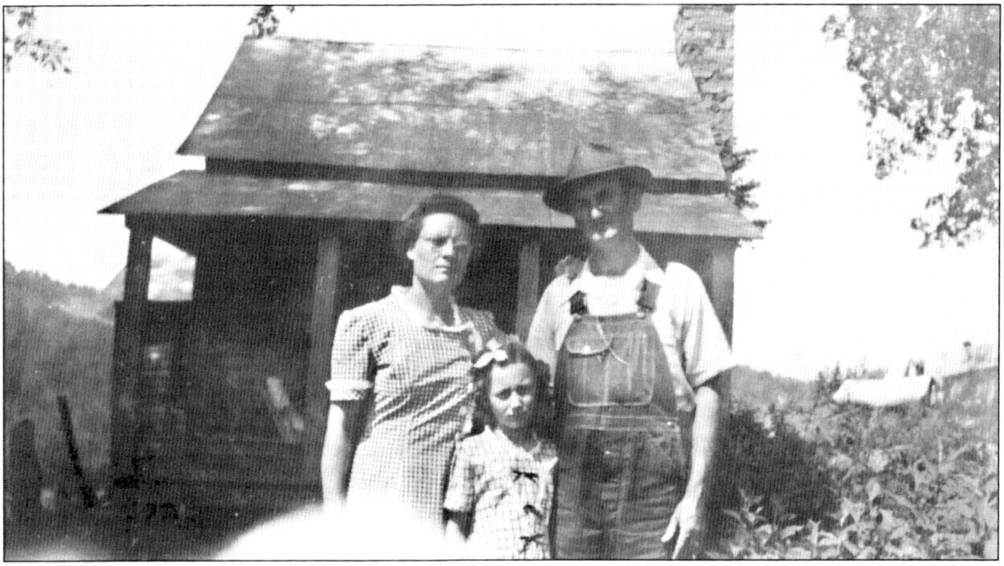

Janie and Jessie Smith with daughter Bobbie are standing around 1940 in front of their home at the mouth of Holmes' Creek where it entered the Caney Fork River. (Courtesy of Ophel Page.)

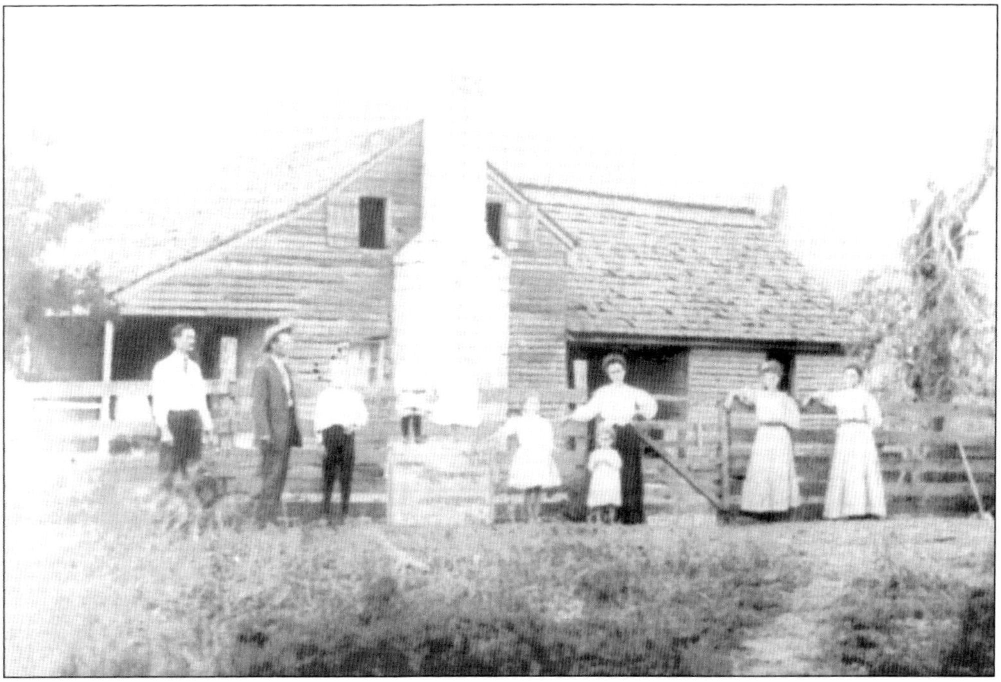

George Bond's family is standing in front of their home at the mouth of Holmes' Creek around 1908. George was a Confederate soldier and had a large family with his first and second wives. This home is now under the lake. (Courtesy of Justin Potter Library.)

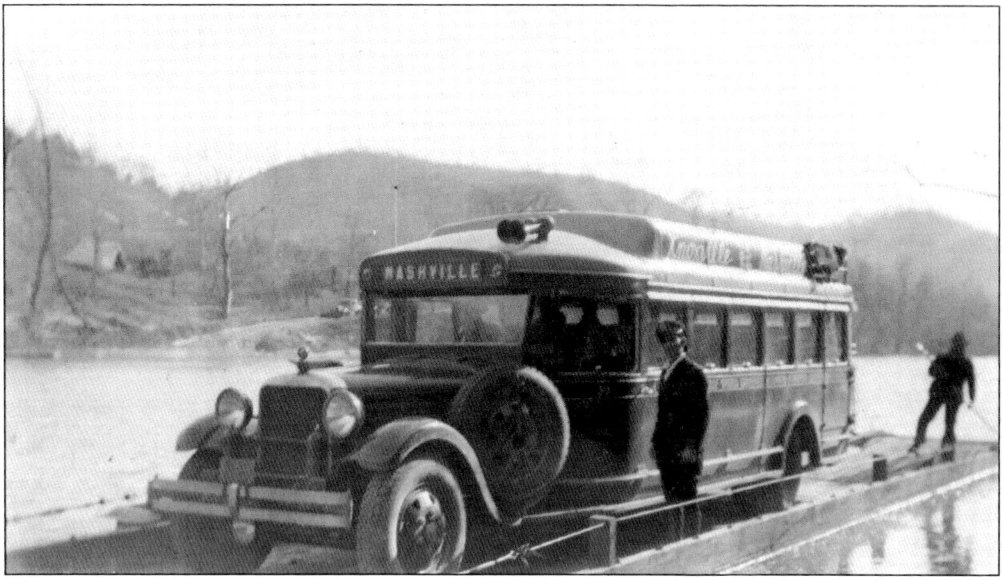

This ferry was used to cross the Caney Fork River for several years before the bridge was built at Sligo. This crossing was around 1927 while the bridge was under construction. The driver of the bus crossing the river is Houston Webb. (Courtesy of Justin Potter Library.)

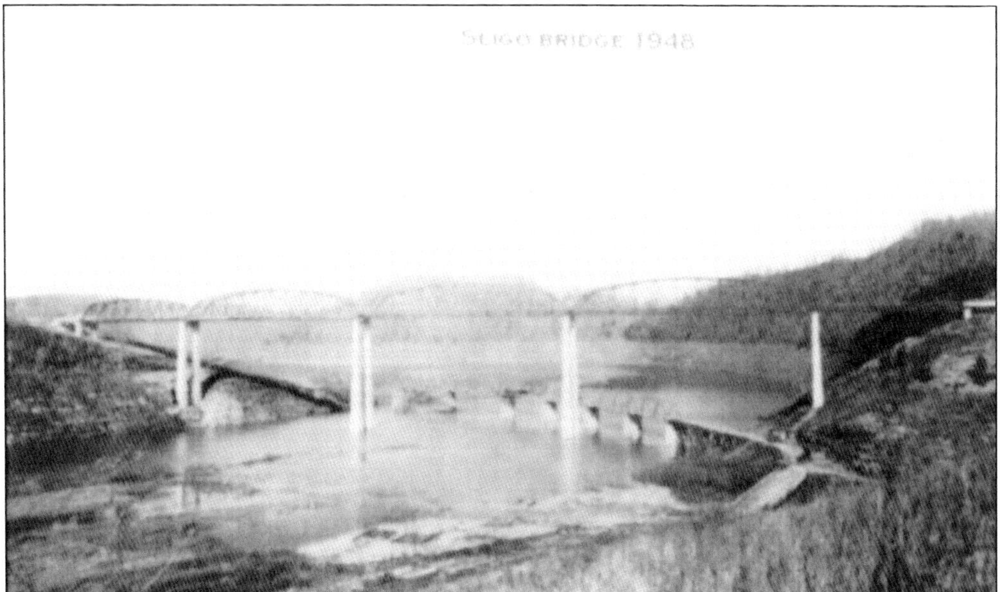

The Sligo Bridge was rebuilt much taller than the old bridge, which is directly underneath. This picture was taken in 1948 as the water is rising after the dam was completed. The site of the old bridge is now under the lake. (Courtesy of Justin Potter Library.)

Harvey Caplinger and wife, Lena (right), with a friend are swimming and boat riding on the Caney Fork River at Sligo around 1940. They lived in Alexandria where they owned a beauty salon and barbershop, later expanded to include a bait shop when they owned Holmes' Creek Boat Dock. (Courtesy of Judy Sandlin.)

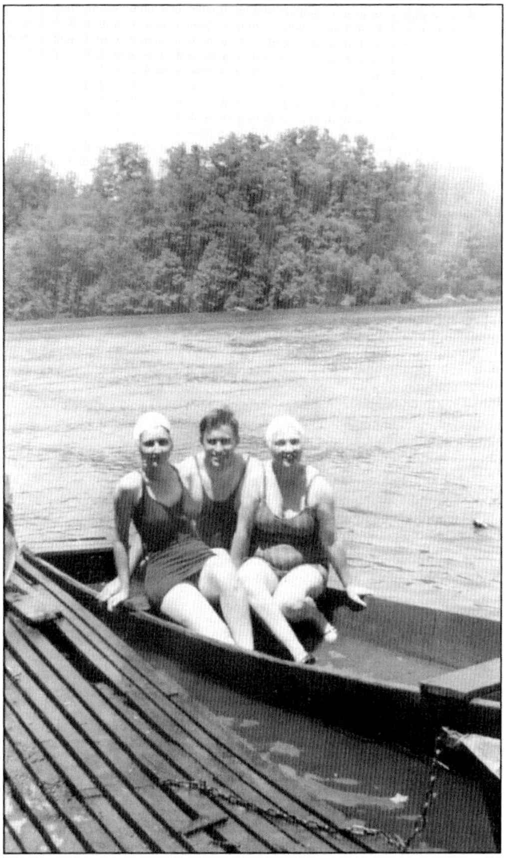

This is the dam construction in the mid-1940s. The US Army Corps of Engineers began the Center Hill Dam in the early 1940s but stopped for a while during World War II. It was eventually restarted and finished by 1948. (Courtesy of Lois Spencer.)

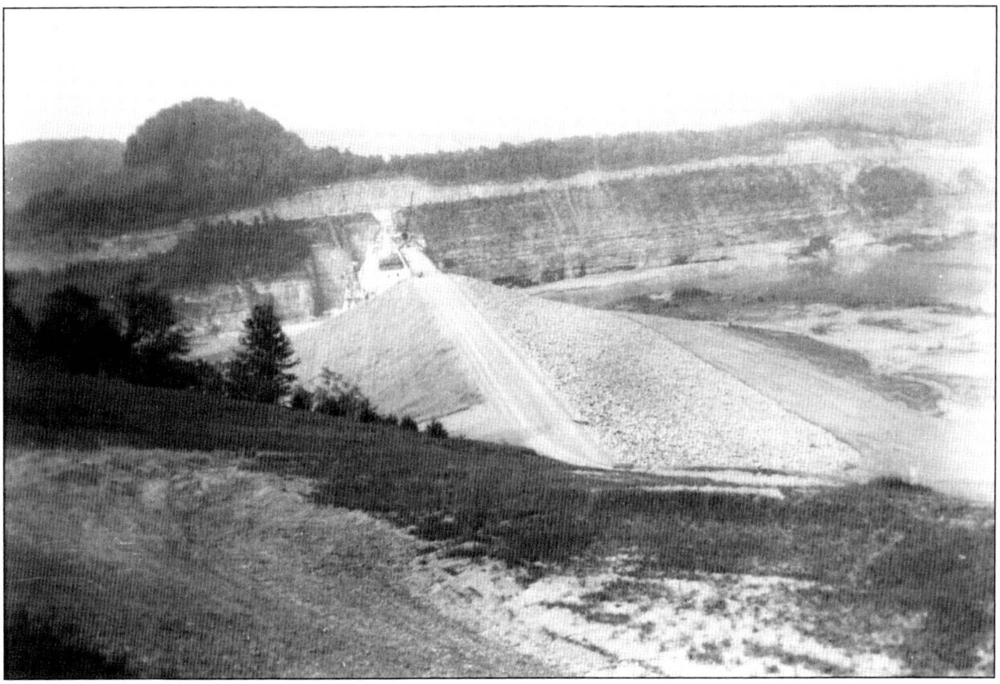

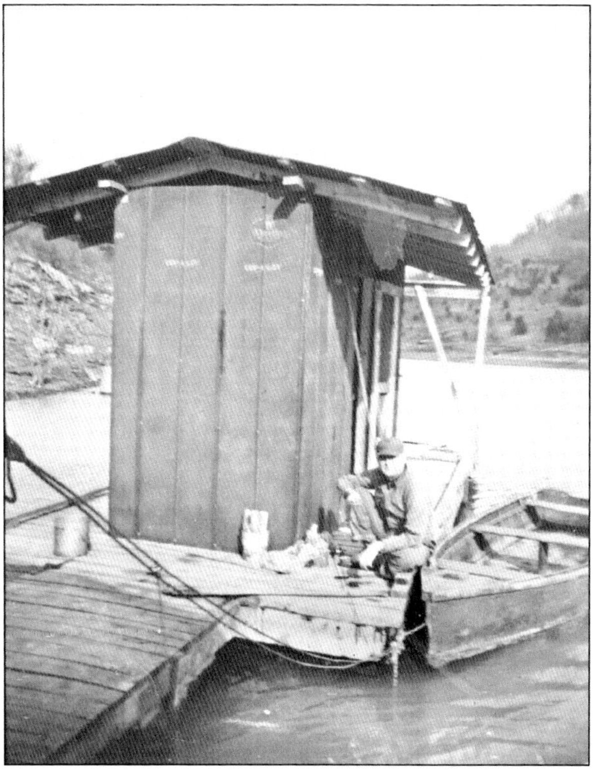

Located on Holmes' Creek and owned by Harvey Caplinger, this is one of the first boat docks after the dam was built and the lake formed in 1948. Boating and fishing soon became a favorite pastime and recreation for people in this county as well as visitors. (Courtesy of Judy Sandlin.)

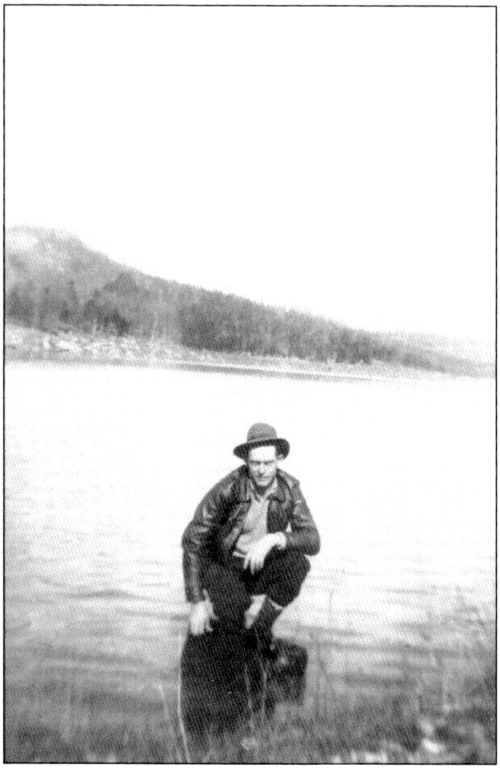

Born in 1917 on Indian Creek, J.B. Taylor had lived on the farm there all his life until the Center Hill Dam was built. He and his wife, Ruth, moved up on higher ground to Hurricane Ridge. Shown in 1949, he is sitting on a log near his old home place, now under the lake. (Courtesy of J.B. Taylor.)

Seven

Old Home Scenes

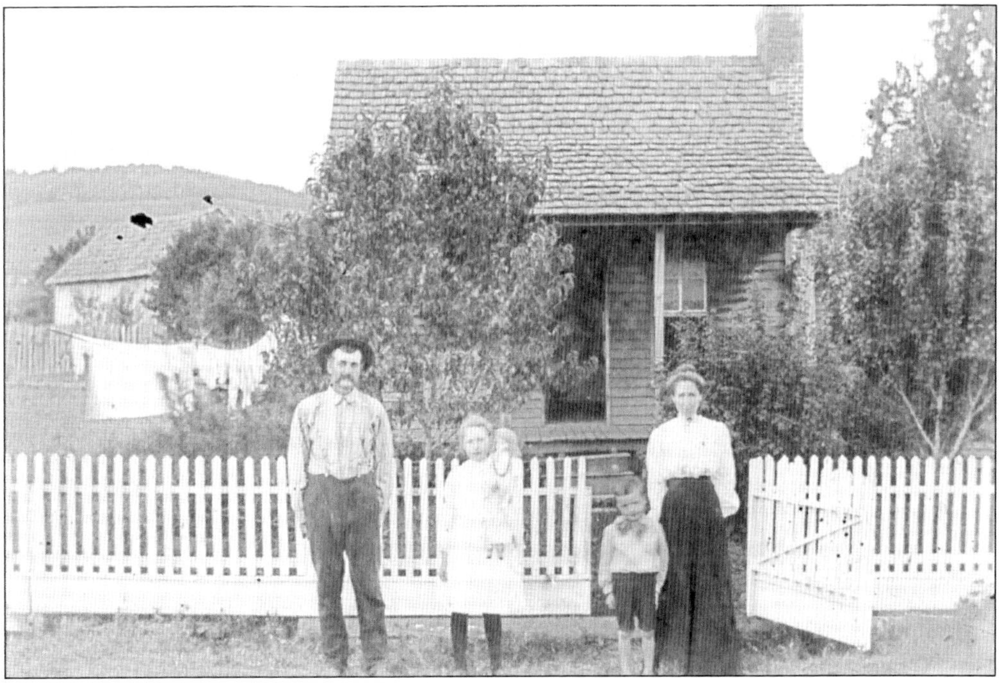

Pictured in 1902 and located just west of Liberty at Forks of the Pike, this is the home place of Thomas Cooper's family. Standing in front of the white picket fence are Thomas and his wife, Melodia, with their daughter Shellie and son Durey. Having had some additions and remodeling, the house is still standing at this location and is owned by Cooper's grandson Robert Robinson. (Courtesy of Robert Robinson.)

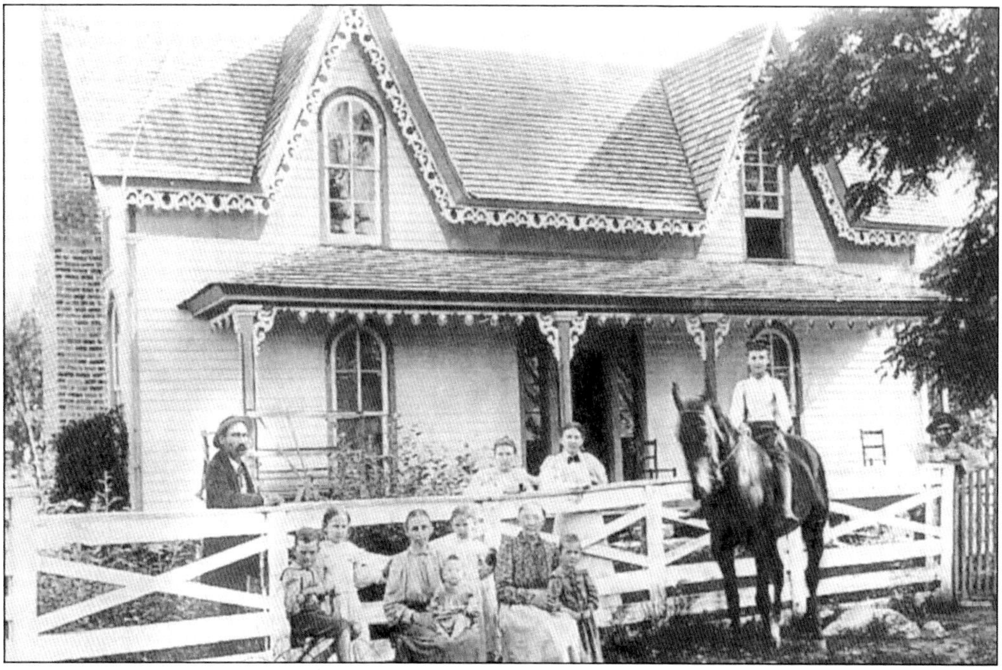

This house was the home of the T.P. Bragg family near the Forks of the Pike at Liberty in 1895. The house was built in 1880 by John Wesley Groom, father of Emma Groom Bragg. Pictured behind the fence are T.P. Bragg and two unidentified women. In front of the fence are, from left to right, John Roy Bragg on the tricycle, Carrie Bragg, wife Emma Groom Bragg holding Dixie Miller Bragg, Hassie Bragg, Mary Elizabeth Alexander Bragg, Thomas J. Bragg, and Clarence Bragg on the horse. Looking much the same with the original trim around the eaves and owned by Mary Ruth Groom, this house is still there. (Courtesy of Mary Ruth Groom and the Bragg family.)

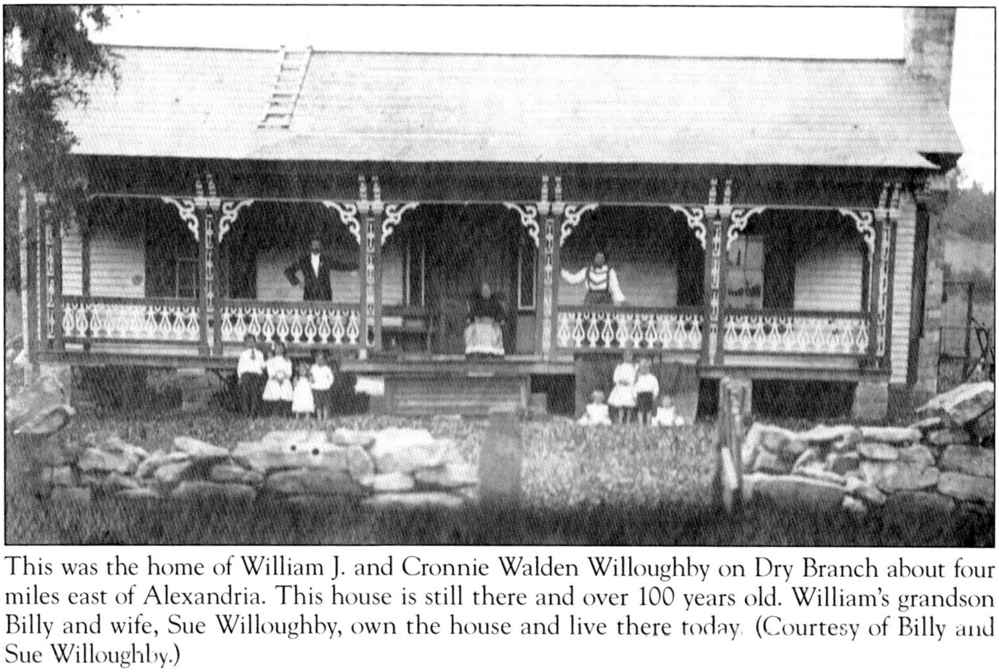

This was the home of William J. and Cronnie Walden Willoughby on Dry Branch about four miles east of Alexandria. This house is still there and over 100 years old. William's grandson Billy and wife, Sue Willoughby, own the house and live there today. (Courtesy of Billy and Sue Willoughby.)

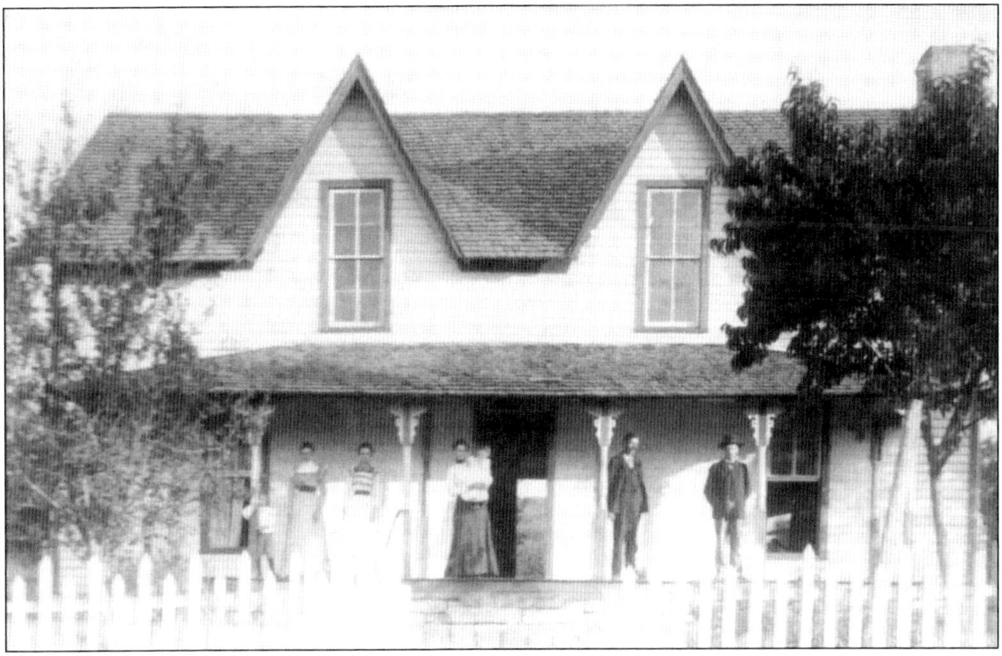

Above, Monroe Willoughby (far right) and his family are standing on the porch of their house on Dry Branch in the early 1900s. Below is the home of one of Monroe's sons John Lee Willoughby and wife, Mintie Nixon (a twin), with children Thelma and Drucie on Upper Helton around 1911. Drucie, the baby in mother's arms, grew up to become a teacher at Alexandria Elementary School for over 40 years. (Both, courtesy of Mac Willoughby.)

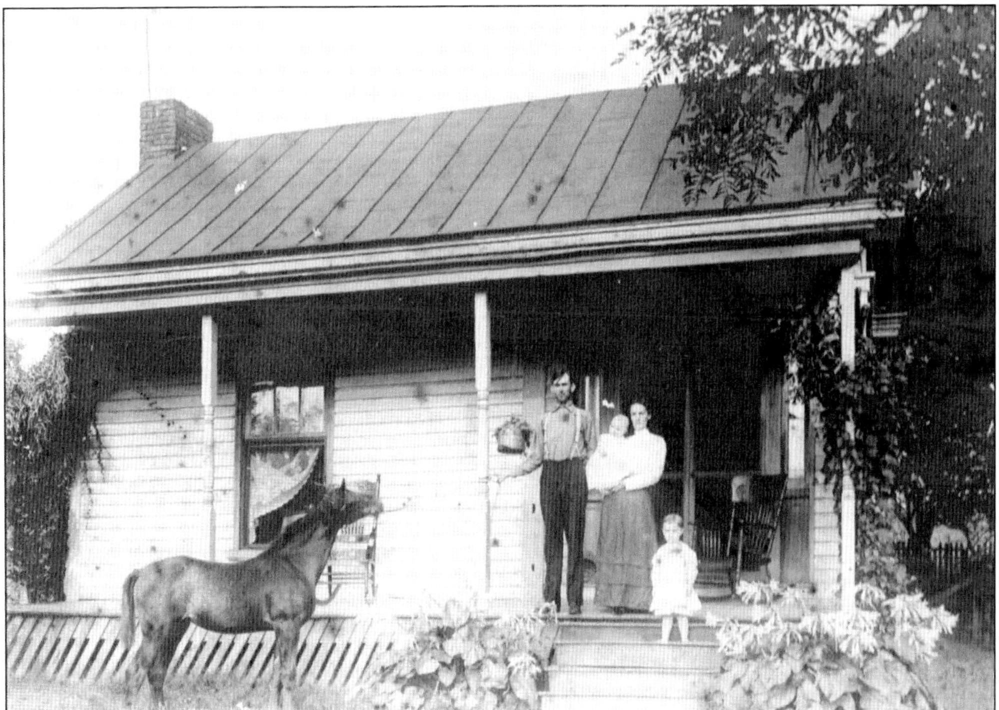

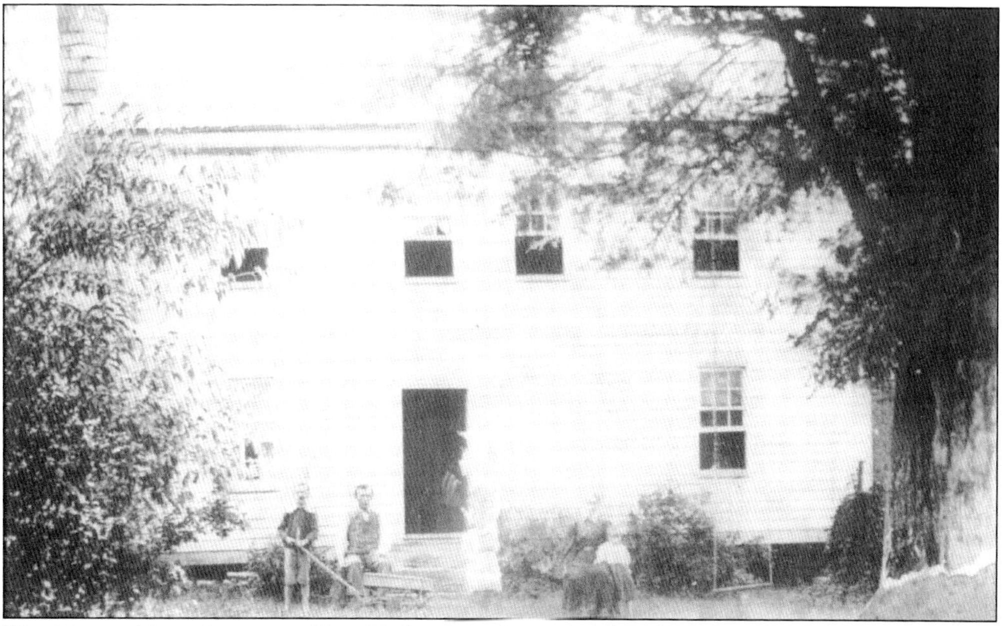

The George Givan home on Clear Fork was built in 1812 by Thomas Dale, Adam's father. The family members pictured in front of the house in 1897 are, from left to right, son Emmons, George, daughter Lena, wife Lella Robinson, and son Seldon. This house is still occupied after some additions and remodeling over the past years. (Courtesy of Justin Potter Library.)

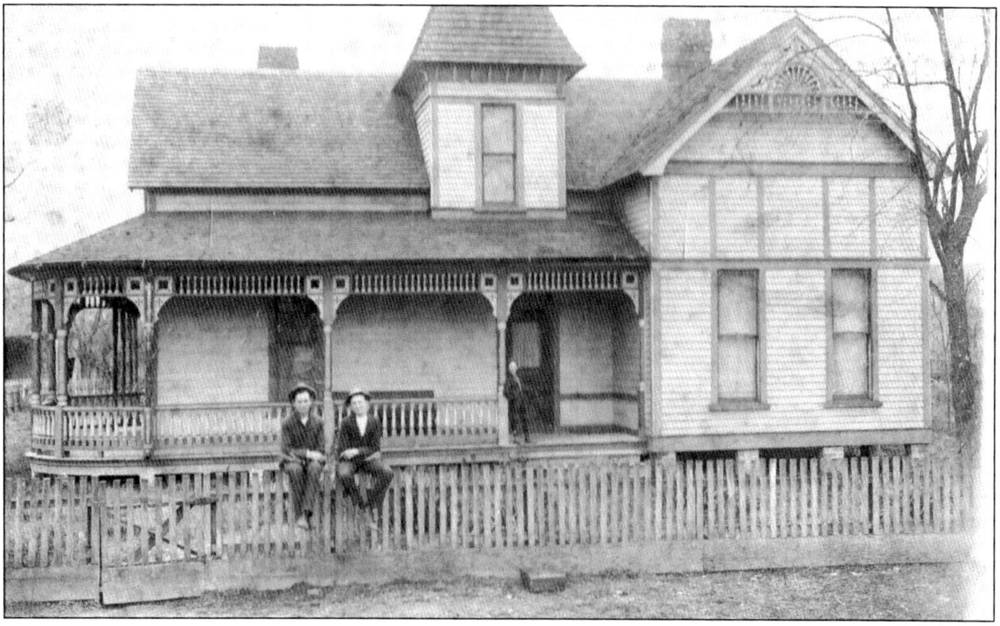

Clarence Moore (left) is sitting on the fence of his home at 111 West Webb Street with an unknown friend about 1904. His little brother, Carlyn, is standing on the porch. This was the home of James B. (Jim) Moore and wife Cartie Webb, sister of local pharmacist F.Z. Webb. At that time, Jim was the clerk and master of the DeKalb County Chancery Court. The house is now the residence of local attorney Jim Judkins; the cupola had been removed by the 1930s. (Courtesy of Tommy Webb.)

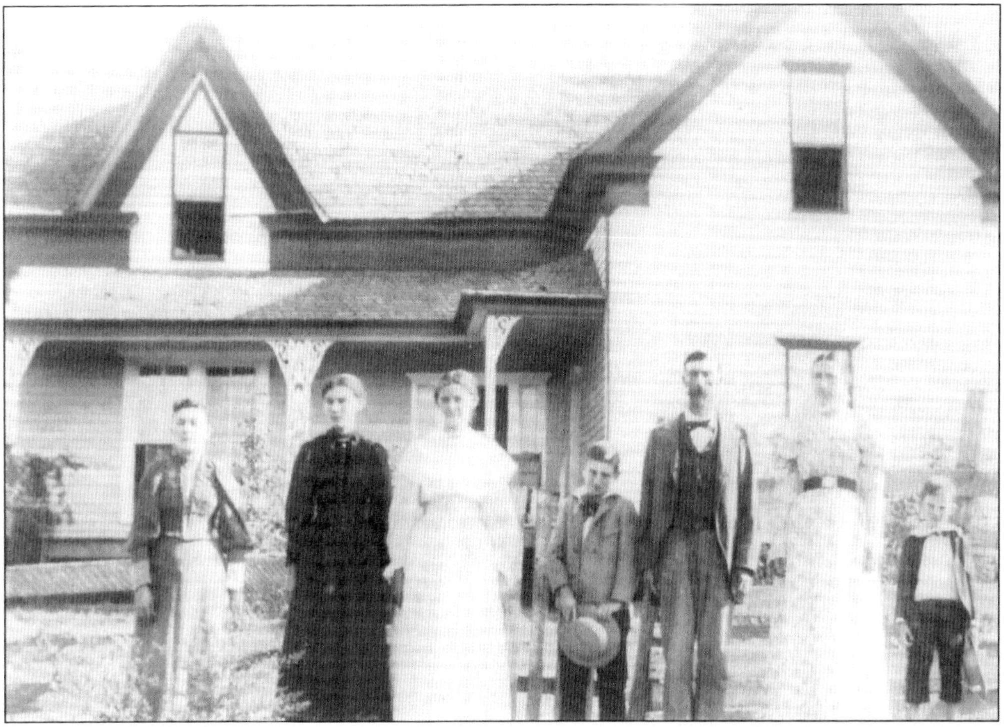

This is the Lycurgas Driver family standing in front of their house in Temperance Hall about 1898. Pictured from left to right are Cleo, Maggie, Era, William L., Lycurgas, Mary Eliza (wife), and Thomas Edgar. Lycurgas was a democrat who served in the Tennessee House of Representatives from 1903 through 1907. His son Thomas Edgar also served in the House of Representatives from 1925 through 1929. (Courtesy of Justin Potter Library.)

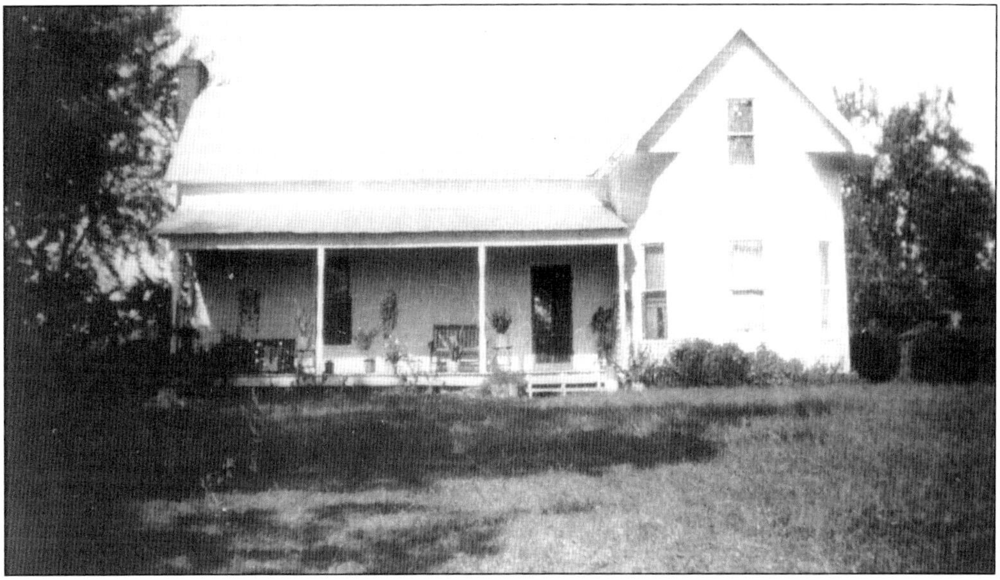

This was the home of Rev. Lemuel W. Beckwith on West Main Street in Smithville. He was the first pastor of the Mt. Herman Baptist church, serving from 1902 to 1912. His grandparents James and Rachael Beckwith were the owners of the Beckwith Inn. (Courtesy of Judy Fuson.)

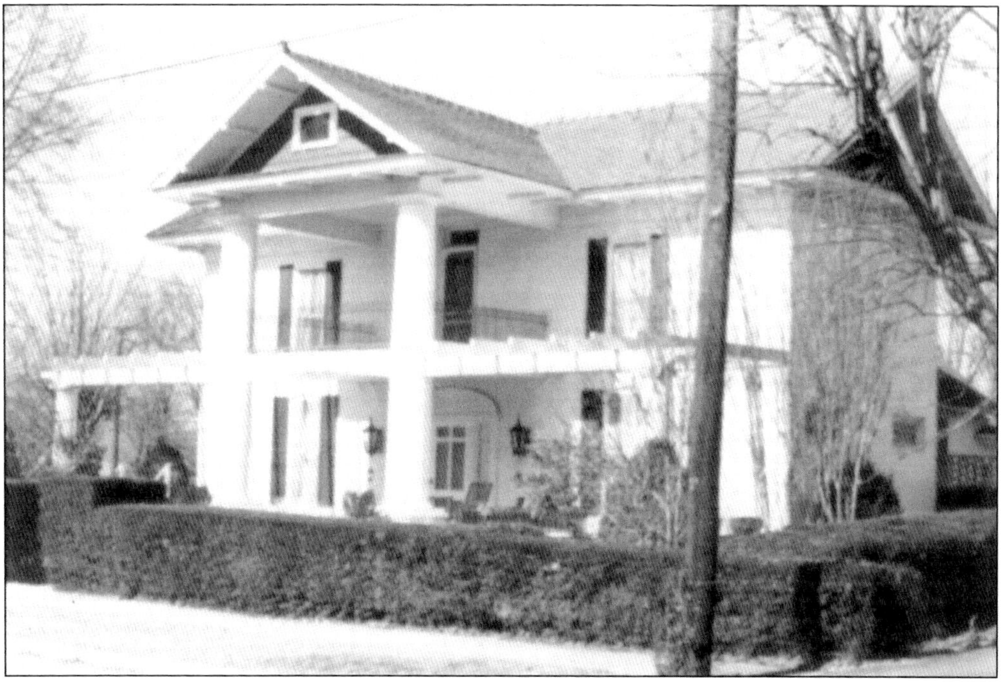

This house was built in 1900 by A.J. Goodson, the grandfather of Joe L. Evins. Joe lived in this home as a boy and after he retired from the US Congress in 1976. This house still stands on the corner of Congress Boulevard and East Main Street in Smithville, and the family still lives there. (Courtesy of Justin Potter Library.)

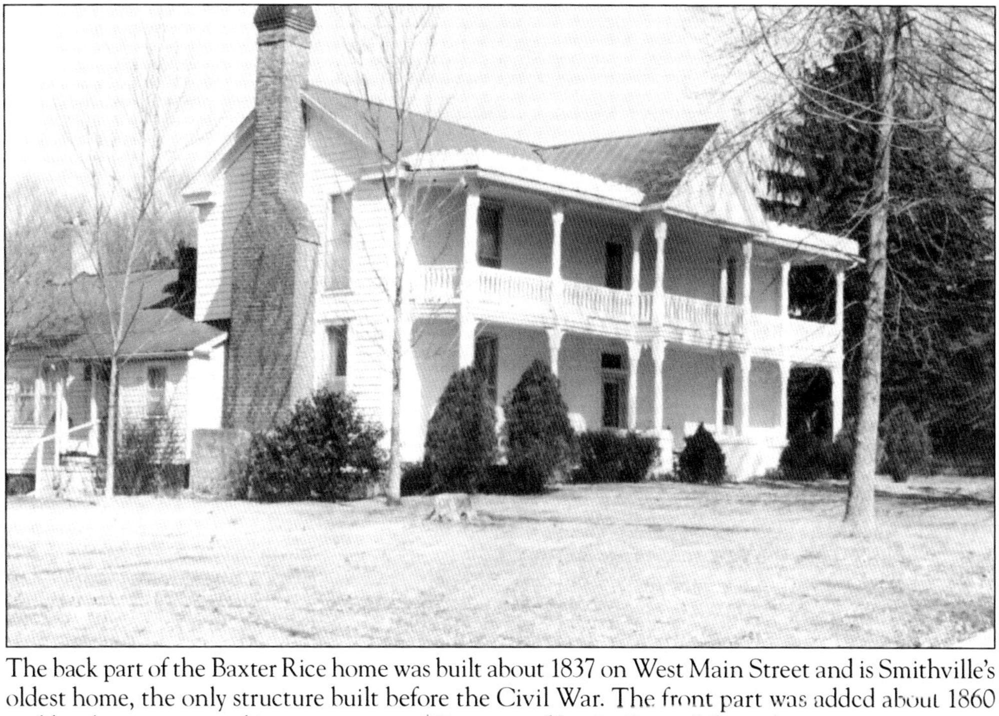

The back part of the Baxter Rice home was built about 1837 on West Main Street and is Smithville's oldest home, the only structure built before the Civil War. The front part was added about 1860 and has been renovated in recent years. (Courtesy of Justin Potter Library.)

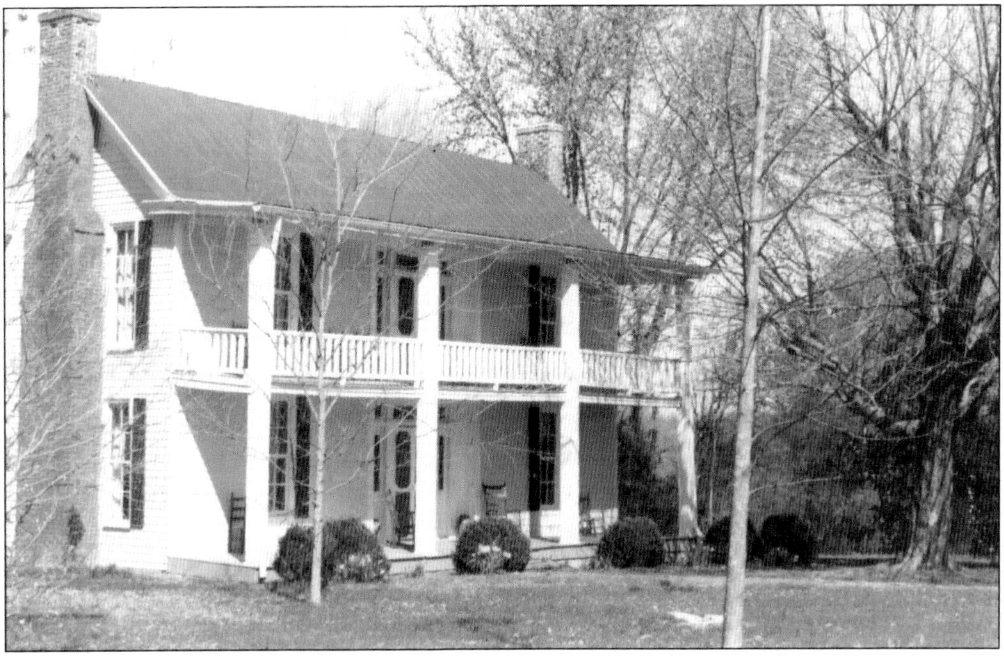

The Thomas G. Webb home on South College Street in Smithville was built in 1879 and was the former home of Sallie Magness Webb, Thomas's great-great-great-grandmother. Thomas Webb, the county historian, taught in various schools in DeKalb County for over 40 years and has worked on genealogy and county history books most of his life. (Courtesy of Thomas G. Webb.)

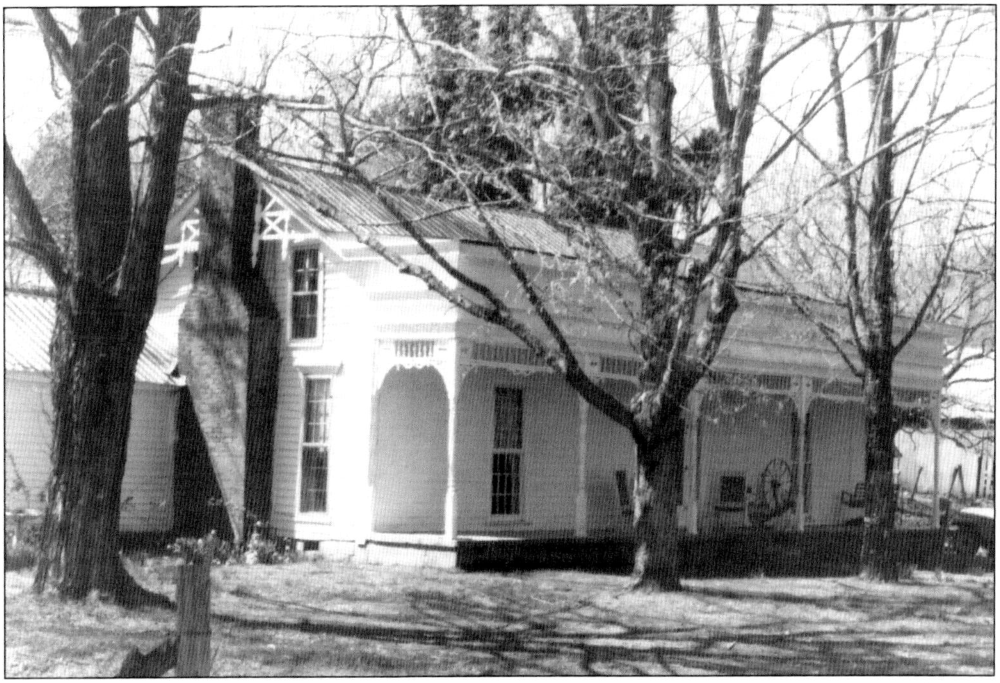

This is the home of Bobby and Barbara Colvert on the old turnpike just east of Dowelltown. This house was used as a hospital during the Civil War, and was occupied in many years by the Beverly Robinson family. (Courtesy of Thomas G. Webb.)

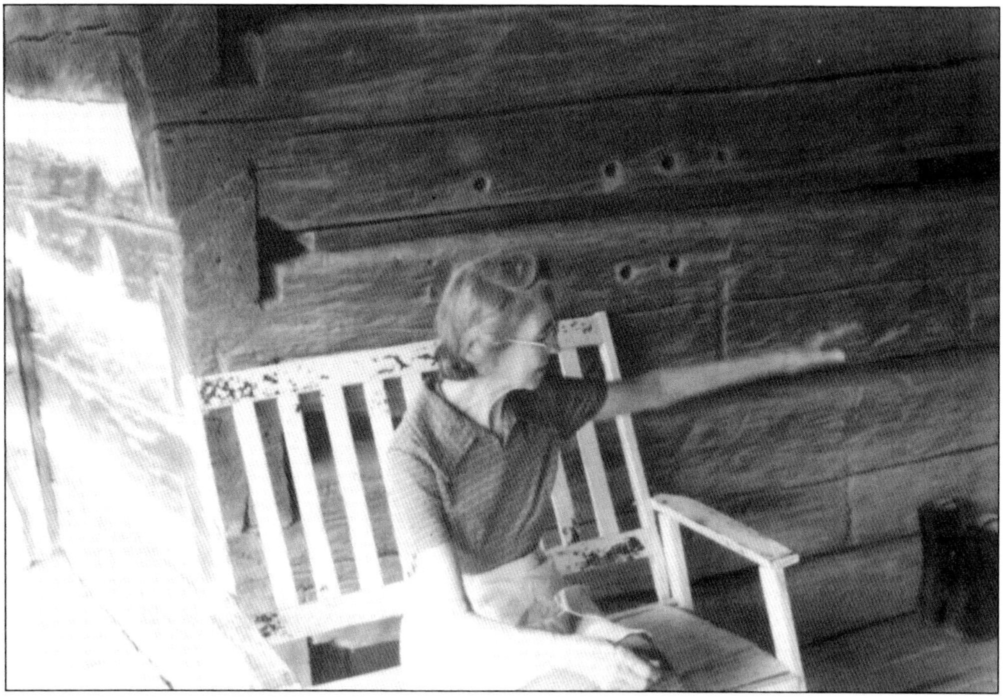

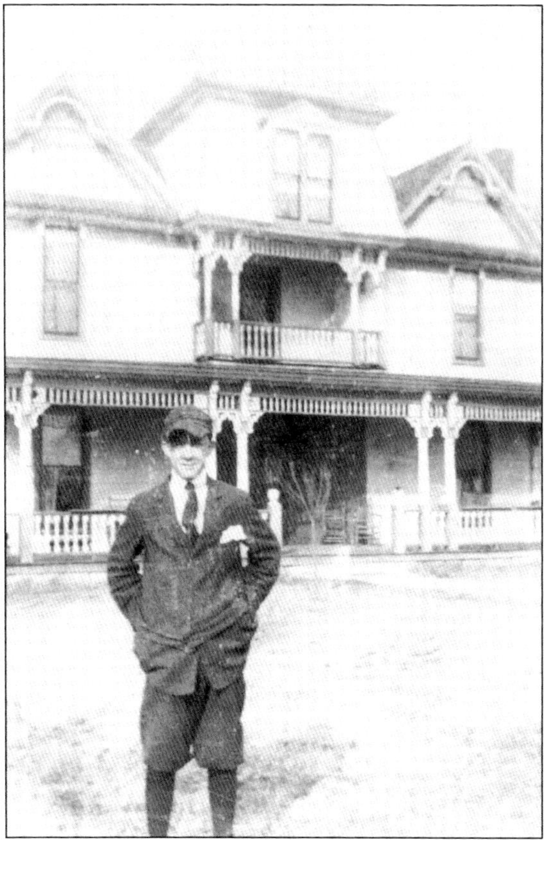

Dovie Carter is sitting in the dogtrot in her old log house on Walker's Creek, east of Alexandria in 1976. This was originally the Jonathan Deadman home, built around 1830, and it still stands today. (Courtesy of Thomas G. Webb.)

Kenneth O. Lester stands in front of his home at 312 West Main Street in Alexandria around 1935. His father operated a general store in town while his mother ran the home and occasionally took in boarders. K.O. began hauling produce for his father from Alexandria to Nashville and eventually established a food distribution business, which is now headquartered in Lebanon, Tennessee. (Courtesy of Bill and Sue Corley.)

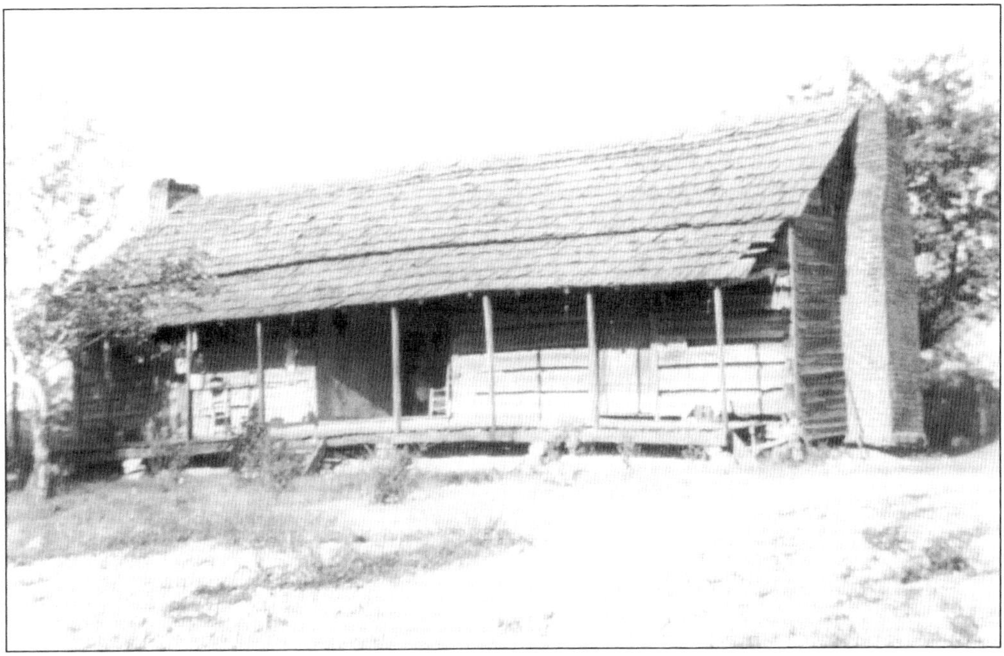

For many years, this was the home of James Monroe and Arminta Young Luna, located in the Young Bend community just next door to the school. Notable is the open section at the center known as the dogtrot. (Courtesy of Thomas G. Webb.)

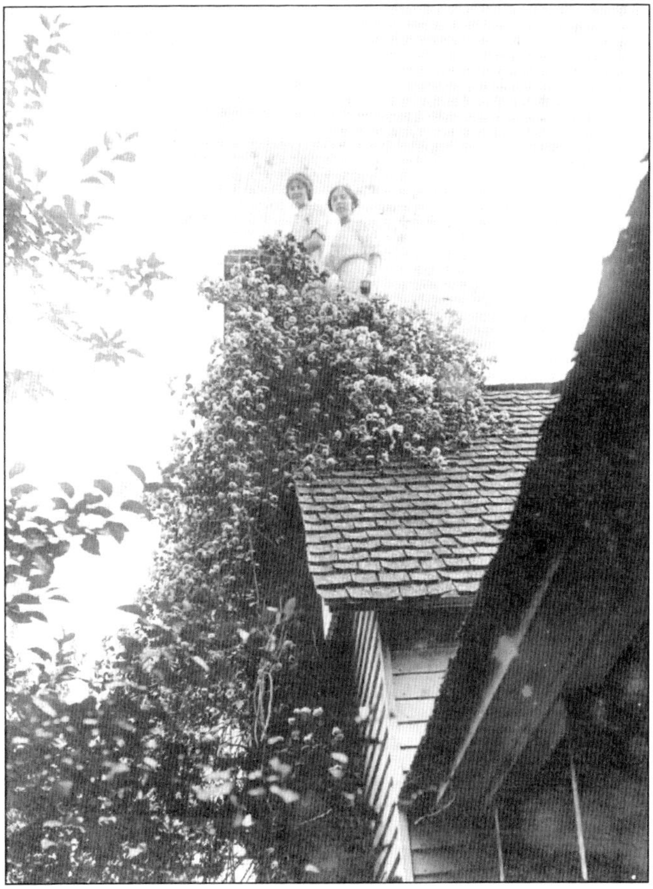

Friends Ola Parker (left) and Emily Beckwith climbed to the top of the Beckwith family's house just west of Smithville to be with the rosebush that had also climbed up the chimney. This was around 1915 when Emily's uncle Tom Beckwith was in the photography business and took many photographs of scenes like this. (Courtesy of Judy Fuson.)

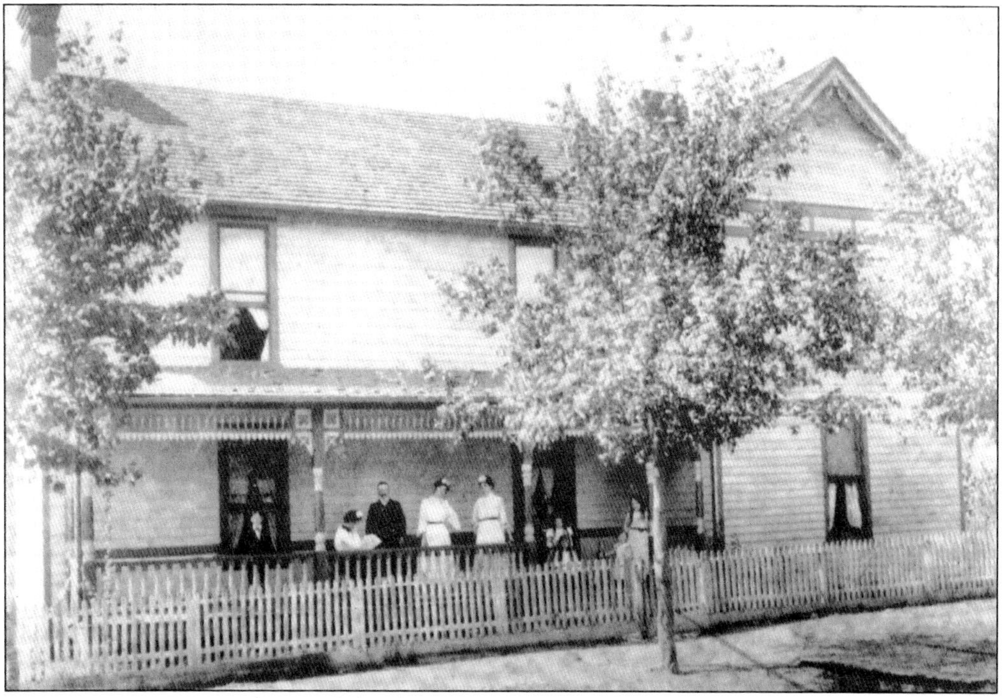

W. Brown Foster is standing with his family on the front porch of their home at 205 West Main Street in Smithville in 1902. Foster was a pearl dealer during the time when pearls were found in the Caney Fork River, and served as the county court clerk from 1898 to 1910. (Courtesy of Justin Potter Library.)

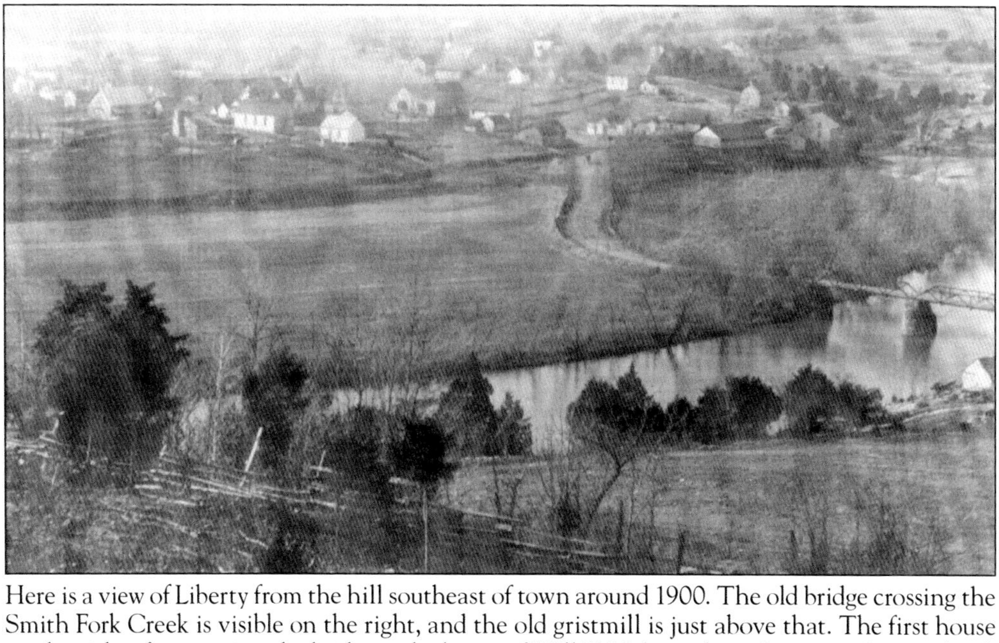

Here is a view of Liberty from the hill southeast of town around 1900. The old bridge crossing the Smith Fork Creek is visible on the right, and the old gristmill is just above that. The first house on the right after crossing the bridge is the home of Will T. Hale, author of a county history book published in 1915. Also in the view are three churches: Salem, Liberty Methodist, and the black Methodist. (Courtesy of Liberty Historic Group.)

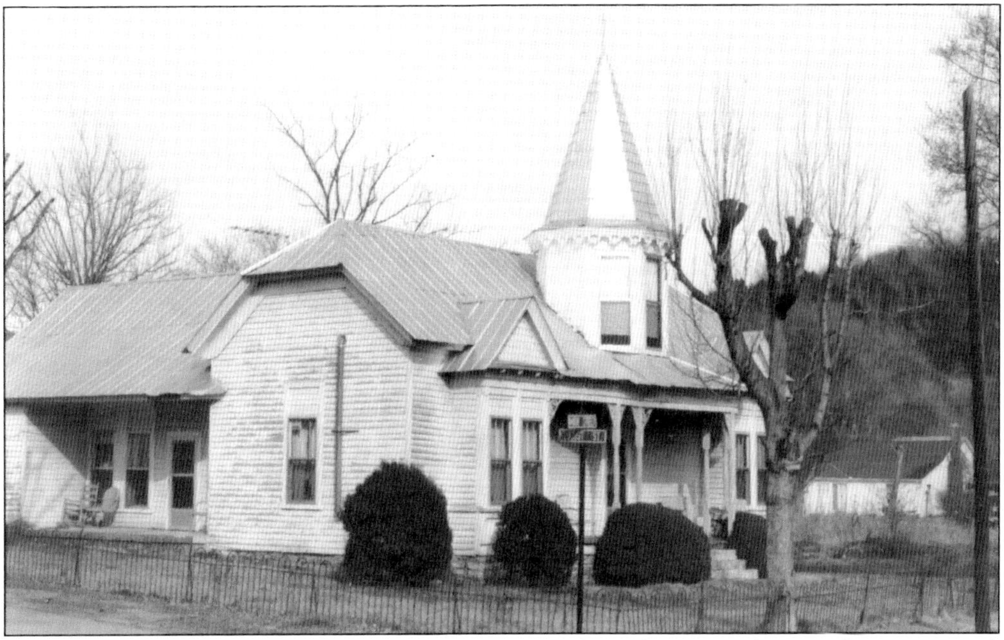

This house containing many interesting features is now the only one in Liberty with an octagonal, tin-covered tower. It was built in 1900 for Dr. Hudson at a cost of $900 and was later lived in by Dr. T.J. and Nette Bratten Jackson. This picture was taken in 1976. (Courtesy of Thomas G. Webb.)

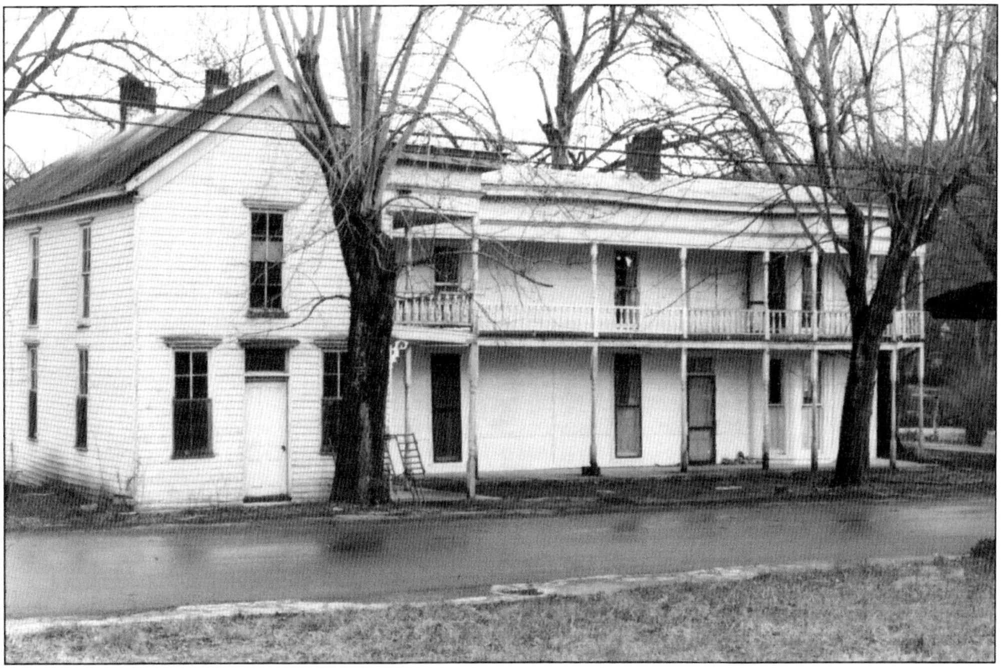

At one time, this building was the Liberty Hotel. George Givan purchased the lot in 1812, and a part of the structure was probably built by 1814. It is not known exactly what time it became a hotel, but the 1860 census lists William H. Whaley as the "Keeper of the Hotel." It is presently the home of Mason Williams's family. (Courtesy of Justin Potter Library.)

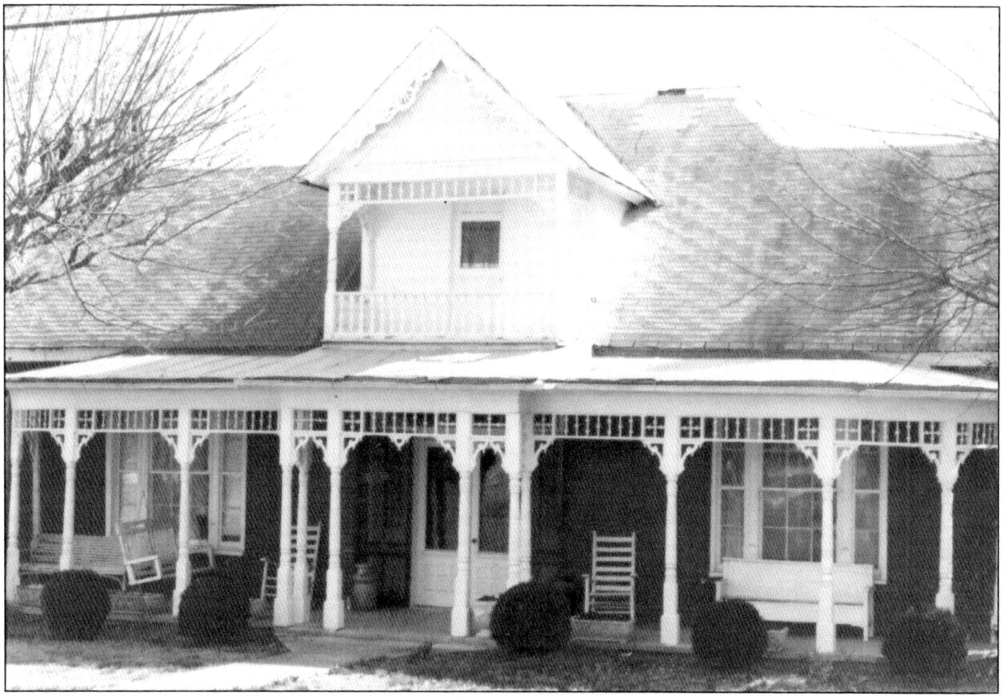

In 1854, Bennett Yeargin lived in the only brick residence in Alexandria, which was probably constructed by his son John who was a carpenter. The house is still standing and is occupied by the Jimmy Mullinax family. (Courtesy of Thomas G. Webb.)

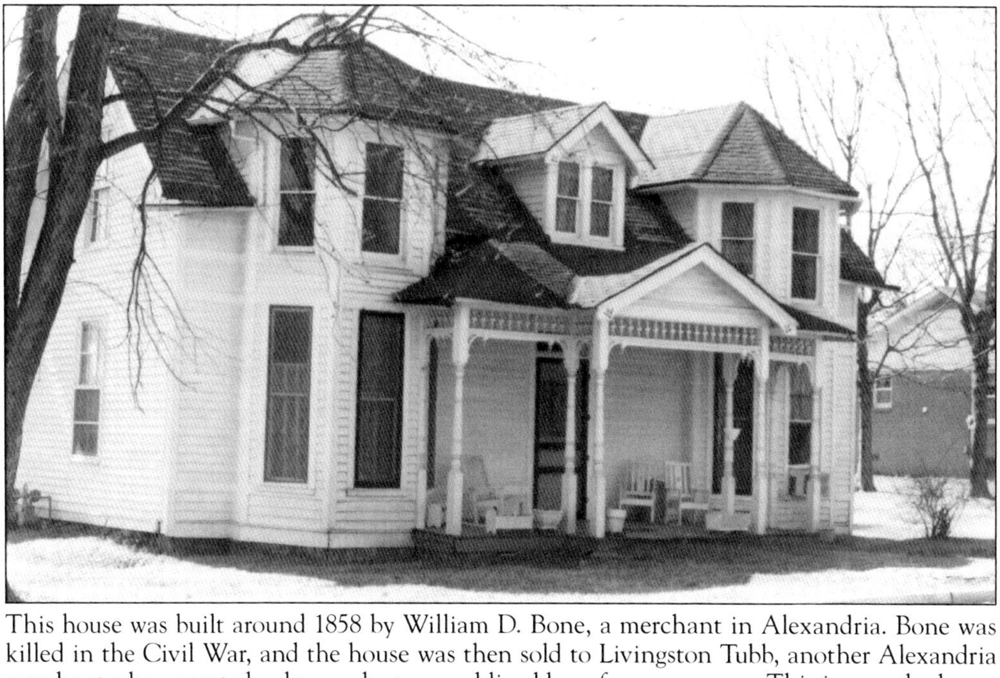

This house was built around 1858 by William D. Bone, a merchant in Alexandria. Bone was killed in the Civil War, and the house was then sold to Livingston Tubb, another Alexandria merchant who operated a dry goods store and lived here for many years. This is now the home of the Bobby White family. White is in charge of registration at the Tennessee State Museum. (Courtesy of Thomas G. Webb.)

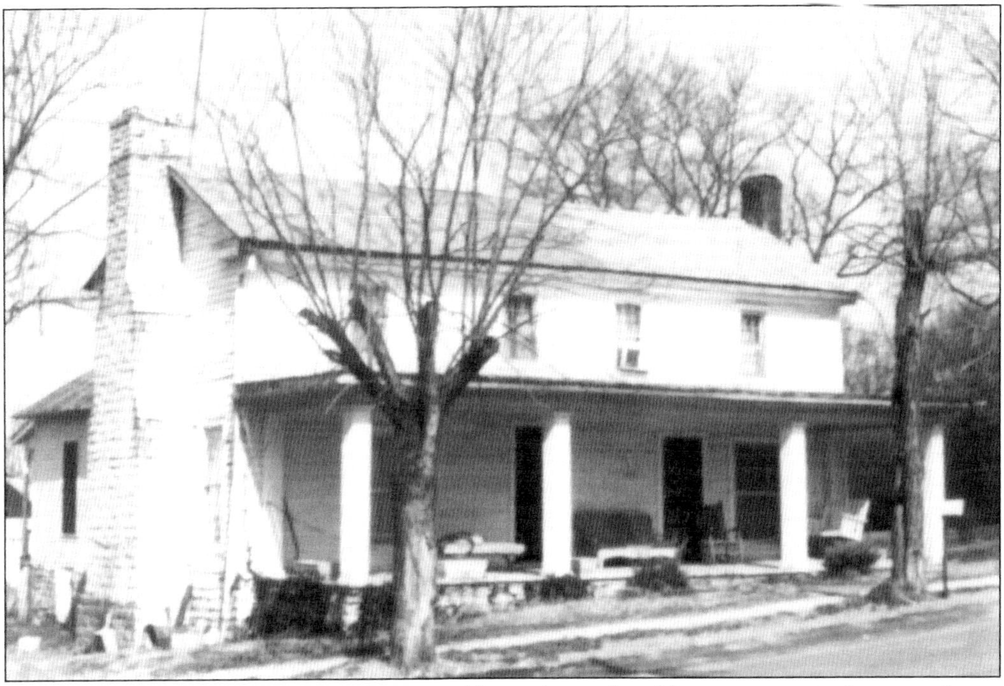

A part of this house on East Main Street in Alexandria is the oldest structure in the town. It was a log house built in 1823 and was once the home of James Goodner, a prominent businessman who operated a tanyard for many years before the Civil War. (Courtesy of Justin Potter Library.)

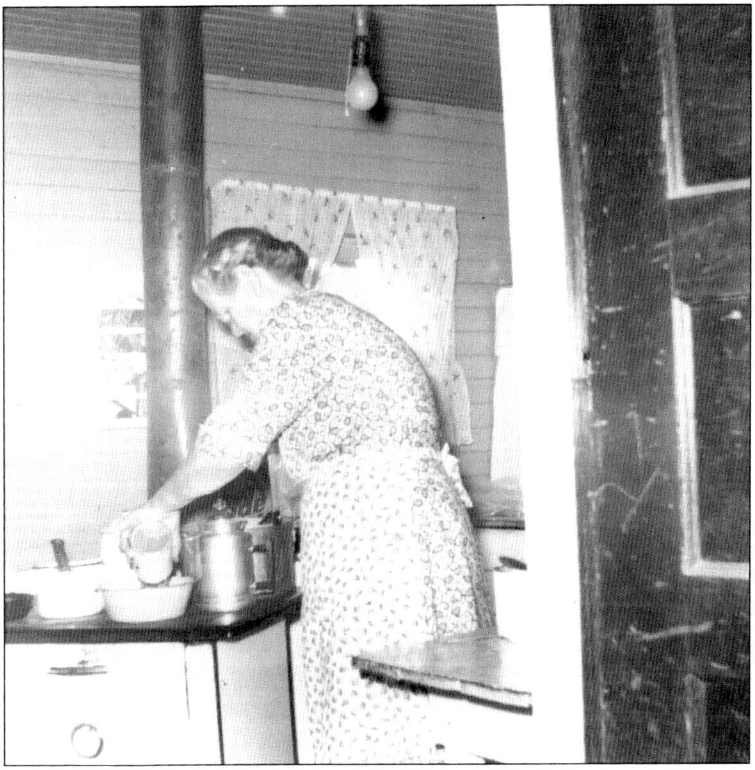

Annie Tramel is shown cooking on a more modern wood stove in her home on West Main Street in Smithville in the 1940s. The early access to electricity in a home was mostly for light. The single light bulb hanging from the ceiling above Tramel was lighting up the kitchen more than ever at that time. (Courtesy of Marguerite Jones.)

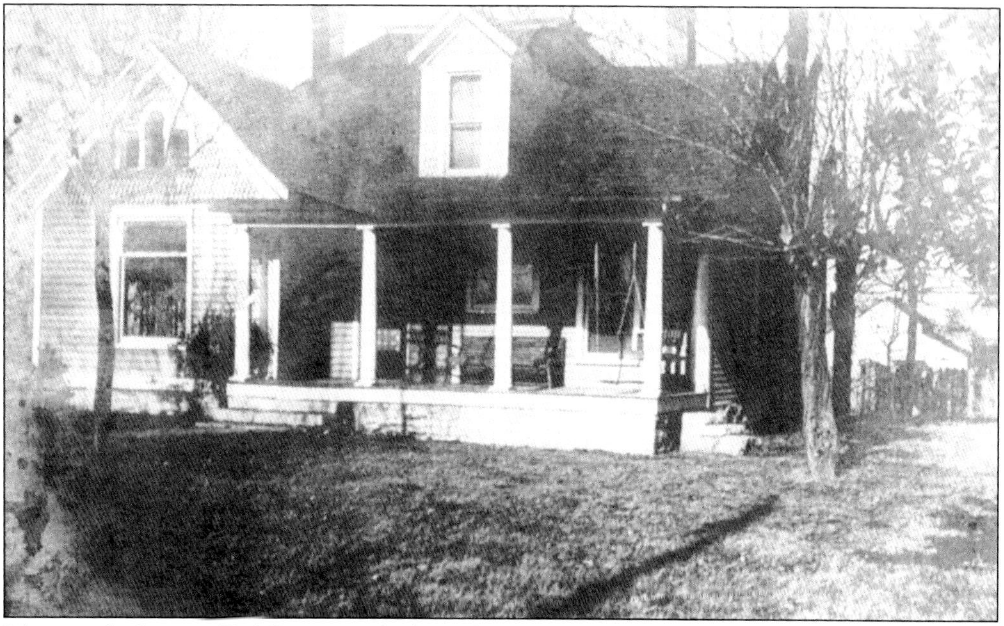

This was the home of Rob Roy, one of Alexandria's prominent residents, who owned and operated the fair at Alexandria for over 50 years. He was a trustee of the Methodist Church, taught the boy's Sunday school class for more than 30 years, and was editor and publisher of the *Alexandria Times* from 1894 to 1918. (Courtesy of Ria Baker.)

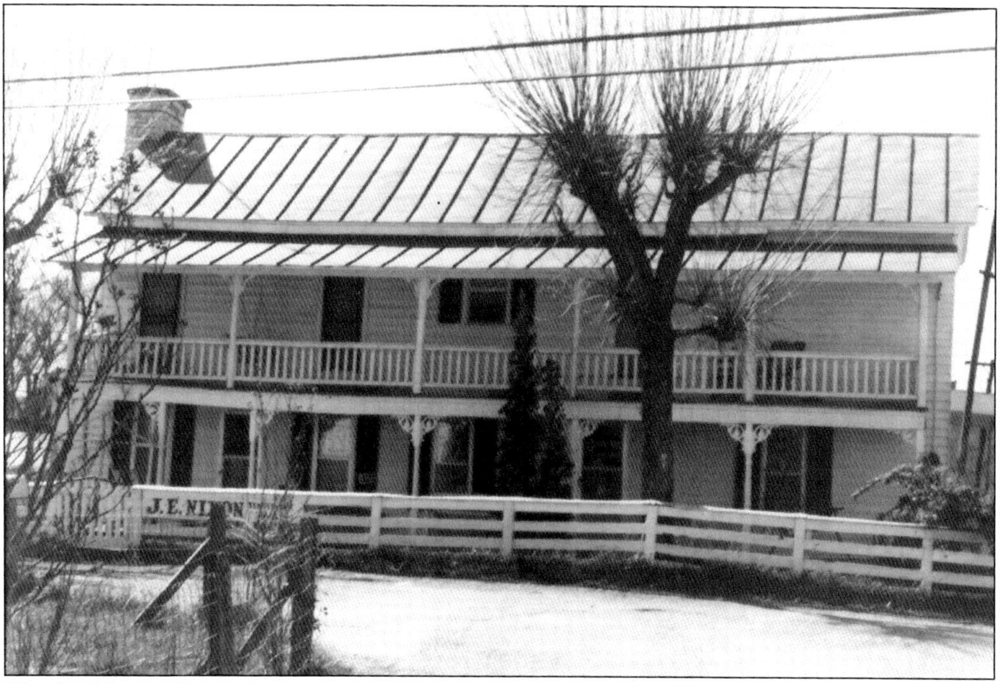

This building still standing in Temperance Hall is the one that gave its name to the town. The Sons of Temperance organized there in 1849 and met on the second floor. The building was later used as a hotel, a store, and a residence. This photograph was taken in 1976. (Courtesy of Thomas G. Webb.)

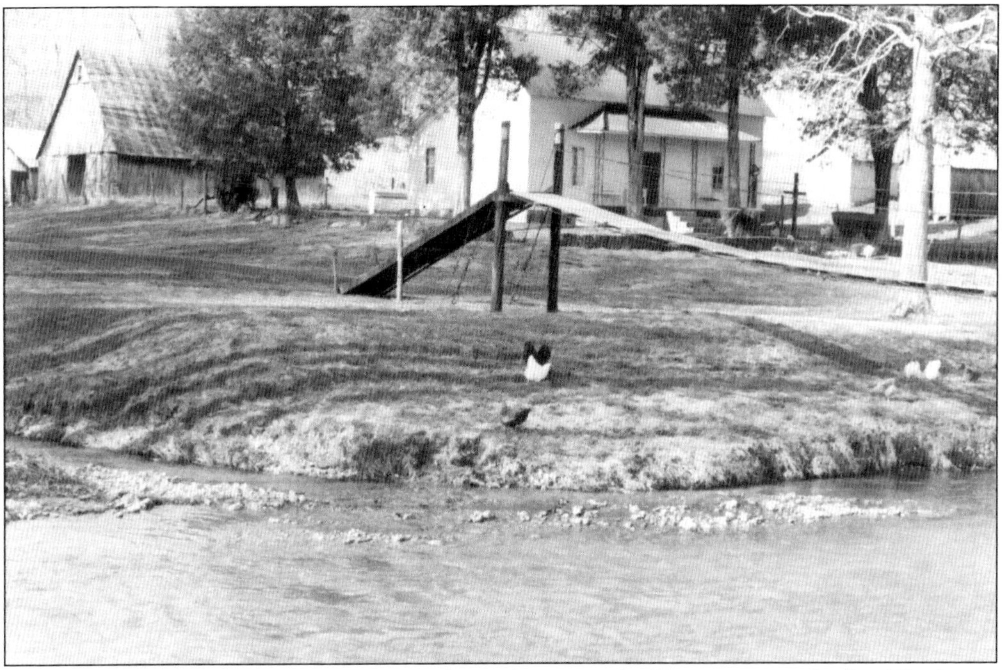

The Chloe Adcock Magness home on Sink Creek was reached by a swinging bridge. The house was built across the creek primarily to keep the chickens at home. It was built by Henry Jefferson Boles in the 1880s and burned in 1986. (Courtesy of Thomas G. Webb.)

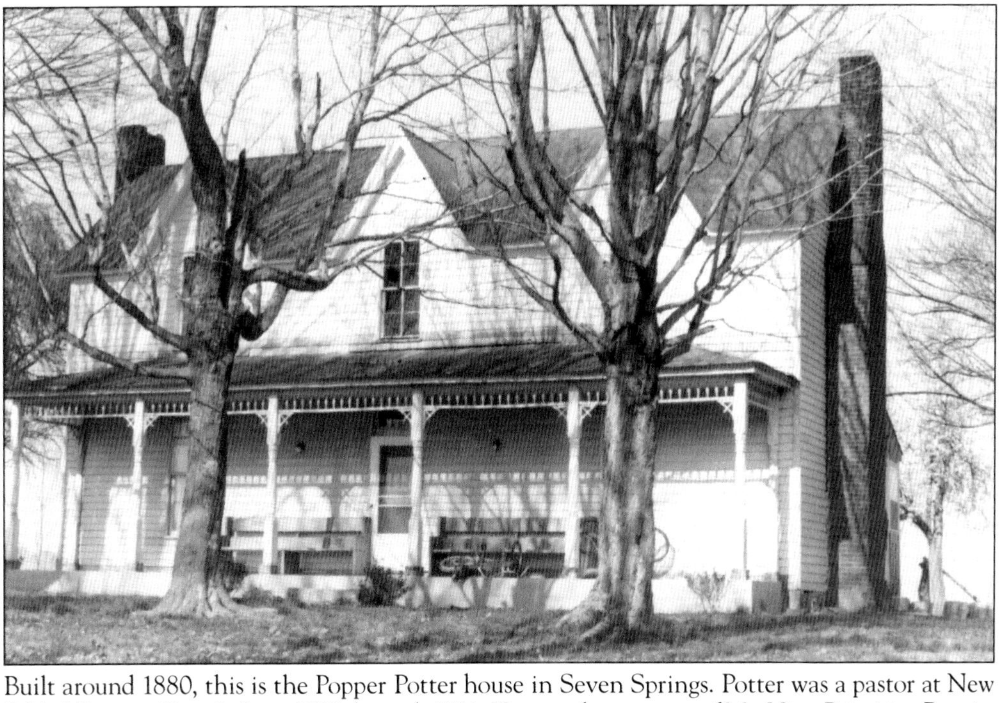

Built around 1880, this is the Popper Potter house in Seven Springs. Potter was a pastor at New Bildad Baptist Church from 1877 through 1911. He was also a pastor of Mt. View Primitive Baptist Church from 1889 until 1906. This picture was taken in 1976; the house is no longer there. (Courtesy of Thomas G. Webb.)

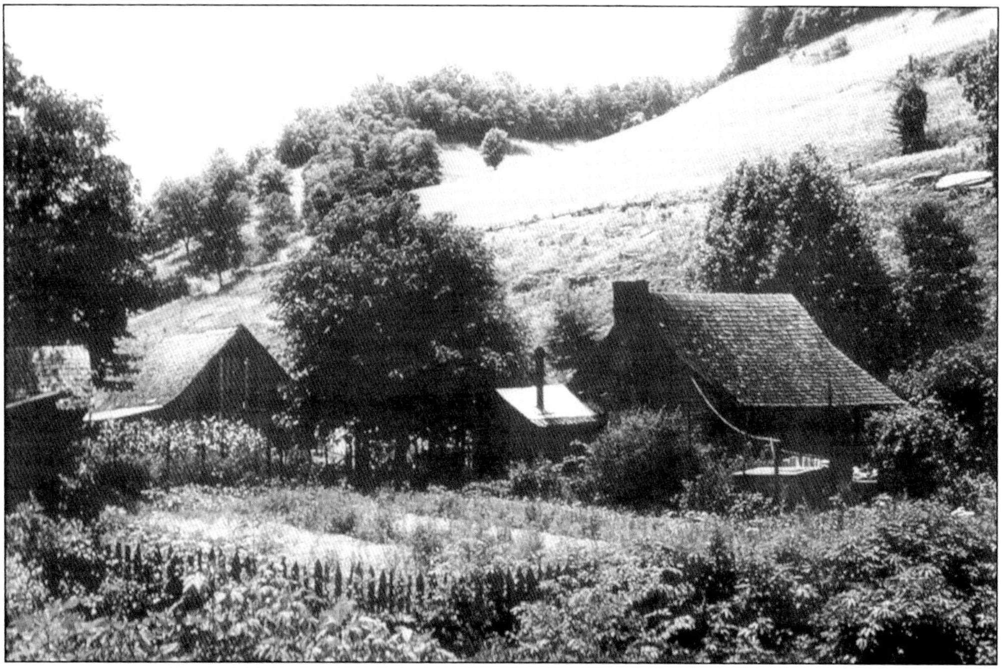

Pictured in 1956, Alvie Mullican's home in Possum Hollow is still standing today. This is at the mouth of Egypt Hollow. (Courtesy of Justin Potter Library.)

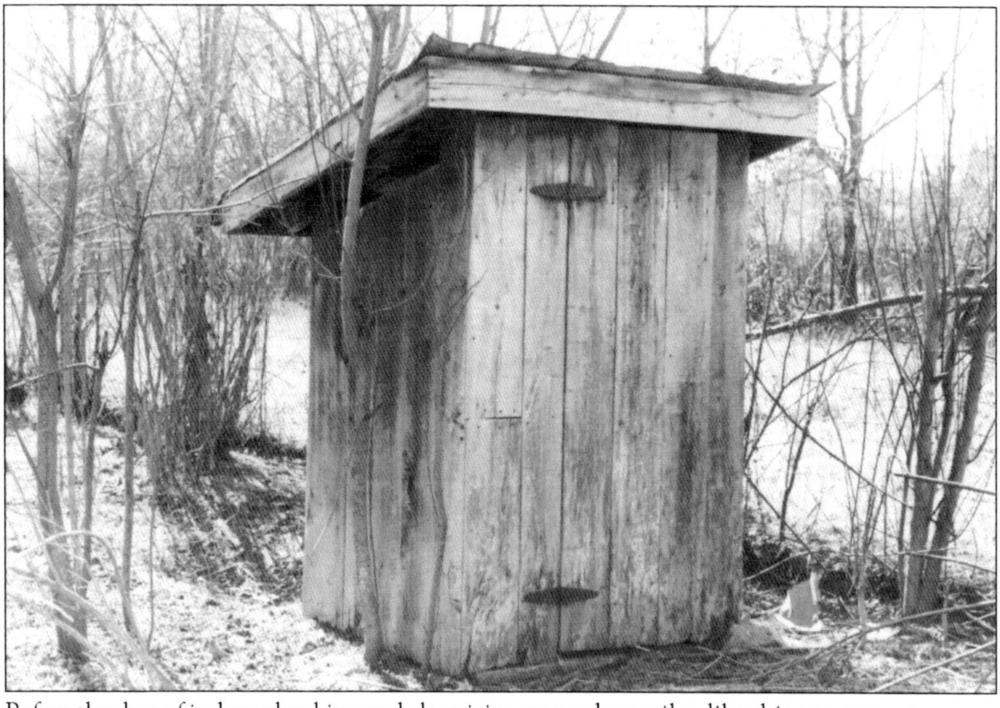

Before the days of indoor plumbing and electricity, an outdoor toilet, like this one, was a common accessory of most every home. This one was at the David J. Atnip home in Smithville, but most of them were not any different for having been built by the Works Progress Administration. (Courtesy of Justin Potter Library.)

Eight

PEOPLE IN PAST TIMES

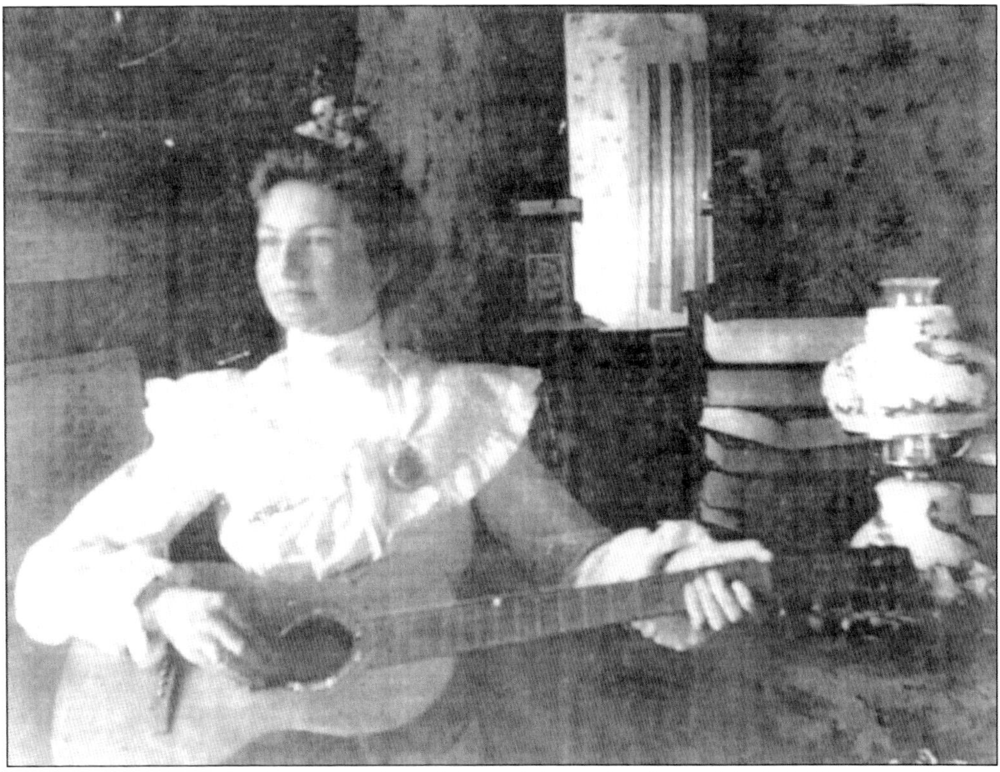

Taken in the late 1800s, this picture shows Minnie Mason, daughter of Dr. Bob Mason and Hatton Wilson Mason of Temperance Hall. Minnie was born in 1886 and died in 1949. She married James Wesley "Jim" Malone and after a few years moved to Fort Lauderdale, Florida, were they lived until their deaths. They are both buried in Salem Cemetery in Liberty. They had three daughters: Ina Mae, Elizabeth Virginia, and Jimmie Lee Malone. (Courtesy of Thomas G. Webb.)

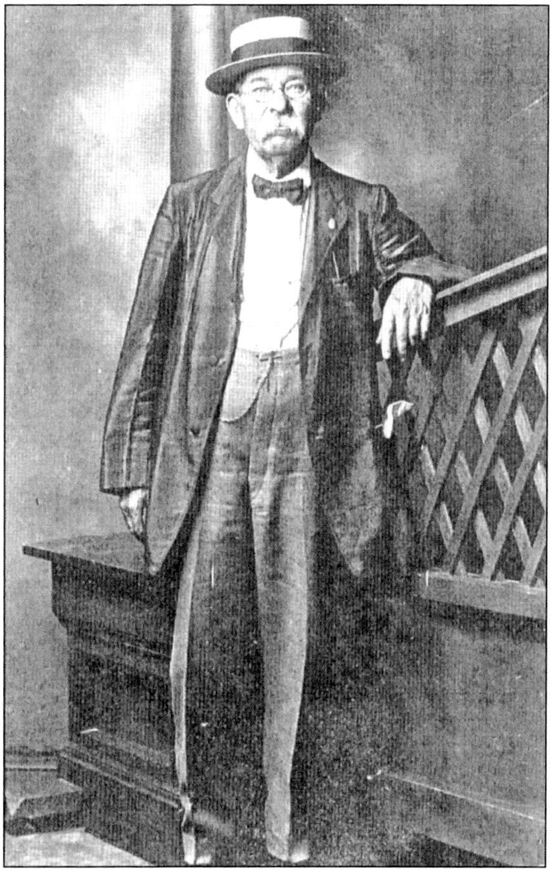

Pictured here, John Fantley Roy was cofounder of the Alexandria Bank and Trust, the pioneer bank of the town and county. The bank was established in 1888 and privately owned by J.F. Roy and Ed Reece with original capital of $10,000. Roy, along with his sons Rob and Frank, owned and operated the bank successfully until the stock market crash of 1929. (Courtesy of Ria Baker.)

This photograph shows the Henry Lucas Winfree family at Long Branch about 1898. From left to right are (first row) Bob, Henry L., Nancy, Emmett Starnes (son-in-law), and wife Josephine with two children; (back row) Sidney, Edgar, and John. The framed picture is of son Willie, who had gone to Texas. (Courtesy of Justin Potter Liberty.)

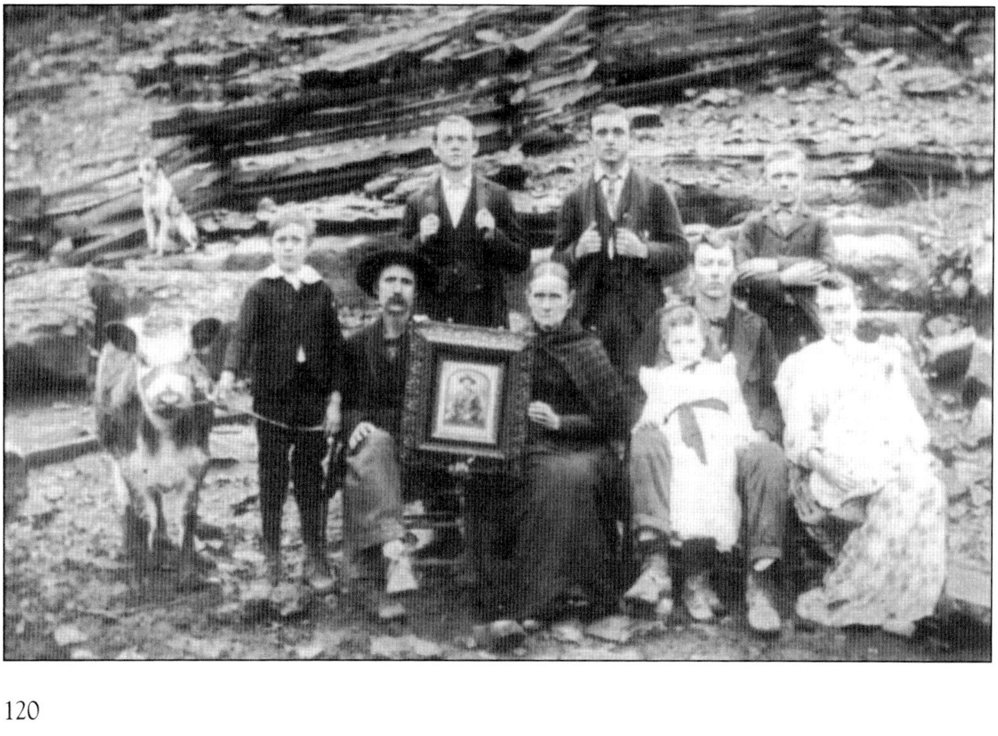

These two little cowboys, Gray Potter (age five) and Tommy Webb (age eight), are taking time out from a hard day of fighting off outlaws to pose for this picture in 1939. Tommy Webb grew up loving history and has worked hard to preserve it in our county. He has written several books about the history of DeKalb County and is the county historian. (Courtesy of Tommy Webb.)

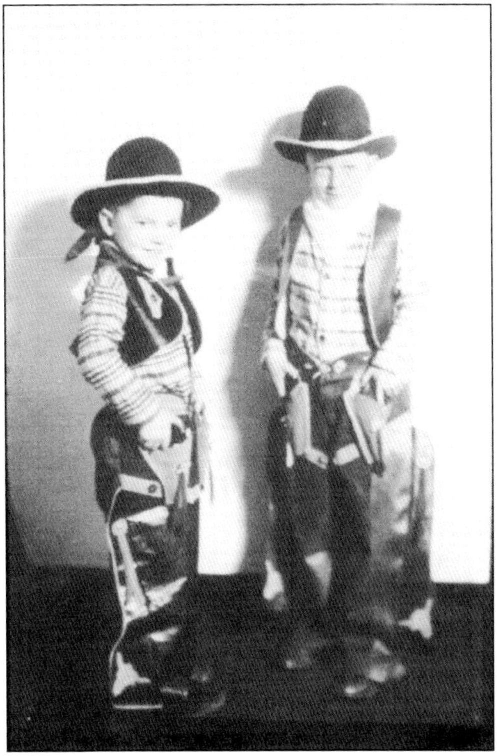

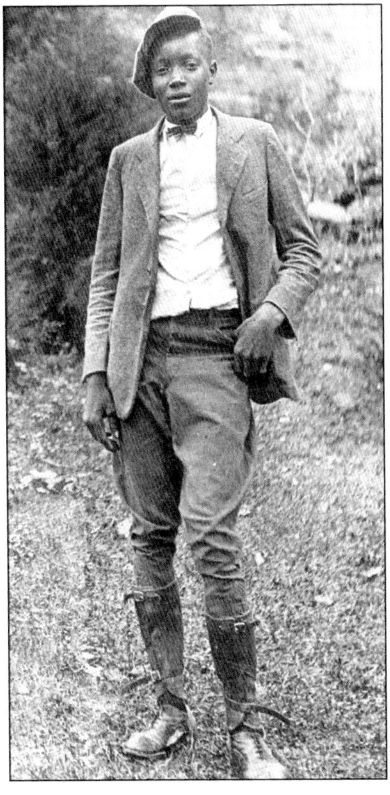

Shown in about 1909, Roosevelt Tubbs was the son of Edd Tubbs and was one of 12 children. The Tubbs family, of Temperance Hall, lived directly behind the United Methodist Church. The family was said to have had as much money in the Temperance Hall Bank as anybody in town but lost it all when the bank failed. Roosevelt was the brother of Inez Tubbs Bass, a well-loved member of the Alexandria community. (Courtesy of Ria Baker.)

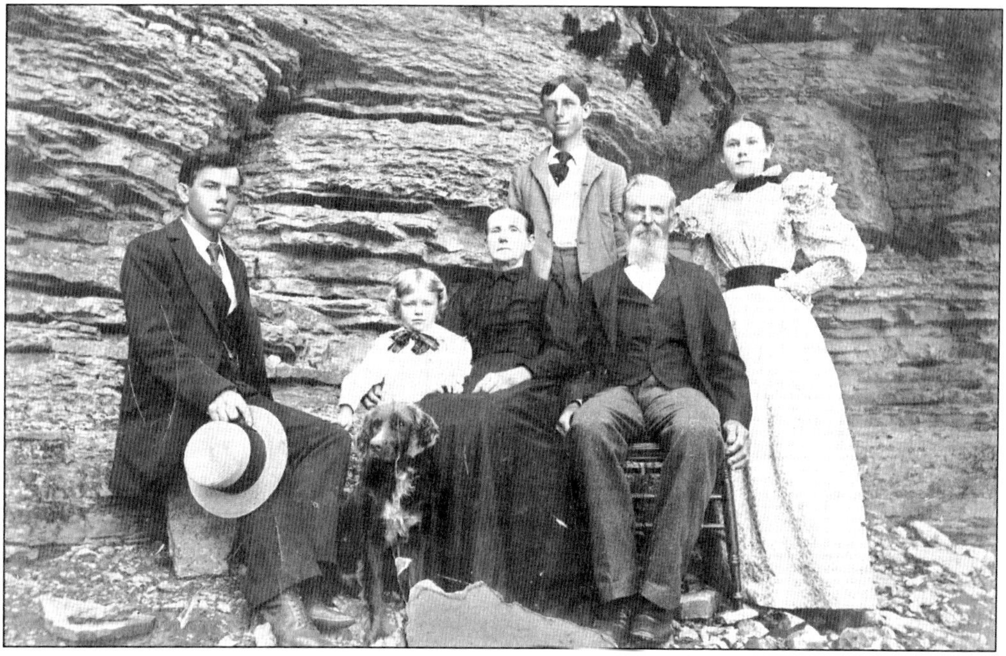

Tom Groom and family lived in the Forks of the Pike area around 1900. They owned a general store as well as a large farm and were prominent members of the community. (Courtesy of Doyle Evans.)

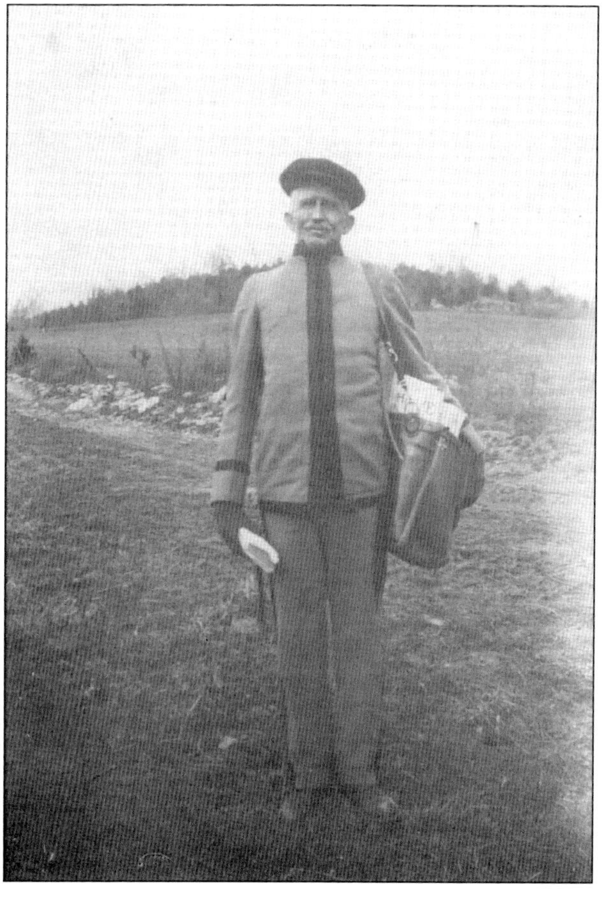

Isaac A. Eaton, born May 11, 1854, carried the mail in rural DeKalb County along the western border. He lived on Edgewood Street in Alexandria and carried mail until his death July 9, 1944. (Courtesy of Pat Parkerson.)

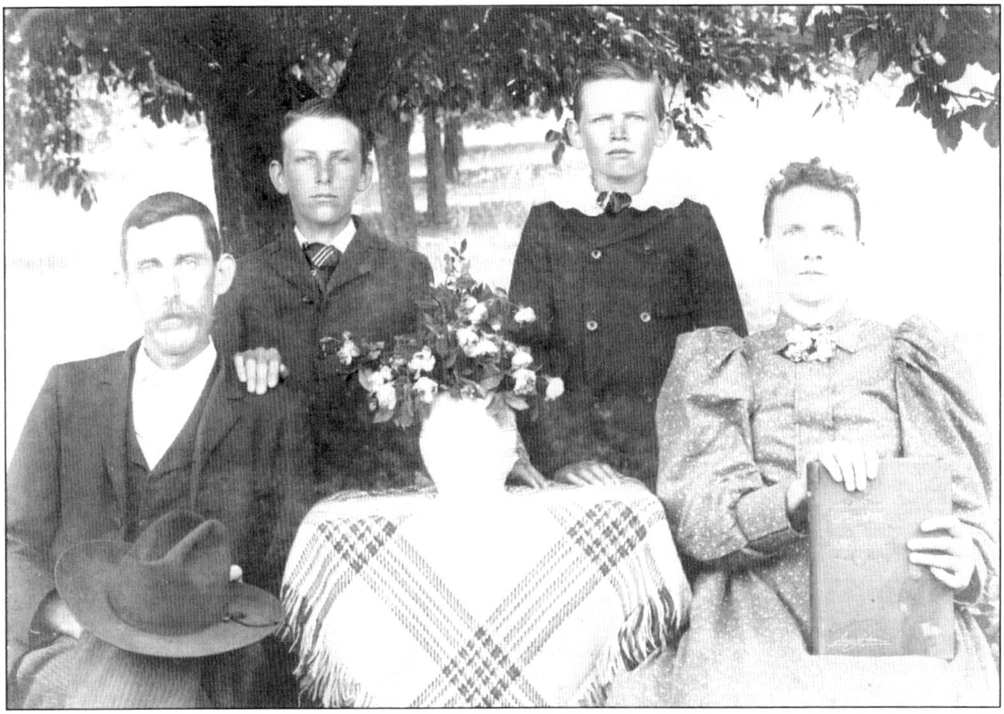

James Monroe Griffith (born in 1859) and his first wife, Matildia Alice (born in 1861), are seen with their children Livingston Lee (second from left) and William Edgar. This family lived in the Jacob Pillow community. (Courtesy of Justin Potter Library.)

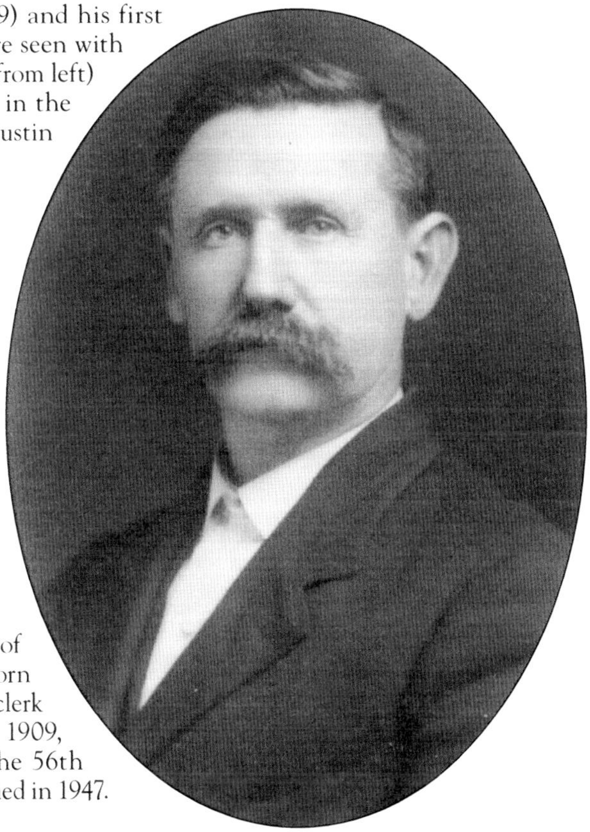

Prominent businessman and member of the community John E. Conger was born in 1859. He served as the county court clerk in the late 1800s and early 1900s. In 1909, he represented DeKalb County at the 56th Tennessee General Assembly. Conger died in 1947. (Courtesy of Justin Potter Library.)

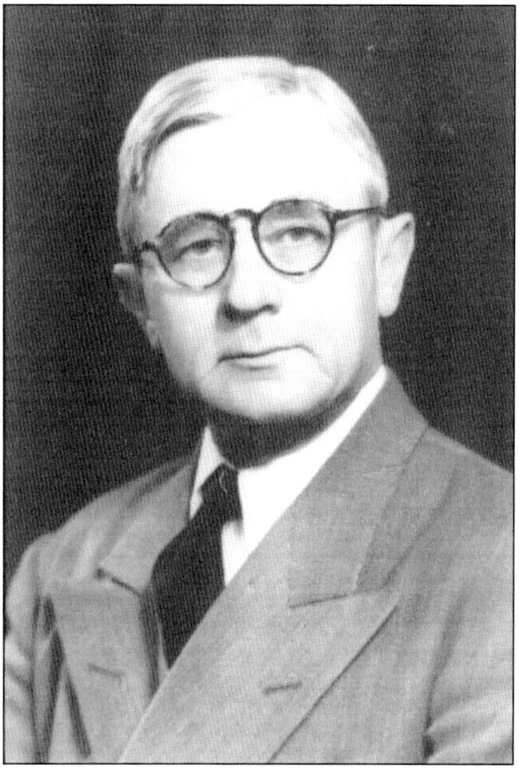

James Edgar Evins (born in 1883) was known as an important civic leader and businessman. He married Myrtie Goodson in 1907 and had sons William Jackson (Dub) Evins and Joseph Landon (Joe L.) Evins. James Edgar Evins served as Smithville mayor and was a state senator for two terms. He was the key in the development of the Center Hill Dam and owned several banks. James Edgar died in 1954. (Courtesy of Justin Potter Library.)

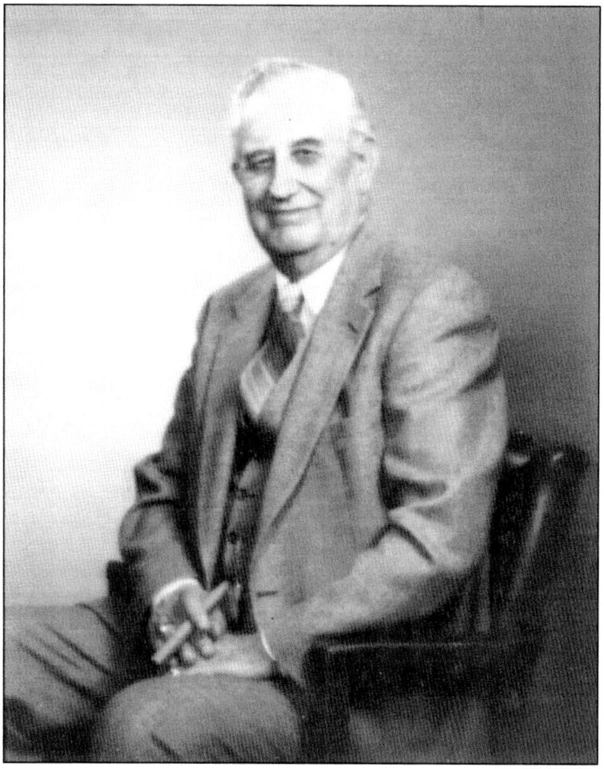

McAllen Foutch, of Alexandria, started a law practice in Smithville in 1938. He served as speaker of the House of Representatives in the Tennessee General Assembly from 1949 until 1953. For years, he was considered by many as the most influential person in DeKalb County politics. (Courtesy of Justin Potter Library.)

E.W. "Eddie" Evins is best known for his banking principles. Believing that a man's word and a handshake stood for something, he was there to help if needed. He served on the DeKalb County Fair Board and Alexandria Lions Club, and he coached local baseball teams. He owned and operated banks in Alexandria, Dowelltown, and Smithville. Much like his grandfather, uncle, and other family members, Eddie loved DeKalb County and worked to make it grow and succeed. Eddie was another true mover and shaker in DeKalb County. (Courtesy of Ria Baker.)

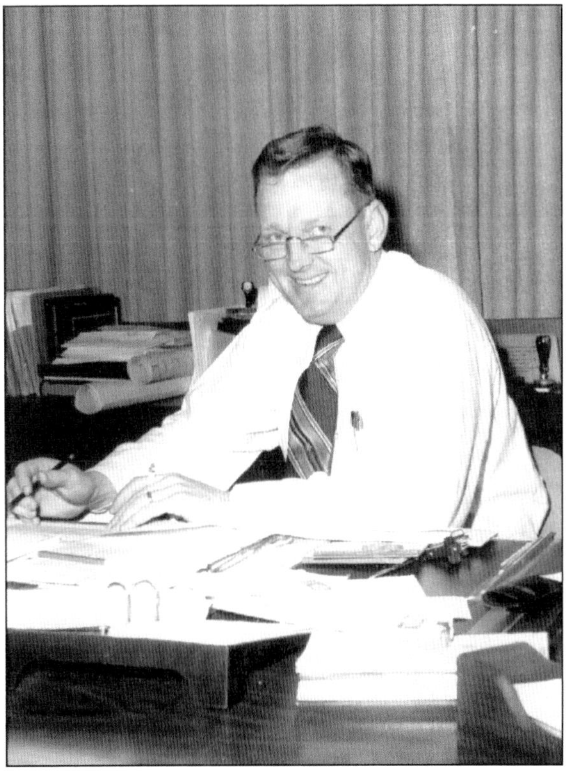

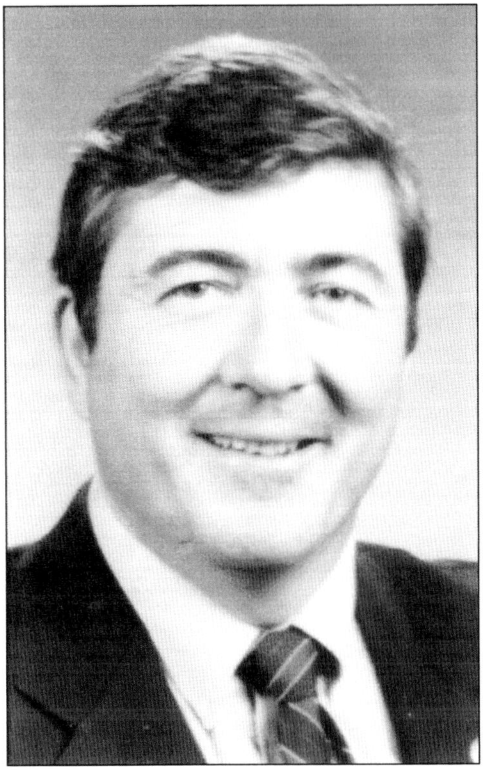

Frank Buck served as a member of the Tennessee state House of Representatives for 36 years, retiring in 2008. Born September 26, 1943, he was the son of John and Georgia Baird Buck. He helped expose a whiskey-for-votes racket operating in DeKalb County. Buck introduced legislation that would prevent legislators from taking so much as a cup of coffee from lobbyists. Frank and his wife Lena are both lawyers and still work together helping their community. Frank Buck is one of the movers and shakers in DeKalb County. (Courtesy of Justin Potter Library.)

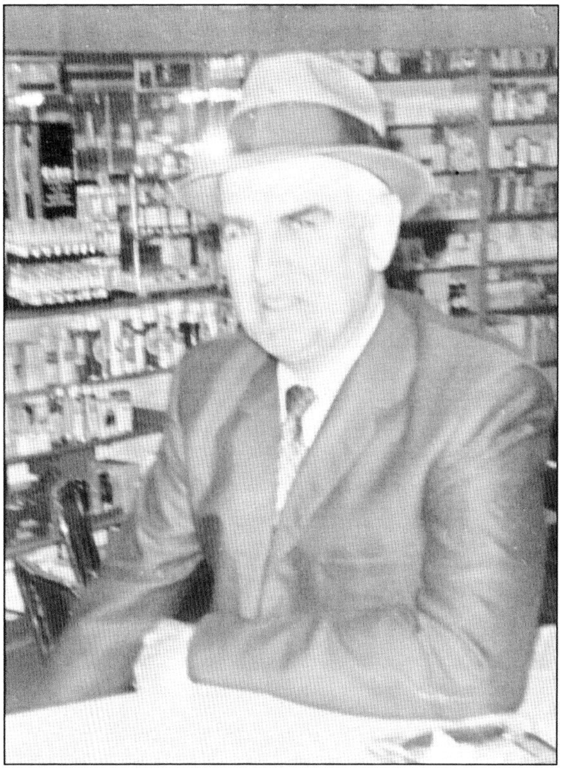

William Clay Avant, a well-known civic leader and postmaster in Alexandria, served his country and his community all throughout his life. As a young man, Clay helped his family run Avant's Funeral Home in Alexandria and taught in area schools. He started the Alexandria Block Plant in the early 1940s. He was elected mayor in 1946 and served for 16 years. He was a DeKalb County Fair director and a key player in establishing the "Down to Earth" All Day Gospel Singing. In 1951, he organized and served as the board president of the DeKalb County Telephone Co-op. He died at age 63 in 1980 and is remembered as a mover and shaker in the Alexandria community. (Courtesy of Jane Avant Fry.)

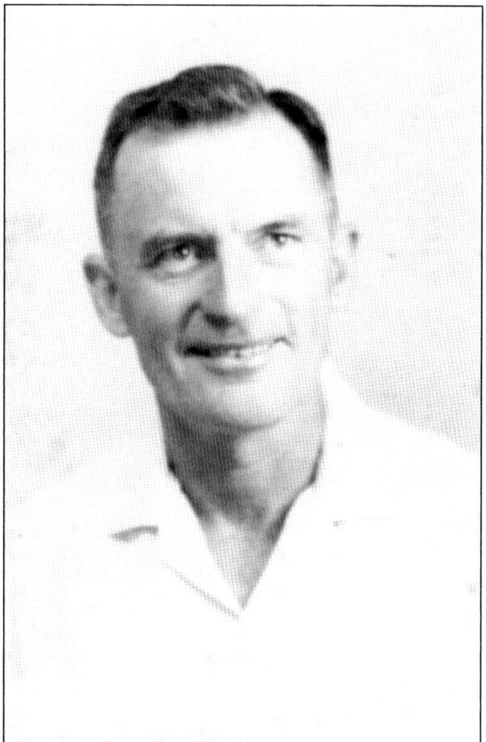

J. Edward "Ed" Hale is the present mayor of Liberty. Elected in 1971, Ed Hale has served his beloved Liberty as mayor for 30 years and counting. In that time, he and his wife, Gloria, have worked hard to help maintain the city's rich historic past and future. In the town of Liberty, Hale has been a much-needed mover and shaker. (Courtesy of Liberty Historic Group.)

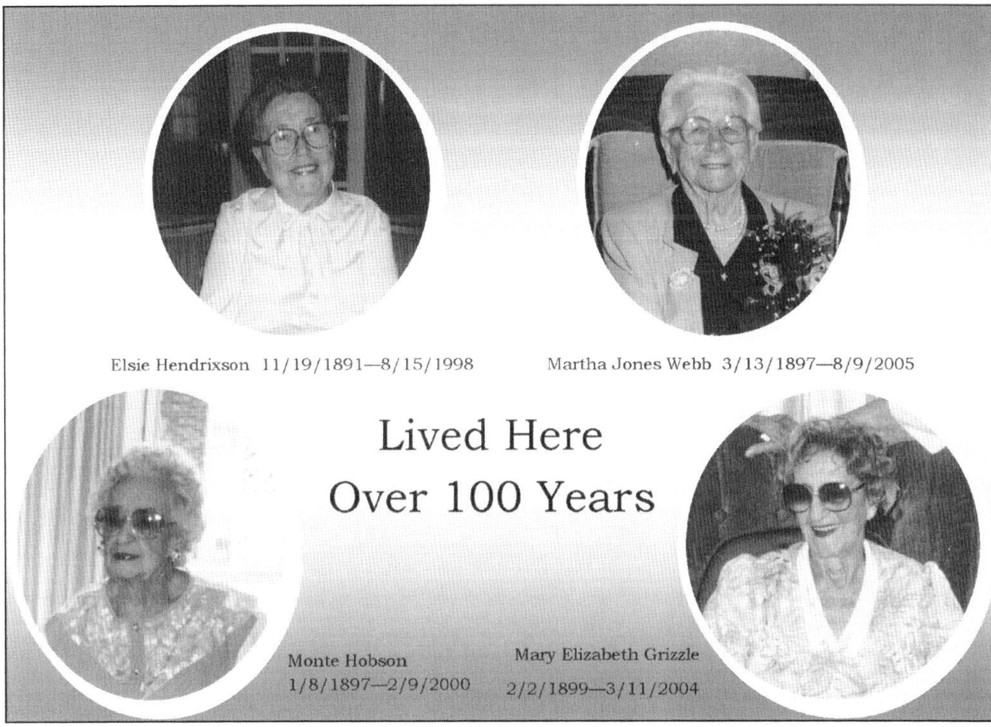

Elsie Hendrixson 11/19/1891—8/15/1998
Martha Jones Webb 3/13/1897—8/9/2005
Monte Hobson 1/8/1897—2/9/2000
Mary Elizabeth Grizzle 2/2/1899—3/11/2004

These ladies were all granted long lives and seem to have enjoyed every year of them. Elsie Evins Hendrixson, of Smithville, lived for almost 107 years. Martha Webb, of the Jefferson community, had the longest life of these ladies, 108 years. Monte Hobson lived 103 years while her sister Mary Grizzle lived 105 years. They were from the Dismal community. The ladies below were younger than those above. Bonnie Taylor lived for almost 101 years, and Allie Fuson just lacked four months of being 102 years old. They were both of the Hurricane Ridge community. Willette Anderson, of Dowelltown and Alexandria, only made it to 100 years plus two months. (Both, courtesy of Linda Fuson, Connie Parsley, Gloria Hale, Robbie Taylor, Ron Paschal, and Judy Fuson.)

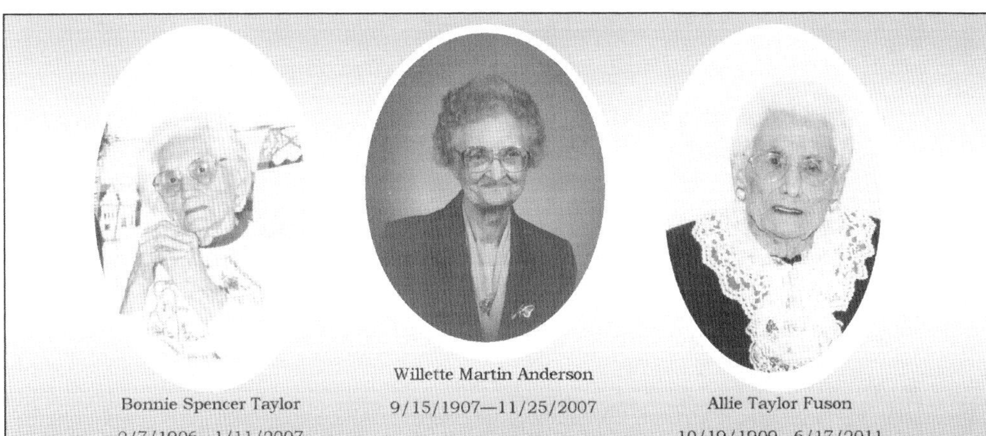

Bonnie Spencer Taylor 2/7/1906—1/11/2007
Willette Martin Anderson 9/15/1907—11/25/2007
Allie Taylor Fuson 10/19/1909—6/17/2011